David Storey
Plays: 1

The Contractor, Home, Stages, Caring

The Contractor: 'A subtle and poetic parable about the nature and joy of skilled work, the meaning of community and the effect of its loss.' *Observer*

Home: 'A sad Wordsworthian elegy about the solitude and dislocation of madness and possibly about the decline of Britain itself ... part of the play's appeal is that Storey leaves it to us to draw our own conclusions ... a play that contains within itself the still, sad music of humanity.' *Guardian*
'Luminous, melancholy and darkly comic.' *Evening Standard*

Stages: 'Storey's haunting new piece ... an elegy for lost times and places, an obituary that has been free-associated by the corpse-to-be ... Storey once said that a play "lives almost in the measure that it escapes and refuses definition". He has always been a writer who hints rather than states, let alone hectors.' *The Times*

Caring, a companion piece to *Stages*, reflects a reassessment and renegotiation of the conflict between life and art.

David Storey: unique in his generation of writers, David Storey's achievements are divided equally between his work as a novelist and as a playwright. Born in 1933, the son of a mineworker, he went to the Slade School of Fine Art in London and had various jobs, ranging from farm labouring and showground tent-erecting to professional rugby league football and schoolteaching. Among his novels are *This Sporting Life*, which won the Macmillan Fiction Award in 1960 and was filmed, *Flight Into Camden*, which won the John Llewelyn Rhys Memorial Prize, and *Radcliffe*, which won the Somerset Maugham Award in 1963. Later novels include *Pasmore*, a Booker finalist and winner of the Faber Memorial Prize, *Saville*, winner of the Booker Prize in 1976, and most recently, *A Serious Man*. His plays include *The Contractor*, *Home* and *The Changing Room* – each of which won the New York Critics Best Play of the Year Award – *In Celebration* which was filmed, *Life Class* and *The Farm*: all of these plays were premièred at the Royal Court Theatre; his two later plays, *Early Days* and *The March on Russia*, were presented at the National Theatre in the 1980s. *Stages* was premièred at the Royal National Theatre in 1992. David ~~~~~~~~~~~~~~~~~~~~~~~~~~~~~~~~in 1956 and has four children.

DAVID STOREY

Plays: 1

The Contractor
Home
Stages
Caring

with an introduction by the author

Methuen Drama

METHUEN CONTEMPORARY DRAMATISTS

3 5 9 10 8 6 4

This collection first published in Great Britain 1992
Reissued in this series 1998
by Methuen Drama
Random House, 20 Vauxhall Bridge Road, London SW1V 2SA
and Australia, New Zealand and South Africa

The Contractor first published by Jonathan Cape 1970
Copyright © David Storey 1970
Home first published by Jonathan Cape 1970
Copyright © David Storey 1970
Stages copyright © David Storey 1992
Caring copyright © David Storey 1992

Introduction and this collection copyright © 1992 by David Storey

The author has asserted his moral rights

ISBN 0–413–67350–2

Random House UK Limited Reg. No. 954009

A CIP catalogue record for this book
is available from the British Library

Photoset in 9½/11pt Sabon by Wilmaset Ltd, Birkenhead, Wirral
Printed and bound in Great Britain
by Cox & Wyman Ltd, Reading, Berkshire

Contents

A Chronology

of plays, novels and poetry

First publication

1960 *This Sporting Life* (novel), pub. Longman (Penguin, 1962). US Macmillan Fiction Award. (Filmed 1963.)
     Flight into Camden (novel), pub. Longman (Penguin, 1964). John Llewelyn Rhys Memorial Prize.

1963 *Radcliffe* (novel), pub. Longman (Penguin, 1965). Somerset Maugham Award.

1967 *The Restoration of Arnold Middleton* (play), pub. Jonathan Cape (Penguin, 1970). First presented at the Traverse Theatre, Edinburgh, 22 September 1966. Royal Court Theatre, London, 4 July 1967. *Evening Standard* Drama Award.

1969 *In Celebration* (play), pub. Jonathan Cape (Penguin, 1971). First presented at the Royal Court Theatre, 22 April 1969. (Filmed 1974.)

1970 *The Contractor* (play), pub. Jonathan Cape (Penguin, 1971). First presented at the Royal Court Theatre, 20 October 1969. Variety Club of Great Britain Best Play of the Year Award. New York Critics Best Play of the Year Award.
     Home (play), pub. Jonathan Cape (Penguin, 1972). First presented at the Royal Court Theatre, 17 June 1970. *Evening Standard* Drama Award. New York Critics Best Play of the Year Award.

1972 *Pasmore* (novel), pub. Longman (Penguin, 1976). Faber Memorial Prize. Booker Prize finalist.
     The Changing Room (play), pub. Jonathan Cape (Penguin, 1973). First presented at the Royal Court

Introduction

At the age of nine I was taken by my elder brother to see a production of *Hamlet* at the Grand Theatre, Leeds. All I recall is one character searching for another along a row of canvas arches, I resisting the temptation to call out that the object of his search was visible to all of us (reading a book) downstage. How absurd it all seemed – and irritating. Pretence.

Afterwards, the last bus had gone (to Wakefield, our home, twelve miles to the south): my brother and I set off to walk through the night – joined on our journey by a young married couple, who had also seen the play – and by two young women who hastily removed themselves from a car which had offered them a lift in the darkened road ahead.

We walked for hours – seemingly until dawn, I, briefly, as we reached the outskirts of Wakefield, carried on my brother's back: my father had informed the police we were missing: much agitation when we arrived: relief, recrimination – or, what might have been missing earlier, the previous evening, in my view: *drama*.

Fifteen years later I was teaching in a school at the back of Kings Cross Station in London. I'd had, by this time, a number of jobs: farm labouring, bus conducting, tent erecting and playing professional football, amongst them. My vocation, however, as I saw it, was as a writer and artist: seven novels had been written and, along with much other work, consistently rejected. Coming home for a half-term weekend break to find yet another rejection slip waiting for me (the eleventh or twelfth for this particular novel) I suddenly had the notion that I might not be a novelist but a playwright: I wanted to get something down in the shortest possible time that would convey my then feelings of frustration and despair.

I wrote a play about a schoolteacher cracking up and called it (appropriately enough) *To Die With the Philistines*. It took three days: the morning after finishing it I was back in front of my class. It provided no immediate solution either to my vocational or occupational problems: indeed, I lost hope in it altogether and for another two years didn't even trouble to type it out. By that time, the above mentioned novel had been accepted and published; the rights had been bought to make a film. The director who was appointed to this daunting task, Lindsay Anderson, asked me if I had ever written a play: I showed him my only endeavour. A production was suggested at the Royal Court Theatre; for one reason or another it never took place. Six years elapsed: the novel I was writing – an ambitious affair, with six principal characters – refused to come together. Something not unlike my schoolteaching despair returned. A letter arrived from the Traverse Theatre in Edinburgh: the director, Gordon McDougall, enquired if a play he had read years ago, as an assistant at the Royal Court Theatre, had ever been produced. If not, he would like to do it.

The play itself had, by this time, been rejected by every subsidised theatre in Great Britain, by all the West End managements to which it had been submitted, and by all the regional and national television companies. Somewhat jubilantly, I sent it off with a suitably revised title, *The Restoration of Arnold Middleton*, and appropriate amendments.

It was performed at the Traverse Theatre in 1966. A year later a new production was mounted at the Royal Court Theatre by Robert Kidd, who had seen the play on its last night while at home in Scotland on holiday – recommending it on his return to the Court. The play transferred to the West End and won an *Evening Standard* Award.

Although I had paid no more than half a dozen visits to a theatre since that childhood *Hamlet*, the stimulation of seeing the play on the Royal Court stage prompted me to write a number of plays in quick succession: the first of these was *The Contractor*, about the erection of a marquee for a wedding; then *In Celebration*, about the return of three educated sons to their working class parents' fortieth wedding anniversary; and *Home*, about a group of people immured in a mental hospital. It was as if a dam had burst: none of the plays took me more than five days to write and, once written, none required more than nominal correction. All three were produced at the Royal Court Theatre over the following two years, directed by Lindsay Anderson – a theatrical partnership which was to continue over the next three decades.

Having worked as a teenager for a tent contractor, the erecting and dismantling of tents had always caught my imagination (and had been used as a 'theme' in an earlier novel, *Radcliffe*). To mount the production on a stage seemed an obvious thing to do (challenging the figment of canvas arches and wholly gratuitous 'searches': there would be no 'plot', merely the actuality – and drama – of work).

Coming to the end of writing this play it occurred to me that the white metalwork table which is left on the otherwise deserted stage provided a basis for the beginning of another play: adding two metalwork chairs (and two characters to occupy the chairs) I assumed the setting was that of a seaside hotel – to discover some way into the conversation of the two increasingly eccentric gentlemen I'd invented that the location was that of a mental hospital. In the original production these two parts were memorably played by John Gielgud and Ralph Richardson – and it was the bringing together of two discernible theatrical traditions (vis-à-vis the Grand Theatre, Leeds – Shakespeare and *Hamlet* – and the Royal Court Theatre, London – *The Contractor*, *Home*), which made this production such a remarkable event.

The Contractor and *Home* have been much performed here and abroad; both of the original productions transferred from the Royal Court to the West End, and both plays were subsequently produced on Broadway. *Stages* and *Caring* were written twenty years and something of a lifetime later. The former might be seen as the resumé of the life of a working class artist who, wisely or unwisely, has dedicated himself to art and to what might be described as an idealised love: following a breakdown, he is visited by members of his family – and others – and inevitably by (climactic) memories of the past.

Caring, on the other hand, was very much written as a play within a play. Not long ago, for instance, playing with a grandson (aged six), I was struck by how important it was to him that the scenario we had 'negotiated' for our game was strictly adhered to: the passion with which our roles were assigned – i.e., not only who was what but who did what, and when, to whom – was more intense than that expended on the game itself – and infinitely more intense when these 'assignations' were deviated from, forgotten or ignored.

Yet – I reflected, later – we do this all our lives: if I love you will you love me? – negotiating roles we would like to have ourselves as well as those by which we would like to be surrounded.

Integral to this 'collusion' is mutual regard: 'caring' to negotiate our roles – and caring, further, to amend them. It was with this 'playing' process in mind that *Caring* came to be written – some fifty years after that nine-year-old boy had watched sceptically one character on a stage at the Grand Theatre in Leeds 'pretending' to search for another – unready, at that age, to accede to the scenario being offered – but now, a lifetime later, acceding to little else – and, in the theatre in general, and in these plays in particular, inviting everyone out there to join him.

David Storey, 1992

THE CONTRACTOR

The Contractor was first presented at the Royal Court Theatre, London, on 20 October 1969. The cast was as follows:

KAY, foreman	Philip Stone
MARSHALL, workman	Jim Norton
EWBANK, the contractor	Bill Owen
FITZPATRICK, workman	T. P. McKenna
BENNETT, workman	Norman Jones
PAUL, Ewbank's son	Martin Shaw
CLAIRE, Ewbank's daughter	Judy Liebert
GLENDENNING, workman	John Antrobus
OLD EWBANK	Billy Russell
MAURICE, Claire's fiancé	Christopher Coll
OLD MRS EWBANK	Adele Strong
MRS EWBANK	Constance Chapman

Directed by Lindsay Anderson

ACT ONE

The stage is set with three tent poles for a marquee, twenty or thirty feet high, down the centre of the stage at right angles to the audience. The poles should be solid and permanently fixed, the ropes supporting them, from the top, running off into the wings. Each pole is equipped with the necessary pulley blocks and ropes, the latter fastened off near the base as the play begins. Two ridge poles, to be used for the muslin, are set between the poles.

Early morning. KAY enters. He's a big man, hard, in his forties, dressed in working trousers and a jacket, not at all scruffy. He's smoking, just off the lorry, and comes in looking round with a professional eye at the scene, at the poles. He tests one of the ropes, checks another, casual, in no hurry.

MARSHALL follows him in a moment later. He's a thin, rather lightweight Irishman, pleasant, easy-going, with no great appetite for work. He's dressed in overalls, well-worn, from age rather than use. He's stretching as he enters, from the ride: arms, legs, back.

MARSHALL. You put these up yesterday, then, Mr Kay?

KAY doesn't answer, going on with his inspection, smoking.

(*Calling off.*) Aye, Fitzpatrick. If you're bringing in your snap can you bring mine with you?

MARSHALL rubs his hands together against a chilly morning, slaps his shoulders.

God, This time of the morning. It shouldn't be allowed.
KAY (*indifferent*). Aye.

EWBANK has entered. He's a solid, well-built man, broad rather than tall, stocky. He's wearing a suit, which is plain, workman-like and chunky; someone probably who doesn't take easily to wearing clothes, reflecting, perhaps,

*the feeling of a man who has never really found his proper
station in life. The jacket of his coat is open as if it's been
put on in a rush.*

EWBANK. You've got here, then.
KAY (*looking up*). Morning, Mr Ewbank.
EWBANK. Morning. God Christ. It's bloody afternoon.
KAY. We had some trouble . . .
EWBANK (*to* MARSHALL). Look . . . look . . . look. Mind
    where you put your bloody feet.
MARSHALL. To God . . . (*Moves them in a hurry.*)
EWBANK. That's grass, is that. God Christ, just look at it.
    (*He presses down a divot.*)
KAY. It must have been from yesterday . . .

*FITZPATRICK enters as EWBANK busies himself with
looking around and pressing down a further divot.
FITZPATRICK is eating a sandwich and in addition to his
own bag of food is carrying MARSHALL's, an old army
shoulder bag. FITZPATRICK is a hard, shrewd Irishman,
independent.*

FITZPATRICK. Is that a ton of lead you have in there,
    Marshy, or the latest of your mother's buns?

He slings the bag to MARSHALL who misses it.

He couldn't nick a tail off a chocolate mouse.
MARSHALL. Nor a cold off a wet morning!

They both laugh.

FITZPATRICK (*catching sight of* EWBANK). Oh, good
    Christ. Good morning. How are you? Good day. Good
    night . . . (*Mumbles on through a ritual of touching
    forelock, bowing.*)
EWBANK. Mind where you put your feet, Fitzpatrick, or I'll
    have them bloody well cut off.
FITZPATRICK. Aaaah! (*Steps one way then another. To*
    MARSHALL.) As long as it's my feet only he's after.

They both laugh.

EWBANK. I came down here . . . Are these all you've got? (*Indicating men.*)

KAY (*calling off*). Bennett!

EWBANK. I've never known such a damn place for eating.

MARSHALL *as well as* FITZPATRICK *is eating a sandwich.*

MARSHALL. It's me breakfast . . . I haven't eaten a thing all night.

FITZPATRICK. Nor drunk a drop of anything, either.

MARSHALL. Now would I do a thing like that? . . . Eating, now, is a different matter.

They both laugh. BENNETT *has come in carrying a ridge pole on his shoulder.*

BENNETT *is a fairly anonymous person, prefers to be inconspicuous, that is, without being overlooked. He'll do whatever is asked of him, no more and occasionally, if he's sure it'll cause no trouble, a little less. His hair is neatly combed and he wears the trousers of an overall and a clean shirt. He, too, as he enters, carrying the ridge pole, has a sandwich in his mouth and, over his other shoulder, a food bag; in his arms he carries the muslin ropes.*

BENNETT (*through sandwich*). Quick! Quick! I'm going to drop it . . .

EWBANK. Damn and blast it, man, look where you're walking . . .

BENNETT. Quick! Quick! It's going on my toes . . . (*He puts the ridge pole down between the first two vertical poles, groaning and then holding his back as he straightens: evidently the root of all his problems.*) Oooooooh . . . ! I should never . . . Oooooooh! (*Holds his back with both hands.*) Rheumatism. Have you ever had anything like it?

EWBANK. Aye. Often.

BENNETT. You have?

EWBANK. When anybody mentions bloody work. I've seen it. Don't worry.

BENNETT. That's right. This place is full of skivers. Just

look at that. (*Looks up at the house.*) It's a damn sight warmer in the cab.

EWBANK. I came down, Kay . . . Just look at this. (*He has examined where he's laid the ridge pole. Now he presses in another divot.*)

FITZPATRICK. That's a lovely house you have there, Mr Ewbank. (*Gestures off.*)

MARSHALL. Beautiful . . . ! Beautiful.

EWBANK. And I'll bloody well keep it that way if I've half a chance.

FITZPATRICK (*to* MARSHALL). He wouldn't be letting us in there, now, that's for sure. To warm up by the fire.

MARSHALL. Toes and fingers . . .

FITZPATRICK. Toes and fingers.

They laugh.

MARSHALL. Just look, to God. (*Holds up his fingers.*) They're dropping off.

EWBANK. I came down to give you all a warning. Before you start. That house, now, is full of people.

MARSHALL (*looks up*). People . . .

EWBANK. Relatives of mine. It overlooks the lawn.

FITZPATRICK. It does. It does. (*To* MARSHALL.) How long's he had it?

EWBANK. And I don't want you, Fitzpatrick, up to your usual habits. Piddling all over the place, for one thing, whenever you feel like it. And language. I'd appreciate it very much, Kay, if you saw to it that they watched their tongues.

KAY. Aye. Right.

FITZPATRICK. You do that, Kay.

EWBANK. And for another thing, Kay: this lawn.

PAUL comes in.

FITZPATRICK. Don't tell me, now. (*Stoops: examines grass.*) He has.

MARSHALL. Numbered every blade.

FITZPATRICK. Lettered every scratch.

EWBANK. Right. I think you know what's what.

PAUL (*to* KAY, *etc.*). Morning . . . Anything I can do . . . ?

PAUL, EWBANK's *son, is a bit slighter in build than his father, feckless, a little uncoordinated, perhaps. He's dressed in a shirt and slacks, the former unbuttoned and showing an apparent indifference to the chill of the morning. His initial attitude, deliberately implanted, is that of a loafer. His hands are buried in his trouser pockets and a cigarette hangs, largely unattended, from the corner of his mouth. His manner is a conscious foil to his father's briskness. He has no particular refinement of accent.*

EWBANK. Aye. You can keep out of the bloody way. Have you had your breakfast?

PAUL. I don't believe . . . (*Thinks.*) No. I'm positive. I haven't.

As he talks he drifts over to the poles, examines them, without taking his hands from his pockets, nods to the men, wandering round.

EWBANK. You can come in then for that. Kay, I don't think you've met my son?

KAY. No . . .

EWBANK. If he gets in the road kick him out of it. It's the only thing he'll understand. Same goes for the rest of the family, too. Get it up. Get it finished. And get away.

KAY (*to men*). Right . . . Let's have the other ridge . . .

MARSHALL. Fitzpatrick . . . I reckon it's up to you and me.

KAY (*to* BENNETT). Side poles . . .

They go, MARSHALL *and* FITZPATRICK *still eating.*

PAUL. I don't mind giving a hand.

EWBANK. Aye, I know what sort of hand that that'll be.

PAUL. I'm very good at this sort of stuff. Though I say it myself.

Takes his hands leisurely from his pockets and, still smoking, stoops and lifts the ridge pole a few inches off the ground. Then he puts it back down.

There, then. What did you think of that?

EWBANK. Bloody astonishing. I'd forgotten you'd got hands on inside them pockets.

PAUL. There's quite a lot of things I've got you haven't seen. I don't know. Some of them might surprise you.

EWBANK (*to* KAY). Surprises. I live from one minute to the next.

He laughs. KAY *gives no expression.*

There are frantic wolf-whistles off.

CLAIRE, EWBANK's *daughter, comes in. Slightly younger than* PAUL, *easy-going yet never anxious to be imposed upon. She's wearing jeans and a sweater which show a regard for practicality rather than fashion. Pleasant. Acts tough.*

CLAIRE. They've started, then.

EWBANK. That's right. They have. Just about.

CLAIRE. How long'll they take? (*Looks at poles, ropes.*)

EWBANK. All day and a bit beyond if you can't keep clear. Now come on. Get in. This's no place here for you . . . The lucky bride, Kay.

KAY. How d'you do? (*Laying out the muslin ropes.*)

EWBANK. How many lasses have you got, Kay?

KAY. Four.

EWBANK. Four! To God. One is well enough for me.

EWBANK *puts his arm affectionately about her shoulder.*

One of each, and they've skint me afore I'm fifty.

PAUL. I don't know. There's still a bit to go.

EWBANK. Aye. So they say. So they tell me.

CLAIRE (*to* KAY). If there's anything you want just let us know. In the house, I mean.

KAY. Right . . .

PAUL (*stooped, hands in pockets*). And if you want an extra hand.

KAY. Aye.

CLAIRE. Yours truly . . . (*Laughs, indicating* PAUL.)

PAUL (*to* CLAIRE). They don't believe me. I'm bloody good at this.

EWBANK. Don't worry. If Kay wants any help he knows where to look for it . . . (*To* KAY.) I'll leave you to it. I'll pop back in half an hour.

KAY. Aye. All right.

PAUL (*to* CLAIRE). D'you wanna fag?

CLAIRE. No thanks . . .

PAUL. Me last one. (*Coughs heavily, to amuse her.*)

EWBANK (*going, confidential to* KAY). I don't mind so much about the piddling. It's just with the house. I have me mother here, you know. And my old man.

KAY. Aye. I understand.

EWBANK. You've got to be able to look out of your own front window, Kay. You understand?

KAY. I'll keep an eye on them.

EWBANK (*looking round*). A grand day for it. No wind. A bit of sun . . .

KAY. Aye . . .

EWBANK (*going, arm round* CLAIRE). Well, lass, how're you feeling?

CLAIRE. Champion.

EWBANK (*pleased*). Champion, is it?

CLAIRE. Aye. That's right.

They go. CLAIRE *laughing,* PAUL *slouching along with deliberate affectation behind, casting a glowering look at* KAY, *coughing, before he finally goes.*

During their departure other sounds have started up outside from MARSHALL *and* FITZPATRICK.

MARSHALL. } Hup, three. Hup, three. Hup, three. Hup, hup, hup . . . two, three, four. Hup, hup, hup, hup.

FITZPATRICK. } Hup . . . two, three, four. Hup, hup, hup, hup.

They enter carrying a ridge pole between them on their shoulders. It's quite light, but they make a routine of it, as if on parade, each carrying at the same time a sandwich in their free hand.

MARSHALL. Four, five, six . . .

FITZPATRICK. Left, left, left . . .

MARSHALL (*to* KAY). Is that Ewbank's daughter, then?

KAY. That's right.

FITZPATRICK. Good Christ . . .

MARSHALL. Aye, now . . .

FITZPATRICK. How could something as beautiful as that come out of something so repulsive?

MARSHALL *laughs. They've put the pole down between the uprights.*

KAY (*going*). All right, then. Let's have the canvas off . . . (*Goes.*)

FITZPATRICK. Nay, steady on, Kay. I've just done a spot of work. It's freezing. Let's have a little look around. Now, then . . . There's the town, from which, earlier in the day, unless I'm mistaken, we ascended. Covered, I'm sad to say . . . (*Stoops to peer at it more closely.*) by a cloud of smoke.

MARSHALL. Impenetrable. (*Eating his sandwich.*)

FITZPATRICK. Not a spot of anything . . . (*Eating too.*)

MARSHALL. On a clear day though . . .

FITZPATRICK. Oh, the view, Marshy, is magnificent. Quite worth the effort, I'd imagine, of coming all the way up here to work.

BENNETT *has come in, dropping down a quantity of side poles.*

BENNETT. Is that Ewbank's son, then?

FITZPATRICK. Is that his daughter?

They laugh. KAY *has returned, bringing in a quantity of side poles which he lays down.*

Who's she getting married to, then? (*To* KAY.)

KAY. I've no idea. (*Goes off.*)

FITZPATRICK. A university man if ever I saw one. (*Still eating his sandwich.*)

BENNETT. Who's that, Fitzie? (*He's shackling the muslin ropes to the muslin ridges.*)

FITZPATRICK. The son.

MARSHALL. The mark of an educated man.

FITZPATRICK. Unlike his bloody old man.

They laugh.

KAY *comes back with more side poles.*

FITZPATRICK. An intellectual. (*Taps the side of his head knowingly.*) You can tell it at a glance.

MARSHALL. Never done a day's work in his life.

They laugh.

BENNETT. A house like that, and you don't need to do any work . . .

MARSHALL. Built up from what . . . ?

FITZPATRICK. The money he never paid us . . .

BENNETT. And a damn sight more besides.

FITZPATRICK (*gestures*).
The windows bright with our sweat
The concrete moistened by our sorrows.

MARSHALL. Did you get that out of the paper?

FITZPATRICK. I did.

KAY. Bloody eating. I've never seen such a place for food. Where's Glendenning? (*Checks BENNETT's shackling of the muslin ridges.*)

BENNETT. He's fastening up the gates.

FITZPATRICK (*imitating, suddenly, a wild and vicious man*). 'Will you keep the gate shut, damn you! Haven't I enough trouble in here wid'out you letting more in besides?'

MARSHALL. Is that what he said? (*Looks up at house.*)

FITZPATRICK. That's right, Kay, isn't it?

KAY doesn't answer but goes on working.

No sooner got the poles up than he comes tearing across the lawn, the dogs yapping at his heels. 'Who the hell left that damn gate open?' I thought he'd fire him on the spot.

MARSHALL. No such damn luck, I'm thinking.

FITZPATRICK. No: no such damn luck. You're right.

They laugh. The tone of this, directed as much at KAY as at anyone else, is that of a casual effort to fill in time, to smoke, eat.

BENNETT. He's not a man to provocate.

They laugh.

KAY. He's a man to come back down here in half an hour. Come on. Come on . . . Glendenning, where the *hell* are you going with that?

GLENDENNING *is perhaps in his early twenties, a good-natured, stammering half-wit. He wears overalls, well-worn but scrupulously clean, and considerably too large for him. A big pair of boots stick out from underneath; something, altogether, of a caricature of a workman. He has entered, carrying a fourteen-pound sledgehammer over one shoulder, and several marquee stakes over the other, crossing over the stage towards the other side.*

GLENDENNING. I . . . I . . . I . . . I . . . I . . . I . . .

MARSHALL (*sings to the tune of 'Down Mexico Way'*). Ay, yi, yi, yi . . . Ay, yi, yi, yi!

GLENDENNING. I . . . I . . . I . . . I'm going to n . . . n . . . n . . . *nnnnn* . . . knock in some . . . *sssss* . . . stakes.

BENNETT Stakes!

FITZPATRICK. Stakes, bejesus.

KAY (*matter-of-fact*). You bloody idiot.

GLENDENNING. W . . . wwww . . . what?

MARSHALL. He said: 'You bloody idiot.'

GLENDENNING. Wa . . .

BENNETT. The stakes, man. The stakes.

GLENDENNING *looks at the stakes. He gazes at them for a while.*

GLENDENNING. W . . . wwww . . . what?

KAY (*going, casual*). Fitzpatrick. Bennett . . . Come on, now. Come on. (*Goes.*)

FITZPATRICK. You don't knock stakes in here.

MARSHALL. You don't at all.

GLENDENNING. What? (*He looks up at the poles.*)

BENNETT. Not in Mr Ewbank's lawn.

MARSHALL. No, no.

FITZPATRICK. He's planted this, he has, with special grass. (*Gestures at house.*) You've to step over it . . . like walking on a cloud. Here, now. Here. Look at this . . .

FITZPATRICK *tiptoes to and fro so that* GLENDENNING *might see.*

KAY (*off*). Fitzpatrick . . .

FITZPATRICK. Come on, now. Let's see you do it.

MARSHALL (*indicating house*). If you can't do it, you know, he'll not have you near the house.

FITZPATRICK (*doing it himself*). Come on, now. Like this . . .

MARSHALL. Do you know what he'll do?

GLENDENNING (*uncomprehending*). W . . . wwww . . . what?

MARSHALL. If he looks through his window and sees you walking about with stakes dangling from your arm?

GLENDENNING *is uncertain, looking from one to the other. Then:*

GLENDENNING. N . . . *nnnn* . . . no.

FITZPATRICK. He'll come out here . . .

BENNETT. And take that hammer . . .

MARSHALL. And drive one right through your . . .

GLENDENNING. Oh!

MARSHALL *has placed a forefinger to each of* GLENDENNING's *temples, pinning his head between.*

FITZPATRICK. Come on, now. Let's see you do it.

MARSHALL. You have to pass the test!

BENNETT. If he's watching, he might just change his mind.

FITZPATRICK, *with something of a gesture, poses on his toes.* GLENDENNING *looks at them, then up at the house.*

FITZPATRICK. Up, now . . . Higher.

GLENDENNING. I can't . . .

MARSHALL. Oh, now. That's not so bad.

FITZPATRICK. He'll be very pleased with that.

GLENDENNING *has scarcely raised his heels.*

MARSHALL. He will. I haven't a doubt.

FITZPATRICK. That's the best piece of toe-walking I've seen in all my life.

BENNETT. For many a year.

MARSHALL. For many a year. You're right.

FITZPATRICK. Do you know, now, what I think he'll
do . . .

KAY (*off*). Bennett . . . !

MARSHALL. He'll come out here . . .

GLENDENNING *still poses, watching them.*

BENNETT. 'Glendenning,' he'll say . . .

FITZPATRICK. 'As a special favour to myself – to myself,
mind – I'd be very grateful if you'd come down here each
morning . . .'

GLENDENNING. M . . . mmmm . . . morning.

MARSHALL. 'To my house . . .'

FITZPATRICK. 'For it just so happens I've been looking for
a man the very likes of you . . .'

MARSHALL. 'A special person . . .'

GLENDENNING. Sp . . . sp . . . sp . . . sssss . . . special.

BENNETT. 'For a job, that is, I have in mind . . .'

FITZPATRICK. 'And for which it seems to me you have all
the necessary qualifications.'

GLENDENNING. Aye!

MARSHALL. Aren't you going to ask him what it is,
Glenny?

GLENDENNING. Aye!

FITZPATRICK. Do you see, now, all those little holes . . .

GLENDENNING. Aye!

FITZPATRICK. Lying all over the grass . . .

GLENDENNING. Aye!

FITZPATRICK. Each one, you know, has a little worm
inside.

GLENDENNING. Aye!

FITZPATRICK. And every time it pops its head out . . .

GLENDENNING. Aye!

FITZPATRICK. I want you to hit it. As hard as you can.
With that. (*Indicates hammer.*)

They laugh. GLENDENNING, *not at all put out, gazes
round at them with a broad smile, pleased.*

KAY *comes back carrying first bag of canvas. He dumps it
down.*

KAY. Bennett. Let's have the canvas off. Fitzpatrick.

FITZPATRICK. Aye, aye, sir.

KAY. And easy with it as it comes. (*To* GLENDENNING.)
You better put those back, lad.

GLENDENNING. H . . . hhh . . . How're you going to k
. . . kkkk . . . keep it up?

FITZPATRICK (*going*). That's a very philosophical
question . . .

He and MARSHALL *go off, laughing.* MARSHALL, *a
moment later, however, comes back.*

MARSHALL. Ay, now. He didn't mention me at all. (*Put
out, he potters with the ropes, checking them with no
interest at all.*)

KAY (*patiently to* GLENDENNING). Mr Ewbank, now –
he's asked us to put no holes into his lawn. (*Presses with
his foot to demonstrate its quality.*)

GLENDENNING. Aye!

MARSHALL. We're going to float it up, Glenny. If we all
stand here, now, and puff together . . . I think we'll be all
right.

KAY (*to* MARSHALL). Come on. You can lift a piece with
me . . . (*As they go.*) You want to leave Glendenning
alone. Have you heard that, now?

MARSHALL. Me! Me? I've never even touched him . . . (*To*
FITZPATRICK *coming in.*) Have you heard him, now?
They're blaming me. Not a damn minute's rest here for
anyone.

FITZPATRICK *and* BENNETT *are carrying in the second
bag of canvas.*

FITZPATRICK. We've left the heaviest piece behind.

MARSHALL (*going*). What?

FITZPATRICK. Couldn't shift it, man. Needs a great big
feller like yourself.

MARSHALL. Oh, to God, now: every time.

MARSHALL, *groaning, follows* KAY *out.* FITZPATRICK
and BENNETT *dump the canvas on the first ridge pole.*
GLENDENNING *watches, nodding, smiling.*

BENNETT. We'll have some trouble here.

FITZPATRICK. What's that?

BENNETT. Running the guys back to the house.

FITZPATRICK. As a matter of topicality. And (*Indicating* GLENDENNING.) between ourselves. What are we going to fasten them to?

They're unlacing the bag, getting the canvas out, obviously familiar with the job. KAY and MARSHALL return with the third bag of canvas, for the rear end of the tent.

BENNETT. You remember yesterday?

FITZPATRICK. Do I not?

BENNETT. After we'd put the poles up and you'd gone back to the yard?

FITZPATRICK. I do. Work for me, Benny, at least, had finished.

BENNETT. He had Kay and myself knocking stakes into . . . Can you guess?

FITZPATRICK (*looks round. Then*). I can not.

BENNETT. The beds.

FITZPATRICK. The beds.

BENNETT. Each one disguised, very nearly, as a flower.

FITZPATRICK. The cunning bastard.

BENNETT. Do you remember the time . . . ? (*Spreading the canvas.*)

FITZPATRICK. I do.

BENNETT. When he made us put up that marquee in a gale at Arsham?

MARSHALL (*spreading out the second bag of canvas with* GLENDENNING). The time it blew away?

FITZPATRICK. 'Come back! Come back wid' you! Come back!'

They laugh.

MARSHALL. He's a very funny feller.

FITZPATRICK. He's amusing, right enough.

KAY. Get it out. Get it out.

FITZPATRICK. What? Right here?

They laugh. BENNETT *and* FITZPATRICK *have spread out the canvas, neatly, either side of the ridge pole.*

MARSHALL *and* GLENDENNING *are doing the same.* KAY *is shackling and spreading the third piece.*

Gradually, in spite of their chatter, the pace of work has begun to assert itself.

MARSHALL (*to* GLENDENNING). No, this way, boy. This way.

BENNETT. Have you noticed?

FITZPATRICK. What? What? What?

BENNETT. New. All of it. (*Indicating canvas, which is clean and white.*)

KAY. He's had the canvas specially made.

MARSHALL. He has. You're right.

FITZPATRICK. Just look now at this stitching. Beautiful.

MARSHALL (*to* GLENDENNING). We'd never get a tent like that, Glenny, if you or I were wed.

BENNETT. And how long have you been married?

MARSHALL. Married? Longer than you can count.

BENNETT *laughs disbelievingly.*

FITZPATRICK (*falteringly*). W . . . w . . . w . . . One . . . T . . . t . . . t . . . Two.

They laugh.

They've begun to attach the rings, fastened to the necks of the canvas, round the poles. They're secured with a bolt, like a collar. The collar itself is then shackled to the pulley rope above and the ridge pole underneath. The guys they fasten off to the 'pegs' in the wings.

BENNETT. Been a bachelor, he has, all his life.

MARSHALL. I have not.

FITZPATRICK. A Protestant agnostic, Marshy. (*Indicating* MARSHALL.)

MARSHALL. That I am . . .

FITZPATRICK. Of mixed parentage, and of a lineage so obscure it'd defy a mouse to unravel it – has been married three times already.

MARSHALL. That I have.

FITZPATRICK. Once to a lady bus-conductor.

MARSHALL. That's right.

FITZPATRICK. Once to a greengrocer's right-hand assistant.

MARSHALL. That is correct.

FITZPATRICK. And once, would you believe it, to a nun.

MARSHALL. She was not.

FITZPATRICK. I could have sworn you said she worked in a convent.

MARSHALL. I did. But she wasn't a nun.

FITZPATRICK. Good God. I hate to think what it is, now, you've been up to.

MARSHALL. She worked inside. In the kitchens.

FITZPATRICK. In the kitchens. No wonder, to God, he's so fond of food.

MARSHALL. I am! Eatin', now, is one of life's greatest pleasures.

They laugh. FITZPATRICK *has been fastening off the guys; so has* GLENDENNING. *The others are working at the shackles at the foot of the poles.*

OLD EWBANK *has come on. In his late sixties, wearing a tweed suit: gnarled. An old artisan. He wanders across absent-mindedly, lighting his pipe.*

OLD EWBANK. Have you seen an old piece of rope lying around? . . . About this length.

MARSHALL. What?

OLD EWBANK. Here. About this thick. (*Makes a circle thumb and finger which he adjusts with some care.*)

MARSHALL. No, no. I don't think I have . . .

OLD EWBANK. Water? You couldn't rot it if you tried.

MARSHALL. Oh . . .

OLD EWBANK. No damn stamina. Resilience: nothing. (*He walks off.*)

FITZPATRICK. And who the hell was that?

MARSHALL. I've no idea. (*Laughs.*)

FITZPATRICK. Well, now. This is the funniest place I've ever seen.

KAY. Right, then . . . let's have it up.
FITZPATRICK. Up?
MARSHALL. Up.
FITZPATRICK. Glenny, now – that's you he means.

They laugh.

KAY. Right, then. Shoulder height . . . fasten off.

Between them, having spread out the canvas – two middle pieces and an end – they haul it up to shoulder height, the sections fastened together by the collars. They fasten the ropes off, through holes in the base of the tent poles, and begin to lace the sheets of canvas together.

MARSHALL *sings, begins to whistle, then*:

FITZPATRICK. There was this place, now . . . where was it? . . . where this feller came in with a little can.
BENNETT. A can?
FITZPATRICK. A can. Full of . . . where were we?
MARSHALL. Full of pennies.
FITZPATRICK. Pennies. Asked Ewbank if he could give him one.

They laugh.

Miles from anywhere . . . wanders up . . .
MARSHALL. 'Have you got one, then, mister?' . . . shakes his can.
FITZPATRICK. Ewbank . . .
MARSHALL. Should have seen him.
FITZPATRICK. Green to purple vertigo in fifteen bloody seconds.

They laugh.

Picks up a hammer . . . 'Here, then . . . '
MARSHALL. Fifty bloody stakes.
FITZPATRICK. Shoves them in his hand . . . 'Here, now. There's a penny . . . knock them in, and I'll pop one in your can.'

They laugh.

They're all lacing now, except FITZPATRICK *who has threaded the muslin rope through the loop hanging from the downstage ridge pole.*

GLENDENNING (*lacing*). If my d . . . d . . . d . . . daughter . . .
MARSHALL. Aye, aye, aye. What's that?
GLENDENNING. If my d . . . d . . . d . . . daughter . . .
FITZPATRICK. If his daughter. I never knew you had a daughter, Glenny . . .
MARSHALL. Nor even a mother.
FITZPATRICK. Nor even a dad.

They laugh.

BENNETT. Where did you find her, Glenny?
FITZPATRICK. In your wage packet on a Friday night.

They laugh.

MARSHALL. If you had a daughter, Glenny?
GLENDENNING. I'd like her go . . . g . . . get m . . . m . . . mmmm . . . married . . . in one of these.
MARSHALL. You would?
GLENDENNING. Aye!
FITZPATRICK. On top, Glenny, or underneath?

They laugh.

BENNETT. Wearing it, Glenny? (*Showing him.*) Or underneath?
GLENDENNING (*uncertain*). Aye . . .
FITZPATRICK. Ah, well. One day, Glenny.
GLENDENNING. Aye. (*He smiles shyly.*) Aye.

FITZPATRICK *takes his place at the lacing.*

KAY. Glendenning . . . (*Calls* GLENDENNING *over to take his place.*) Get on with it, Bennett. (*Going.*)
BENNETT. It's always me. Always me. Did you notice that? It's always me he's after.

KAY *has gone off.*

FITZPATRICK (*lacing*). Kay, you know, is a married man.

They look off as they work.

MARSHALL. He is?

FITZPATRICK. He has four daughters, each one of them a bit bigger than himself.

BENNETT. D'you hear that, Glenny? There might be one of them in there for you.

GLENDENNING. Ah . . . I w.w . . . w.w . . . w.w . . . wouldn't want one of Kay's lasses.

MARSHALL. Which one would you like, Glenny?

GLENDENNING. I w . . . w . . . wouldn't mind the one they have in there. (*Gestures at house.*)

They laugh. GLENDENNING *is very pleased.*

BENNETT. She's already spoken for is that, Glenny.

FITZPATRICK. Though I'm thinking if she hasn't set eyes on Glenny here she might very well change her mind.

They laugh.

GLENDENNING (*carried away*). Th . . . th . . . th . . . there's many a slip twi . . . twi . . . twi . . . twixt c . . . c . . . c . . . cup and l . . . l . . . l . . . l . . . lip!

BENNETT. There is, lad. There is.

MARSHALL. Now then, where have I put me rubber hammer? (*Looking anxiously round.*) Me hammer, Glenny. And me glass nails.

GLENDENNING. Sh . . . sh . . . sh . . . shall I look in the cab?

MARSHALL. Aye. Aye, you do that. I'll be in a fix without –

BENNETT. Glass hammer in the cab, Glenny. And rubber nails in the back.

GLENDENNING *goes.*

FITZPATRICK. Aye, now. That's a sight that'd turn a donkey round.

KAY *has come in with a huge bag of walling on his shoulder. Tips it down at one side. With him, too, he's brought the four quarter guys.*

KAY. Come on. Come on. Haven't you finished yet?
Where's Glendenning wandering off to?
MARSHALL. He's fallen in love, Kay.
FITZPATRICK. With the lady of the house.

They laugh.

MARSHALL. She was only a tentman's daughter
But she knew how to pull on a guy.
KAY. Glendenning: come on, here!

GLENDENNING *has come back on.*

MARSHALL. Ay, now. Ay, now. I believe he hasn't found
it.
BENNETT. Did you get it, Glenny?
FITZPATRICK. Don't tell me I'll have to do without.

GLENDENNING *laughs, indicating he's seen the joke.*

MARSHALL. Here I am now, stuck waiting. Can't move
another step without.

GLENDENNING *shakes his head, still laughing, swaying
from side to side, his hands hanging, clenched, before him.*

KAY. Get all the guys fastened off, Glendenning.

*They go on lacing up the canvas which is done by
threading loops from one side through eyelets on the
other. KAY positions and fastens on the quarter guys.*

FITZPATRICK. Ay, now. I'm dying for a smoke.
MARSHALL. Do you think they're watching from the
windows? (*Looking at the house.*)
FITZPATRICK. Do I not?
MARSHALL. Toes and fingers.
FITZPATRICK. Toes and fingers.
KAY. *Glendenning!*
BENNETT. Bloody cold. Just look. (*Shakes his fingers.*)

GLENDENNING *is still standing there, swaying,
grinning. The men turn round to look.* BENNETT *has
finished his lacing and has gone over to finish*
GLENDENNING's.

KAY. What the *hell*, Glendenning, do you think you're doing?

GLENDENNING *still grins*.

MARSHALL. Ay, Glenny, lad, you don't want to get the old feller upset.

GLENDENNING (*pleased*). I w.w.w . . . w.w.w . . . w.w.w . . .

BENNETT. Nay, Glenny . . .

GLENDENNING. You're nnn . . . nnnnn . . . not going to trick mmmm . . . mmmm . . . me again!

KAY. I said fasten off the ropes.

GLENDENNING. You're mmmm . . . going to mmmmm . . . blow it up. Mmmmm . . . Marshall told me.

KAY. God Christ.

KAY *unlaces the walling bag, forestage. He turns away in disgust. The others laugh, more to themselves in order not to provoke* KAY *unduly.*

Bloody lunatics. It'll be the day in this place when they hire a bloody man.

MARSHALL. Now, Glenny. You've got Mr Kay upset.

GLENDENNING *nods, smiling broadly.*

FITZPATRICK. Nay, nay, Glenny, lad. No joking. Mr Kay wants you to examine all the ropes. The stakes are hidden in the flower beds. Just see if they're fastened on . . . One little rope now round each petal.

They laugh. GLENDENNING *smiles confidently, pleased, still swaying, his hands clenched before him.*

KAY. You see how it ends up, Fitzpatrick. Rubber nails. Glass hammers.

MARSHALL. Nay, fair's fair. Glass nails it was.

FITZPATRICK. And a rubber shaft.

They laugh.

KAY. You go, Marshall. You started it.

MARSHALL. What?

The men laugh as MARSHALL sets off to fasten on the guys.

There's only one person does any work round here. (*To GLENDENNING.*) Can't you see? Stuck in front of you. Geee . . . ! (*Smacks his hand against his own forehead.*)

The men laugh, FITZPATRICK doubled up.

KAY (*indicating lacing*). Pull it tight. Pull it tight.
FITZPATRICK (*to MARSHALL*). Pull it tight, Marshy.
MARSHALL. Pull it tight I shall.

BENNETT *laughs.*

They've begun to put in the side poles now: one at each corner of the tent, and four more at the 'quarters', i.e. at the point where the laced edges meet. On to these quarter poles they fasten the quarter guys, already clipped to the 'pegs' by KAY.

FITZPATRICK. Have you seen his wife?

BENNETT *looks round.* FITZPATRICK *gestures at the house.*

Ewbank's.
BENNETT. Don't think I have.

MARSHALL *laughs.*

FITZPATRICK. If I had a wife like that I wouldn't spend my time, now, making tents.
BENNETT. No?
MARSHALL. Concrete shelters, I should think more likely.

They laugh.

FITZPATRICK. What do you say, Kay?
KAY (*putting in the downstage corner pole –
   FITZPATRICK is putting in the other*). Either way, one wife, after a couple of years, is very much like another.
FITZPATRICK. Is that so, now. Is that a fact?
KAY. It is.
FITZPATRICK. You've seen old Ewbank's wife, then, Marshy?

MARSHALL. What? What? Where's that? (*Looking quickly round.*)

They laugh.

FITZPATRICK. Bloody nig-nog, man.

MARSHALL. Oh. Aye.

FITZPATRICK. You don't think much to her, Marshy?

MARSHALL. Do I not? (*Laughs.*)

FITZPATRICK. Seen better, have you, Marshy?

MARSHALL. Seen better? I should think I have.

BENNETT. And where would that be, Marshy?

MARSHALL. Around, I think. Around.

BENNETT. Around? Around where, then, Marshall?

MARSHALL. One or two places I have in mind.

They laugh.

BENNETT. The places Marshall hangs around I'd be surprised if you'd find a woman there at all.

FITZPATRICK. Is that a fact, now, Benny. I'm not so sure of that.

MARSHALL. Won't find Bennett there, now: that's for sure.

FITZPATRICK. Find Bennett some places I wouldn't care to mention.

They laugh.

Seen him one night . . . now, where was it? . . . taking out his dog.

MARSHALL. A dog!

FITZPATRICK. Fine little mongrel . . . Black and white, now . . .

MARSHALL. Wags its tail.

FITZPATRICK. Wags its tail, you're right.

KAY. Right, then . . . are you ready? Let's have you underneath.

The canvas has been stood up now around the edges and the men have started scrambling underneath, moving on all fours to get to the ropes by the poles.

FITZPATRICK (*underneath*). Ay, get off! Get off!

There are cries and laughs as they horse around.

BENNETT (*underneath*). What're you doing . . .
MARSHALL (*underneath*). Aaaah!
FITZPATRICK (*underneath*). Get off! Get off!
BENNETT (*underneath*). Give over!

A burst of laughter.

KAY (*underneath*). Are you ready?
MARSHALL (*underneath*). Aaaah!
KAY (*underneath*). Are you ready?
MARSHALL (*underneath*). Aaaaaaaah! (*A great scream.*)
FITZPATRICK (*underneath*). Okay. We're ready, Kay.
MARSHALL (*underneath*). Aaah. Get off!
KAY (*underneath*). Right. Glendenning. Have you got hold
of a rope?
GLENDENNING (*underneath*). I . . . I . . . I . . . I . . . I've
mmmm . . . got one!
FITZPATRICK (*underneath*). It's not a rope he's got hold
of, Mr Kay.

A burst of laughter from underneath.

KAY (*underneath*). Are you right? Then pull together.
BENNETT (*underneath*). Pull together!

Another burst of laughter.

KAY (*underneath*). Heave . . . Heave . . . Heave!

FITZPATRICK *and* MARSHALL *pull together at the one
pole:* 'Heave! Heave! Heave!'

GLENDENNING *and* BENNETT *pull together at the
second pole:* 'Heave! Heave! Heave!'

KAY *pulls alone at the nearest pole, one rope in either
hand.*

FITZPATRICK (*underneath*). Don't pull too hard, now,
Glenny.
MARSHALL (*underneath*). You might do yourself an hurt.

They laugh, pulling up.

*Slowly the canvas is drawn up to the top of the poles and
the men come into view.*

KAY. All right. Get in your side poles and tighten up your quarter guys.

The ropes are fastened off: threaded through holes in the pole for that purpose, then knotted, the men going to put in the side poles as they finish, hoisting up the edges of the tent.

MARSHALL. Rubber poles, Glenny. Make sure they bend. (*Demonstrates.*)

GLENDENNING. Aye! (*He laughs, fitting in the poles like everyone else.*)

FITZPATRICK at one point, as he goes past, grabs GLENDENNING's backside, off-hand, whistling.

Aaaah!

BENNETT. Keep at it, Glenny.

MARSHALL. Never knew you were fond of animals, then, Bennett.

FITZPATRICK. Don't think he is, to tell the truth.

MARSHALL. Persecution.

FITZPATRICK. Persecution.

KAY. All right. All right. Just get 'em in.

FITZPATRICK. Get 'em in, there, Marshy.

MARSHALL. Get 'em in, I shall.

KAY has started 'dressing-off' the ropes, i.e. wrapping them off, naval fashion, around the foot of the poles.

FITZPATRICK (*sings*). It's that man again . . . It's that man again. (*Whispers urgently to GLENDENNING.*) Glenny! Glenny! Glenny!

Gestures to GLENDENNING: aproaching danger, trouble, watch it, careful . . . burlesque. Whistles shrill, toneless tune.

EWBANK has come in. Stands there, watching, intent.

FITZPATRICK (*sings drunkenly as he works*). 'I was staggering home one night . . .'

MARSHALL (*sings*). 'As sober as a newt . . .'

FITZPATRICK. 'When I should see a sight
    You'd think was rather cute . . . '

MARSHALL joins in the chorus.

MARSHALL.
    '*White* elephants, *pink* elephants,
    Hanging on the wall . . .
    O . . . oooo . . . oh, what a palaver,
    Fifty-one feet tall . . . '
EWBANK (*to* BENNETT). That's not some bloody field
    you're digging up. Just look at this here. Go steady, man!
    Go steady! Kay! (*Presses in divot.*)
KAY. Right . . . (*Dressing downstage pole.*)
EWBANK (*to* MARSHALL). Walling. Walling! God Christ.
    They stand about as if they were paying *you*!
KAY. Aye . . . Walling.
EWBANK (*to* GLENDENNING). And look! Look! Look!
    Look! Look! Look! Look! Look! Look! Don't walk
    around as if you were at home. God damn and blast. Just
    look at this . . . !
GLENDENNING. I'm . . . I'm . . . I'm . . . I'm . . . I'm . . .
EWBANK. That's all right, then.

*The men have begun to hang the walling, hooking it up
on the rope that underlies and is sewn into the lower edge
of the canvas.*

That's a nice bit of canvas, Kay.
KAY. It is. (*Nods, looking up at it.*)
EWBANK. They don't make them like that no more.
    (*Gestures at tent.*) 'Least, not if I can help it. (*Laughs at
    his own humour.*) It'd be too damn expensive.
KAY. Aye. It would.
EWBANK (*pleased, contemplating*). Would you believe it?
KAY. Aye?
EWBANK. It's the first time I've hired a bit of my own
    tenting. It'll go down in the books you know. Pay meself
    with one hand what I tek out with the other.
KAY. Aye! (*Laughs dutifully.*)
EWBANK. I'll never do it again. Never. Never have to.

KAY. No. Well. It's worth making a splash.

EWBANK. Splash? By God, this is a bloody thunderclap! It's not just the tent I'm paying for. God, Christ. I wish it was. No. No. (*To men.*) Hang it! Hang it! Hang it! Hang it! *Hook it up!* That's what they're there for. (*To KAY.*) Three or four hundred people here. Bloody string orchestra. Waiters. Chef. I could buy four marquees with what I've laid out here . . . Ah, well. That's another matter. (*Looks round, examining canvas.*) Let's hope it keeps fine. Have you got the lining?

KAY. It's on the truck . . .

EWBANK. No marks on it, Kay. And no marks on this either. (*Indicates canvas.*) Four lasses, eh?

KAY. Aye . . .

EWBANK. They'll cost you a packet. If I had four I'd set 'em to work and retire. (*Laughs. Wanders round, examining.*) Four. And I can't even manage one. And none of 'em married?

KAY. No, no. They're still at school.

EWBANK. By God. If you had the benefit of my experience you'd never set a lass at school. God Christ, they're only good for one damn thing. And for that you don't have to read a book.

KAY (*laughing*). Aye.

EWBANK. You've kept your eye on them relieving themselves, have you?

KAY. Aye. They've been all right.

EWBANK. I don't give a damn myself. I've told you that already. But I can't have the old lady looking out of the window and not knowing where to put herself. (*To* MARSHALL.*) Leave that side alone. You want it open to bring the floor in. (*To KAY.*) I noticed on the truck, Kay. That floor costs a bloody fortune. When you put it on you want to load it near the front. If a bit drops off it's done. That's a lovely bit of sewing. (*Looking up.*) Look at that seam. (*Reads.*) 'Made by F.Ewbank to commemorate the wedding of his daughter Claire.' My wife chose it.

KAY. The tent?

EWBANK. The bloody name, Paul. That's another of her choices . . .

BENNETT. Shall we get the battens in, Kay?

KAY. Aye. Start fetching them in. And watch the walling.

The men, as they finish off the walling, leaving the one side open, go off to fetch in the battens which they begin to lay out on the floor.

BENNETT has raised the muslin ridges a few inches, fastening them off to enable the battens to go underneath. The ropes for raising these are threaded by FITZPATRICK and BENNETT before the canvas is raised.

CLAIRE has come in. Wanders round. FITZPATRICK whistles a tune.

EWBANK. Do you know how many tents we have out this week?

KAY. Quite a lot, I know.

EWBANK. Thirty-four. And that's just about the lot. If the wind gets under this we'll have some trouble. It blows like a bloody hurricane up here.

KAY. It's a lovely view.

EWBANK. Aye. It is. Whenever you can see it. At one time, do you know, there was nothing in that valley but a farm, a mill, and half a dozen houses. And what're you doing out here you wouldn't be better doing somewhere else?

CLAIRE has been wandering round the edges of the tent, looking around, slow . . . only now has she been noticed by EWBANK.

CLAIRE. They're coming out to have a look. (*To* KAY.) See how you're getting on.

EWBANK. We're all right. We don't need no helpers. (*Looks off.*)

CLAIRE (*to* KAY). Best to keep him on his toes.

KAY (*laughs*). Aye. (*He is dressing the second pole.*)

EWBANK. They don't need any supervision. Not with Kay. How long've you been with me? Three years. That's about as long as anybody in this place. They don't stay long. I employ anybody here, you know. Anybody who'll work. Miners who've coughed their lungs up, fitters who've lost

their fingers, madmen who've run away from home.
(*Laughs*.)

As the men go in and out they gaze over at CLAIRE,
FITZPATRICK *still whistling his tune whenever he
appears*.

They don't mind. They know me. They can soon get shut.
I've the biggest turnover of manual labour in this town. I
take on all those that nobody else'll employ. See that? (*He
indicates the inscription on the tent*.)

CLAIRE. You'll look well if we put it off.

EWBANK. Put it off? You'll not get this chance again. Not
from me. Not from him either. (*He thumbs off, to* KAY.)
She's marrying a bloody aristocrat, Kay. He's so refined if
it wasn't for his britches he'd be invisible.

CLAIRE. Not like somebody else we know . . .

EWBANK. Oh, she doesn't mind. Frank by name and frank
by nature. If they don't like it they soon get shut. Have
you ever seen a straight line, Bennett?

BENNETT. A straight line?

EWBANK. Well I have, man, and that's not one of them.
(*He indicates the rows of battens they're laying across the
floor*.) By . . . ! Just look at this. Grass. Grass. Fitzpatrick!

FITZPATRICK. Yes, sir.

EWBANK. Don't bloody well sir me or I'll fetch you one
round your ear. I'm not too old. Rest them . . . *rest* them
. . . gently. (*To* KAY *and* CLAIRE.) The trouble I take.
What for? I might as well be shoving up a circus. (*Then,
looking up at the tent*.) I'm going to like this tent. Do you
know? I'm going to like it, very much.

PAUL *has come in and had a look around, hands in
pockets*.

PAUL (*to* EWBANK). Do you know. For one minute there, I
thought I'd come in to find you working.

EWBANK. I am working.

PAUL. I heard you. From the house.

EWBANK. My work's done here. I'm a bloody artisan, I am.
Not a worker. (*To* KAY.) He's never believed that, Kay.

And he's a . . . Well, I don't know what he is. He's
supposed to be a summat.

PAUL (*to* KAY). I'm a drain on his pocket for one thing. He
must have told you that.

EWBANK. Aye. For one thing. And as for another . . . Aye,
well. Least said, soonest mended. (*To* MARSHALL.) Have
you got that level? I don't want no ups and downs.

PAUL (*to* CLAIRE). How are you feeling?

CLAIRE. All right. (*Laughs.*)

PAUL. I don't know. (*Thumbs at* EWBANK *behind his back
then looks up at the tent.*)

CLAIRE. It's going to be very nice.

PAUL. Lovely.

CLAIRE (*gesturing at tent*). Why, what's the matter with it?

PAUL. Nothing.

CLAIRE. Nothing.

PAUL (*broadly*). We don't get married every day.

CLAIRE. Let's all thank God for that.

PAUL (*to* KAY). I'll give you a hand if you like.

KAY. Well, I don't know . . .

PAUL (*broadly*). I've done it before. I know a bit about it.
(*Gestures at* EWBANK.) When I was younger he used to
let me help him, for half a crown an hour. Did the work
of three men. Quite a saving.

KAY. I reckon it must have been at that.

PAUL. Well, then. Let's set about it. (*He goes, joining the
men fetching in the battens.*)

EWBANK (*to* KAY). I'm off in. I'll leave you to it before the
rest of 'em arrive. (*Gestures at house.*) Is there ought you
want while I'm at it?

KAY. No, no. We'll be all right.

EWBANK (*to* CLAIRE). Working under t'boss's eye. They
none of them like it.

CLAIRE. That's going to be the floor, then.

EWBANK. That's right. This time tomorrow you'll be
dancing over it light as a feather.

CLAIRE. Let's hope you're right.

EWBANK. Nay, damn it all. I wish I had my time over
again, I do. (*To* KAY.) I'm off in, then. (*To* CLAIRE.) Are
you coming with me?

CLAIRE. I think I better.

EWBANK (*to* KAY). Here, come with me, lad. I'll show you what I mean with that bloody load . . . (*Going.*)

KAY glances round then follows EWBANK who goes out with his arm absent-mindedly round CLAIRE's shoulders.

PAUL has come in with his battens: he's followed by GLENDENNING, laying them side by side.

PAUL (*to* GLENDENNING). What's your name, then?

GLENDENNING. G . . . G . . . G . . . G . . . Glenny!

FITZPATRICK. That's Glenny.

MARSHALL. He's a bit soft in the head.

GLENDENNING. I . . . I . . . I . . . I . . . Aye. I am. (*He laughs.*)

BENNETT. Takes all sorts to make a world.

PAUL. That's right. It does. What do you think of this one, then? (*Indicates tent.*)

BENNETT has started to bring in the sections of polished floor, beginning to lay them on the battens.

FITZPATRICK. A bit of all right, boy.

MARSHALL. Your old man can make a tent when he wants to.

PAUL. That's right. He can.

FITZPATRICK. There's not many of them around these days.

PAUL. What's that?

FITZPATRICK. Butterflies with caps on.

They laugh.

PAUL (*to* GLENDENNING). Will you give us a lift with that?

GLENDENNING. Aye. Aye! I will.

PAUL. Do you like working here, Glenny?

GLENDENNING. I . . . I . . . I . . . Aye!

PAUL. Yes?

GLENDENNING. Aye . . . I . . . I . . . I . . .

MARSHALL (*sings*). Ay, yi, yi, yi . . . Ay, yi, yi, yi . . .

GLENDENNING. I . . . I . . . I couldn't nnnnnn . . . get a job anywhere else.

PAUL. There's not many places.

GLENDENNING. They w . . . w . . . w . . . won't have you if you're o . . . o . . . off your head.

PAUL. Are you off your head?

GLENDENNING. Aye! (*Laughs pleasantly.*)

FITZPATRICK. You'd never have believed it.

They laugh.

GLENDENNING (*to* PAUL). W . . . w . . . w . . . what do you d . . . d . . . d . . . do, then?

PAUL. Me?

GLENDENNING. F . . . f . . . f . . . for a living.

PAUL. Well, I'm a sort of a . . . No, no. I'm a kind of . . . I don't do anything at all as a matter of fact.

GLENDENNING. Oh, aye!

PAUL. You fancy a bit of that, do you?

GLENDENNING. Aye! (*Laughs.*)

MAURICE *comes in.*

PAUL. Ah, well, Glenny. Each one to his trade.

GLENDENNING. I . . . I . . . I . . . I . . . I'd like to give it a g . . . g . . . g . . . go, though! (*Laughs.*)

PAUL. Aye, well. That's a privilege few of us can afford, Glenny.

MAURICE *has come in while they're working, wandering round until he comes to* PAUL.

MAURICE *wears a jacket and flannels, a bit crumpled. He's tall, perhaps with a moustache: fairly ordinary and straightforward.*

FITZPATRICK. Can we do anything then, to help?

MAURICE. Oh, I belong here as well. (*To* PAUL, *casual.*) I thought I better warn you. There's your Grandad on his way.

PAUL (*carrying on working*). Aye. (*He's bringing in and laying sections of polished floor.*)

MAURICE. Have you seen her anywhere around?

PAUL. She was here just now. A few minutes ago.

MAURICE. This is where all the doo-dah's going to be?

PAUL. Seems so.

MAURICE. I can't see why we couldn't have had it in the house.

PAUL. He says there wasn't room.

MAURICE. There seems plenty room to me.

PAUL. You know Frank.

MAURICE. By name and nature.

They laugh.

I suppose it means a lot to him.

PAUL. A bit of his own tenting over his head.

MAURICE. I suppose it does. You haven't got a fag, have you?

PAUL. I'm working. (*To* MARSHALL.) Have you got a fag to spare?

MARSHALL. Me? No. Never. (*Scandalized, he turns to* BENNETT.)

BENNETT (*instant*). No. Not one at all.

FITZPATRICK. Here. Have one of mine.

PAUL. This's the blushing bridegroom.

FITZPATRICK. I thought as much.

MAURICE (*lights up from* FITZPATRICK). I'll fetch you one out of the house if you'll hang on.

FITZPATRICK. S'all right. Just put it on me wages.

They laugh.

MAURICE. Good God. (*Coughs.*)

FITZPATRICK. S'all right. I make them up meself. Good Irish baccy, there is, wrapped up in that.

MARSHALL. Swept up, that is, from some of the best bar-rooms in the town.

They laugh, still working.

FITZPATRICK. No, no, now. He's having you on.

MAURICE. Let's hope you're right. (*To* PAUL.) If I didn't feel so exhausted I'd have given you a hand.

PAUL. I know the feeling.

MAURICE. I don't know. What are we supposed to do in here, for instance?

PAUL (*shrugs*). Dance around. Look jolly.

MAURICE (*surreptitiously putting out cigarette*). It's a lot of fuss.

PAUL. It may never happen again. You might be lucky.

MAURICE. Aye. Let's hope you're right . . . What's the matter with him?

While they've been talking, GLENDENNING has gone out and returned carrying his fourteen-pound sledgehammer, proudly, over his shoulder. Now, smiling, he marches up and down for PAUL's benefit.

PAUL. He's a . . . Well done, Glenny.

GLENDENNING (*pleased*). Aye!

KAY has returned; with him are OLD EWBANK and OLD MRS EWBANK, in her sixties, a small, practical, homely person.

OLD MRS EWBANK (*to KAY*). If we're in the way just let us know . . .

KAY. No, no. It's all right by me.

FITZPATRICK (*calling to GLENDENNING*). Hup, two, three, four . . . Right a . . . a . . . a . . . about—*turn!* By God. They ought to make him a bloody general.

OLD MRS EWBANK. You're having a look as well, Maurice?

MAURICE. Surveying the scene of battle.

OLD MRS EWBANK. Oh, now. Get on.

MAURICE. Best to take precautions.

PAUL drifts back to work.

OLD MRS EWBANK. We're having a struggle – now he's seen the tent – to keep him retired. (*Indicating OLD EWBANK whose arm she holds.*)

OLD EWBANK. What?

OLD MRS EWBANK (*shouting*). We have a struggle keeping you retired.

OLD EWBANK (*to MAURICE*). Good God. I am. We've never had this damn fuss before.

OLD MRS EWBANK. It'll sink in, don't worry.

FITZPATRICK (*in background*). Hup, two, three, four . . .

Hup, two, three, four . . . Lee . . . eeeeft wheeee –
eeeeeeel!

KAY. Glendenning, for Christ's sake. Put that hammer
down.

MARSHALL. You want to watch how you speak to him,
Kay. Or he'll fetch you one with that right over the head.

Nudges PAUL.

KAY (*to GLENDENNING*). Come on. Come on, now. Let's
have this floor down.

*Gently, KAY takes the hammer from him. Smiling,
pleased, GLENDENNING joins the others.*

FITZPATRICK. The army's the place for you, Glenny, all
right.

MARSHALL. Frighten the bloody enemy to death.

OLD EWBANK *has crossed to BENNETT, who is
working assiduously at the floor, and continues to do so.*

OLD EWBANK. You know what I used to be?

BENNETT. What? (*Looks up startled.*)

OLD EWBANK. Rope-maker. (*Pauses for effect.*) You see
all the ropes that hold up this tent?

BENNETT. What? Aye . . . (*Looks up.*)

OLD EWBANK. I made 'em!

BENNETT. That's very good.

OLD EWBANK. No. No. Not for good. The ones I made're
all worn out. Started making tents in my old age. Passed it
on.

BENNETT (*working*). Ah. Yes.

OLD EWBANK. You haven't seen the old man?

BENNETT. Old man?

OLD EWBANK. The gaffer. (*Waits for BENNETT to nod,
mystified.*) That's my son. He owns all this now. He made
it.

BENNETT. Aye?

OLD EWBANK. The tent.

BENNETT. Aye . . .

OLD EWBANK (*suddenly*). Ropes. That's my trade. Nowt
like it.

PAUL (*calling*). I should get him out of here, Gran. Something's likely to fall on his head.

A section of floor, in fact, has narrowly missed OLD EWBANK's *head.*

OLD MRS EWBANK. I will. I will . . . I never knew you were employed here, Paul.

PAUL. I don't know . . . Got to find your natural level, Gran.

OLD MRS EWBANK. I've heard that before, I think, somewhere else —

PAUL. Aye. I believe you have. (*Laughs.*)

OLD EWBANK (*to* BENNETT). The best education money can buy. That's my grandson. Oxford. Cambridge. University College. All the rest. Ask him about anything and he'll come up with an answer.

BENNETT. Oh. Aye . . .

OLD EWBANK. Not got his father's skill.

FITZPATRICK (*joining in*). No?

OLD EWBANK. Sure? I am. He couldn't thread a needle. Have you seen the way that canvas is cut? (*To* OLD MRS EWBANK.) . . . What is it?

KAY. Come on, Fitzpatrick. Let's see you stuck in.

OLD EWBANK. I've come up for the wedding. Otherwise I wouldn't be here.

BENNETT. Ah, yes.

OLD MRS EWBANK (*to* OLD EWBANK). It'll soon be time for dinner.

OLD EWBANK. I'll what?

OLD MRS EWBANK (*shouting*). Dinner.

OLD EWBANK. Good God, we've only just got up.

They go out slowly, OLD MRS EWBANK *taking his arm.*

FITZPATRICK. A fine old man.

MARSHALL. One of the great old-timers.

BENNETT (*to* PAUL). He has a very high opinion of yourself.

PAUL. Has he? I know the thing you mean.

They laugh.

MAURICE (*to* PAUL). I'll be off then. See you in the house.
(MAURICE *goes.*) Thanks for the cigarette.
FITZPATRICK. Not at all. (*To* PAUL.) A college man.
PAUL. Yes?
FITZPATRICK. Yourself. I could see it at a glance.
PAUL. Well, then. That's pretty good.
FITZPATRICK. I've always fancied that, you know, myself.
Books. Study. A pile of muffins by the fire.
MARSHALL. A pile of what?

They laugh.

FITZPATRICK. And the bridegroom feller. The one that's
such a great one with the cigarettes.

They laugh.

PAUL. A doctor.
FITZPATRICK. A doctor! By God.
MARSHALL. Fitzie's always fancied himself as that.
FITZPATRICK. Aye. The stethoscope is my natural weapon.
There's not many a thing, now, that I couldn't find with
that.

They laugh.

Most of the floor is now in, though GLENDENNING *and*
KAY *could still be bringing in the last,* BENNETT,
MARSHALL, FITZPATRICK *and* PAUL *going round*
fitting the polished sections into place, on top of the
battens.

And your sister's been a nurse?
PAUL. That's right.
FITZPATRICK. Ah, yes. A hospital, now. You can't go
wrong with that.
PAUL. And yourself?
FITZPATRICK. Me? Why, I'm like the rest of them.
MARSHALL. An honest working-man.
FITZPATRICK. That's right.
MARSHALL. Born and bred in Ireland!
FITZPATRICK. Like every one before me.
PAUL. And . . . (*Indicating* MARSHALL.)

MARSHALL. Marshall.

FITZPATRICK. It's the funniest Irish name I've ever heard.

MARSHALL. My mother was a decent Irish woman.

FITZPATRICK. That's not what she told him, now, when she met his grand old man.

They laugh.

BENNETT (*at a gesture from* PAUL). Oh, I'm good old English stock.

MARSHALL. Stock, did he say?

FITZPATRICK. English born, English bred:
Long in the leg, and thick in the head.

They laugh.

BENNETT. Done a bit of everything.

MARSHALL. He has. And everybody, too.

They laugh.

BENNETT. And I end up in a place like this.

PAUL. Why's that?

BENNETT. I don't know.

MARSHALL. He likes the fresh air: coming through the windows.

BENNETT. Fresh air. (*Laughs.*) You get fresh air all right, inside that cab.

MARSHALL. Empire-builders! That's us!

They laugh.

The floor now is laid, smooth squares of parquet that slot together over the battens.

The men pause, resting.

BENNETT (*tousles* GLENDENNING's *hair*). How's old Glenny? He's the only one of us that doesn't hold a grudge.

GLENDENNING. Ay . . . ay . . . Aye! (*Laughs.*)

BENNETT. Glass hammers and rubber nails. All day long. Never remembers.

MARSHALL. Does it in his sleep I shouldn't wonder.

GLENDENNING. I . . . I . . . I . . . Aye! I do!

MARSHALL. Nearly caught him this morning sticking stakes in your dad's green grass.

FITZPATRICK. Aye. We did. That'd have put the kibosh on it, Glenny!

BENNETT. He's a good lad at knocking in stakes. You should see him with that hammer. Isn't that right, Glenny?

GLENDENNING. Aye! (*Laughs.*)

MARSHALL. Hits it once in every four.

FITZPATRICK. Damn great pit you find, with a little stake sticking up inside.

BENNETT. He's a good lad.

KAY (*coming back*). Have you finished off that flooring? Bennett. Fitzpatrick. Can you carry in the lining?

FITZPATRICK. Nay, steady on, Kay. We've had no snap for hours.

KAY (*getting watch out*). Get the lining in, then you can have it. Best get it under cover, then we'll be all right.

FITZPATRICK. Ah, come on, Glenny . . .

MARSHALL. And where's he been the last half hour?

FITZPATRICK. Tipping it back, no doubt, with number one . . . (*Mimes drinking.*)

They laugh. KAY *takes no notice.*

KAY. Marshall. Come on. Let's have you . . . (*As* PAUL *makes to follow.*) There's your mother looking for you outside . . .

From outside come FITZPATRICK, MARSHALL, *etc., saying, 'Morning . . . Good morning', and* MRS EWBANK's *pleasant reply, 'Morning . . .'*

MRS EWBANK comes in as men leave: a pleasant, practical-looking woman in her middle forties, not smart but certainly not dowdy.

PAUL. We were just fetching in the lining . . .

MRS EWBANK (*looking around*). I thought I'd just pop out . . . Don't worry. I won't get in the way. It's not often I see one of your father's tents go up.

PAUL. No . . . I suppose not.

MRS EWBANK. It's going to look very grand.

PAUL. So they say.

MRS EWBANK. How have they been getting on?
(*Indicating the men who've gone outside.*)

PAUL. All right.

MRS EWBANK. This wood . . . (*Walking over the floor.*) A few years back one man got a splinter in his hand, left it unattended . . .

PAUL. Turned septic . . .

MRS EWBANK (*looks up*). He had to have one of his fingers off.

PAUL. Dangerous job.

MRS EWBANK. Yes.

She walks on after a moment, looking round. Sees inscription overhead, on the canvas.

I didn't know he'd written that.

PAUL. All done by stencils.

MRS EWBANK. Is that it? (*Gazes up at it.*)

PAUL. Takes it all to heart.

MRS EWBANK. Yes. He does. (*Pause.*) Why? Don't you like it? (*Casual, pleasant.*)

PAUL. I don't know. (*Shrugs, laughs.*) I suppose I do . . . Frank by name . . . (*Imitates EWBANK's voice.*)

MRS EWBANK. But not by nature.

PAUL. No?

MRS EWBANK. No.

From outside come the voices of the men.

FITZPATRICK (*off*). To you . . . (*Sing-song.*)

MARSHALL (*off*). To me . . .

FITZPATRICK (*off*). From me . . .

MARSHALL (*off*). From you . . .

FITZPATRICK (*off*). Here you are, Glenny . . . Ooooops!

Laughter off.

MRS EWBANK. Is there anything we can get them?

PAUL. Probably a pot of tea would go down very well.

Pause.

MRS EWBANK. Are you going off, then?
PAUL. Off?
MRS EWBANK. When all this is over.
PAUL. Suppose so.
MRS EWBANK. Where to?
PAUL. Don't know . . .

Pause.

MRS EWBANK. Suppose you'll let us know.
PAUL. Yep.
MRS EWBANK. Well, then . . . I'll see about the tea.
PAUL. Don't worry . . . (*Holds up his hands.*)
MRS EWBANK. No, no. (*She smiles.*)

She goes out as the men come in, bringing three bags of muslin with them.

FITZPATRICK (*off*).
I knew a man called Glenny
Who went to spend a penny:
He got inside,
And tried and tried –
But found he hadn't any. (*Entering.*)

The men burst into laughter, putting down the bags, GLENDENNING smiling, pleased.

MARSHALL. There was a man Fitzpatrick . . .
FITZPATRICK. He wouldn't know a poem if he saw one.
MARSHALL. Who sat on an egg to hatch it:
He sat and sat,
BENNETT. And sh . . . at and sh . . . at.
MARSHALL. But found he hadn't cracked it.

They laugh among themselves, KAY coming in last.

KAY. Right, then . . . You can break it up.
FITZPATRICK (*to* PAUL). Kay, you know, is a very conscientious man. Always does as he's told. Keeps strictly to instructions.
KAY. It's a damn good job there's somebody here to do something. (*They're going.*)

MARSHALL. It's right. It's right. Value for money is his motto.

FITZPATRICK (*arm round* GLENDENNING *as they go*). Grub at last, Glenny.

GLENDENNING. Aye!

FITZPATRICK (*winking to* PAUL). You'll see the bloody sparks fly now.

They go, leaving PAUL *alone.*

Their laughter and shouts fade outside.

FITZPATRICK (*off*). Here, Glenny. Have a snap at that!

Laughter.

It grows silent.

PAUL *stands gazing round at the interior, grows abstracted. Sits on bag of muslin, arms resting on knees. Begins to whistle quietly to himself: a slow, rather melancholy tune.*

After a while lights slowly fade.

Curtain.

ACT TWO

The muslin is being taped to the muslin ridges which have been raised to shoulder height. Most of the muslin now has been taped, and most of it has been laced – in the same manner as the canvas before it.

The men work minus GLENDENNING and KAY.

FITZPATRICK. Do you know. I never fasten one of these without thinking of my mother.

MARSHALL and BENNETT laugh.

MARSHALL. Why's that, Fitzie?
FITZPATRICK. I don't know. I don't know. I'd go a long way, now, to find that out.

KAY has come in.

KAY. All right, then. Let's have it out.
FITZPATRICK. Out?
MARSHALL. Out.
FITZPATRICK. Out we shall.

They draw the muslin out on either side: a thin drape in green, yellow, and white, each band of colour is perhaps two feet or eighteen inches in width: the seams are ruched.

There are three pieces in all, corresponding to the three pieces of canvas: one piece between each of the three poles (1 and 2) and the end piece (3) at the back of the stage.

Having laid it out across the floor the men go back to complete the lacing.

MARSHALL (*looking around*). Where's Glenny, then? He's taking a long time to take them cups back.
FITZPATRICK. When you give Glenny a job he likes, he gives it his full attention.

They laugh.

KAY. I wish I could say the same for yourself. Now get on with your lacing.

FITZPATRICK glances at MARSHALL. They laugh.

MARSHALL. Kay. It's lovely stuff. It is. It is . . . Made too, if I'm not mistaken, specially for the occasion.

FITZPATRICK. I remember the first day I came here, now, to work. At the beginning of the summer.

MARSHALL (*looking at the sky*). It's damn near the end of it now.

FITZPATRICK. Except in the army, I'd never seen a tent before.

BENNETT. Aye!

FITZPATRICK. We were driven out of the town, on one of the trucks . . . Up the valley, past a lot of trees and hills. And suddenly . . . looking down . . . this field. Full of tents. White canvas, everywhere you looked.

MARSHALL. Big as a balloon.

FITZPATRICK. Big as an elephant . . . Aye.

They work for a moment in silence. Then:

When we got down there, and we got out of the cab . . .

MARSHALL. One of the favourites . . . Not riding on the back.

FITZPATRICK. I stood there, looking up at them and thinking, 'It's a damn great pity it is, to take them down at all.'

MARSHALL. I remember that day very well. Almost four hours before he did a stroke of work himself.

They laugh.

KAY. Fitzpatrick, get on with your bloody lacing.

MARSHALL *and* FITZPATRICK *exchange glances, then laugh.*

MARSHALL. Four daughters!

They laugh.

FITZPATRICK *has begun to sing as he works.*

MARSHALL. Where were you working, then, Kay, before you came to Ewbank's?

KAY. I was working.

BENNETT. Kay was in the nick. Isn't that right?

KAY *doesn't answer.*

MARSHALL. Well, I never knew that. Is that right, then?
BENNETT. It is.

FITZPATRICK stops singing.

FITZPATRICK. In the lock-up, Kay, were you?

KAY doesn't answer but continues lacing.

MARSHALL. And what was he in for? If that's not the wrong thing to ask.
BENNETT. I don't know. You better ask him.

MARSHALL laughs.

FITZPATRICK. Come on, now, Kay. What did they put you in for?
KAY. Get on with your lacing.
MARSHALL. Ah, come on, now, Kay. Aren't you going to give us a clue?
FITZPATRICK. Was it animal, vegetable, or mineral?

They laugh.

KAY. I was sent up . . .
MARSHALL. Aye?
KAY. For not minding my own business. (*Factual: goes on working without being distracted.*)
FITZPATRICK. Is that a fact? (*To the others.*) God damn it: we deserve to be put inside an' all.

They laugh.

MARSHALL. Kay . . . you . . . me . . . Glenny.

Following KAY's lead, they hook the corners and quarters of the muslin up, in the same fashion as the canvas was first raised on the 'quarter' and corner side poles. It hangs in a great loop now across the flooring.

FITZPATRICK. Ah, it's a great life if you can afford it.
MARSHALL. And what, now, is that?
FITZPATRICK. A wife . . . home . . . children.
MARSHALL. Hot chocolate.
FITZPATRICK. Hot chocolate.
MARSHALL. Toes . . .

FITZPATRICK. Toes . . .
MARSHALL. Fingers.
FITZPATRICK. Fingers.
KAY. All right, then . . . Let's have it up.

The men have scrambled underneath, the muslin billowing as they reach the ropes.

Are you ready?
BENNETT. Ready . . .
MARSHALL. Ready, Mr Kay.
FITZPATRICK. Ready, Mr Kay; you're right.

They laugh.

KAY. Right, then . . . together.

They haul up the muslin, fastening it off.

MARSHALL. *Christopher!* Just look at that!

GLENDENNING *has come in, looking pleased, standing to one side and eating, so that they all might see, a very large bun.*

As they turn to look across he smiles dazedly at them, eating.

FITZPATRICK. Eating on the job, Mr Kay! Mr Kay! Glendenning here is eating a big fat bun.
BENNETT. Did you nick it from the house, Glenny?
GLENDENNING. No . . . n . . . n . . . no. (*He shakes his head.*)
FITZPATRICK. Then where . . . then what . . . then what*ever* have you done with ours, Glenny?

GLENDENNING *happily shakes his head.*

MARSHALL. He's eaten it!

GLENDENNING, *happy, dazed, smiling, still eating, shakes his head again.*

BENNETT. I don't understand, Glenny. Do you mean to say, the lady of the house . . .
MARSHALL. Herself . . .

BENNETT. Gave you a bun? And didn't give us one – as well?

GLENDENNING. I . . . I . . . I . . . Aye! (*Nods happily, putting the last large fragment into his mouth.*)

The men start taping up the muslin to the sides of the tent. It's hung in such a way that it hangs slightly, billowing in, a soft lining to the tent.

FITZPATRICK. Well, I'll be damned. I will.

GLENDENNING *nods at them, smiling.*

MARSHALL. And not a bite to share between us.

KAY. Glendenning, make yourself useful. Pick up the bags.

GLENDENNING *still gazes at them, smiling.*

Glendenning. Have you heard?

GLENDENNING. Aye! (*Happily goes to work.*)

FITZPATRICK. Well, I'll be damned. I *will* be damned. All this time I've been thinking: Glenny is a friend of mine. If I have *one* friend in this big wide world, it's Glenny. All the rest I can do without.

GLENDENNING. I . . . I . . . I . . . Aye!

MARSHALL. It's a great and terrible disappointment. I shall never get over this. I shan't. (*He gets out his handkerchief, dabs his eyes, wipes his nose . . .*)

FITZPATRICK. Aye. This really is the end. For sure.

KAY. Keep your folds even. Space it out. Space it.

MARSHALL. Work your fingers to the bone. Break your back. Crack your head. And out there, all the time, Glenny is cramming his face with buns. It's more than anyone could stand.

GLENDENNING *is pleased with all this, no more so than with* MARSHALL's *attempts at crying: he watches, smiling, anxious for them to go on.*

KAY (*going*). Bennett . . . Give me a hand in with the furniture.

BENNETT. I think Kay's greatest disappointment in life –

prison sentence apart – is for him not to see me working – hard. (*Follows* KAY *out.*)

FITZPATRICK *signals* MARSHALL.

FITZPARRICK. By God, and I could have done with that bun, Marshy. My stomach's trembling here from lack of food.
GLENDENNING (*laughing*). Aye!
MARSHALL. When I get a bun myself – *which I shall* – not a crumb of it will I give away.
FITZPATRICK. No, no. Not a drop.
MARSHALL. At least, not to a *certain person* whom I shall not go to the trouble of puttin' a name.

KAY *and* BENNETT *come back in carrying white metalwork chairs and tables.*

FITZPATRICK. No, no. That's a fact.
MARSHALL. The one I have in mind has cream on.
KAY (*to* BENNETT). Come on. Let's have some more inside.
BENNETT. Bloody hell . . . (*Groans to himself.*)

KAY *and* BENNETT *go out.*

FITZPATRICK. With a strawberry on top.
MARSHALL. And thick jam inside.
FITZPATRICK. With a touch of apricot.
MARSHALL. About as big as a Christmas pud. (*Shapes it.*)

GLENDENNING, *as he listens, loses his smile. For a while he watches them concernedly then, slowly, he turns away.*

FITZPATRICK. Aye. Aye. I know just the shop. They sell them by the score. God, it takes half an hour to get through one of them.
MARSHALL. And that, mind you, is just the start.
FITZPATRICK. Aye. Aye. The rate we work, the money we earn, we s'll have enough for half a dozen.
MARSHALL. I can just see it, sitting there. Waiting to be eaten up.
BENNETT (*coming in with* KAY, *with another table*). Oh,

now you're not letting them get on top? (*To* GLENDENNING.)

GLENDENNING *is still turned away, slowly picking pieces up.*

MARSHALL. Ah, Fitzie, now. Just look.

FITZPATRICK. He's . . . Why? . . . (*Stepping round so that he can look in* GLENDENNING's *face.*) You're not wishing, now, that you'd given us a bit of that?

KAY *and* BENNETT *go out again.*

MARSHALL. He's wishing now he'd broken off a bit. Perhaps, even, as much as half.

FITZPATRICK. Or more.

MARSHALL. Or more. Come on, now, Glenny . . . I was pulling your leg.

GLENDENNING *is immobilized, standing now with his head hanging down.*

FITZPATRICK. Why, you've gone and made the feller roar.

MARSHALL. I have?

FITZPATRICK. There are tears streaming from his eyes.

MARSHALL. And nose.

FITZPATRICK. And nose.

BENNETT (*carrying in a tin of polish and rag*). You want to leave the lad alone.

GLENDENNING *has begun to shake his head slightly, turned away, wiping his eyes and sobbing.*

KAY (*coming in with another table*). Look out. Look out. He's here.

FITZPATRICK. Kay is ever such a conscientious feller. It just shows the benefits, now, of being put inside. (*Going.*)

They laugh.

FITZPATRICK *goes.*

BENNETT (*crossing to* GLENDENNING). Ah, now, Glenny. Don't take it so much to heart.

GLENDENNING *shakes his head. He goes.*

MARSHALL *laughs.*

BENNETT. You want to leave him alone!

MARSHALL. Jump on your bloody head. (*Faces up to him, then darts away, laughing.*)

EWBANK has come in behind them, watching them.

EWBANK. *Get your boots off that bloody floor!* God Christ. Just look at him. Studs and half a ton of earth sliding about on top of it.

BENNETT is standing at the centre of the polished floor.

Get your boots off, off, off, off, off, off, if you're going to stand on it.

KAY. Bennett. We'll work this side. You work that. (*Indicating BENNETT should take his boots off.*)

BENNETT. Me?

It's evident, though not too much, that EWBANK has had a drop.

MARSHALL. His socks are full of holes, Kay.

FITZPATRICK (*entering with polish*). He hasn't got no socks.

They laugh, starting to polish.

MARSHALL. If he takes his boots off in here there'll not be one of us left alive.

EWBANK (*swaying slightly*). I take it that that lining's not been hung right yet.

KAY. No. No.

BENNETT. Bloody hell . . . (*He's begun to take his boots off, sitting on the polished floor.*)

FITZPATRICK has begun to sing, drunkenly.
GLENDENNING has come back in.

FITZPATRICK. We hash a good night to . . . night . . .

MARSHALL. We'll have a good one to . . . morrow . . .

FITZPATRICK. We hash a few drops to . . . night . . .

MARSHALL. We'll have a few more to . . . morrow . . .

EWBANK (*head craning back*). Aye. That's going to look very nice.

EWBANK *has become aware of* GLENDENNING, *walking, drooped, at a snail's pace.*

KAY. They've been having him on . . .

EWBANK. Ay, ay, ay . . . Do you hear that, now. Do you hear?

FITZPATRICK. Aye. Aye. (*Ruffling* GLENDENNING's *hair.*) You're all right, aren't you?

EWBANK. I'm not having you tormenting that lad. A bloody half-wit. You ought to have more common sense.

MARSHALL. Aye. Aye. We should.

EWBANK (*has tripped up*). God damn and blast . . . Glendenning. Give me a hand with this. (*Picks up the bag he's tripped over.*)

KAY. What's the *matter* with Fitzpatrick?

FITZPATRICK *is doubled up, laughing.*

MARSHALL. It's the smell. Bennett, for God's sake.

BENNETT. My feet are all right.

KAY. What?

BENNETT. I wash them. Every night.

MARSHALL. Soap and water.

FITZPATRICK. Soap and water.

EWBANK *has sent* GLENDENNING *out.*

MARSHALL. You could make a collander of his socks. Just look at them. Bennett, don't you have a wife?

KAY (*to* FITZPATRICK). If you find it so damn funny no doubt you'll tolerate your own.

MARSHALL. No. No. Don't ask him that. I'd rather be annihilated by Bennett than by Fitzpatrick. (*Looks up to the sky.*) If it has to come, O Lord, let it not be at the feet of my friend, Fitzpatrick.

EWBANK. Just watch that floor. Watch it. It's a precious thing is that. (*To* KAY.) I've sent Glendenning down to the shop.

FITZPATRICK (*to* MARSHALL, *polishing*). I hope, not for another tot.

EWBANK. What's that?

FITZPATRICK. I say: he's about the only decent one we've got.

MARSHALL. I hope to God it's nothing lethal: matches or a packet of cigarettes.

MARSHALL and FITZPATRICK laugh, polishing.

EWBANK. Have you levelled off that floor?
BENNETT. We have.

MARSHALL and FITZPATRICK have begun to sing the drinking song in quiet voices.

PAUL has come in, in shirt-sleeves hanging loosely down, his hands deep in his pockets, standing in the door, stooping slightly.

PAUL. I've had me snap. I've had me rest. Now. Where would you like me?
EWBANK (*looking up*). There's nowt in here for you, lad.
PAUL. I don't mind. I'll give a hand.
EWBANK. There's no need.
PAUL. No, no. I understand. Nevertheless . . . I'll do whatever it is I'm able.

He goes to dress the muslin ropes on the main poles.

EWBANK. Marshall. Fetch in the walling. You can start hanging that.

MARSHALL gets up and goes out.

EWBANK (*to KAY*). Keep that evenly spaced there, Kay.
KAY. Aye. We'll have it straight. Don't worry. (*Arranging muslin.*)

EWBANK stands gazing round, a little helpless.

EWBANK. Aye, well . . . (*Looks at his watch.*) I'll look in again in a few minutes. I shan't be long. (*He goes.*)

MARSHALL comes in with the sack containing the muslin walling.

BENNETT (*working with his back to the door*). Has he gone?
MARSHALL. You can breathe again, feller. (*To PAUL.*) No disrespect, mind, to you at all.

PAUL. No. No. None at all.

FITZPATRICK. What're you going to be at the wedding, then?

PAUL. Oh, I don't know . . .

FITZPATRICK (*cheerful*). Not the best man, then?

PAUL. I might well be that.

They laugh.

FITZPATRICK. What did you study at the school, then?

PAUL. Nothing much.

MARSHALL. Nothing much, to God. You better not tell him that. (*Gestures at house.*)

They laugh.

MARSHALL *has got out the muslin walling and starts to hang it.*

FITZPATRICK (*loud*). I've always fancied myself, you know, as a criminal lawyer . . .

MARSHALL. He's very good at that. Knows it from the inside . . .

They laugh.

FITZPATRICK. No, no. I'm too old now, to go to school, and too damn poor to bother.

MARSHALL. But then, you know . . . Talking of criminality . . .

FITZPATRICK. That's right . . .

MARSHALL (*to* PAUL). You were probably not aware that you were working in the presence of one such man himself.

FITZPATRICK. You are. I bet you didn't know it.

MARSHALL. A fair-minded, decent feller like yourself, coming in here, hoping to find himself among his equals. Only to discover, behind his back, that one of *them* had crept in unnoticed.

PAUL (*laughing*). And who's that?

FITZPATRICK. Why, none other than – himself. (*Gestures at* KAY.)

BENNETT. I wish you'd pay a bit more attention to this here. Just look at the bloody floor. (*Polishing.*)

FITZPATRICK. Attention, now. Attention.

KAY (*to* BENNETT). Watch that walling . . . Fitzpatrick. I hope you're going to rub that floor. (*He goes to dress one of the remaining muslin ropes.*)

BENNETT. Oh, God. My bloody back. (*To* PAUL.) Have you ever suffered from rheumatism?

PAUL. I don't think I have.

BENNETT. One of the worst diseases known to man.

FITZPATRICK. Bloody indolence, more likely.

BENNETT. What's that?

FITZPATRICK. I say, you get it all the time.

BENNETT. I do. (*Holds his back, groans.*) God.

FITZPATRICK (*to* PAUL). On the other hand, what we haven't discovered – and speaking purely as a man familiar with nothing but his own profession –

MARSHALL snorts.

is, what crime this person, this man, who has inveigled himself into our presence, what crime it is, precisely, that he's committed.

MARSHALL. I hope it was nothing indecent to do with little girls.

FITZPATRICK. Good God. Crimes of that nature I cannot stand.

MARSHALL. I can't bear to read a word about them in the papers.

FITZPATRICK. I sincerely hope – I sincerely hope, Marshall – that it's nothing I'd be afraid to mention to me mother.

They laugh.

Come on, now, Kay. Between these four walls – or three and a half to be exact – what manner of crime was it that you committed? Were you driven to it by the pressures of the world; or is it simply that you're a rotten *sod*?

They laugh.

Kay is a very hard man. You'll get nothing out of him. He didn't suffer all that, you know, in vain. (*Friendly.*) Isn't that right, Kay?

KAY, *unmoved until now, has gone on with his work, not even looking up. Now, however, he pauses. He looks up very slowly. Then:*

KAY. And what sort of suffering have you done, Fitzpatrick?

FITZPATRICK. Suffering? By God. I'm suffering every day.

MARSHALL *laughs, snorting.*

MARSHALL. All day. Seven days a week. Fifty-two weeks in the year.

KAY. Aye. Between one bottle and another. One bar-room and the next.

FITZPATRICK. Me? I hope you heard all that. I wouldn't touch a drop of liquor.

MARSHALL *snorts again.*

I mean, dropping no names, Kay, and all that there and that, aspersions of that nature would be better cast in a different direction altogether.

FITZPATRICK *gestures at the house.*

KAY. Some people have a grievance. And some of them haven't.

FITZPATRICK. And what is that supposed to mean?

KAY *looks at PAUL, then looks away.*

The others look at PAUL.

PAUL. Don't mind me. I'm easy.

KAY. Bennett. Mind that walling.

FITZPATRICK. Are you frightened of telling us something, Kay?

KAY. If you want to work, Fitzpatrick, work. If not, the best thing you can do is to clear off altogether. (*He returns to hang and arrange muslin walling.*)

FITZPATRICK. Ay. Ay, now. Those are very strong words. (*To MARSHALL.*) Very strong words indeed.

MARSHALL. If it wasn't for the fact that no trade union would have us . . .

FITZPATRICK. I'd repeat that to the man in charge.

MARSHALL. The top official.

FITZPATRICK. Right away.

MARSHALL. Intimidation . . .

FITZPATRICK. Suppression of the right to labour.

KAY. You wouldn't know a piece of work, Fitzpatrick, if you saw it. The bloody lot of you . . . (*Gestures at the house.*) Poor sod.

GLENDENNING *has come in, eating a bar of chocolate.*

FITZPATRICK. Now, then. Now, then. Now, then. What have we got here?

MARSHALL. Come on, now, Glenny. Are you going to let us have a bit of that?

BENNETT. What is it you're eating, Glenny?

GLENDENNING. O . . . O . . . O . . . O . . . Oh, a bit of stuff.

FITZPATRICK. A bit of stuff, is it?

GLENDENNING. Ch . . . ch . . . ch . . . ch . . . ch . . . ch . . .

MARSHALL. And have you brought us some of it back?

GLENDENNING. I . . . I . . . I . . . I . . . I . . . I . . .

MARSHALL (*sings*). Ay, yi, yi, yi . . . Ay, yi, yi, yi . . .

BENNETT. You have, then?

GLENDENNING. Aye!

FITZPATRICK. Chocolate!

GLENDENNING, *happy, hands out pieces of chocolate, breaking them from the bar.*

BENNETT. Ah, he's a good lad is Glenny.

FITZPATRICK. I hope he's washed his hands.

They laugh.

KAY. You better get on with a bit of the walling, Glendenning. (*Looks over at* PAUL.)

MARSHALL. Currying a bit of favour, Kay.

FITZPATRICK. Don't give him any of your sweets, Glenny.

MARSHALL. And don't get too near.

They laugh.

GLENDENNING *starts hanging the muslin wall.*

In the doorway CLAIRE *and* MAURICE *have appeared.*
They stand on the threshold, looking in. They make some
comment to one another and laugh as they watch PAUL
working, dressing the muslin ropes.

MAURICE. Are you enjoying yourself, man?
PAUL. What? (*Looks up.*) I don't know. (*Stands up from the*
floor where he's been kneeling.) I've no idea.
MAURICE (*to* CLAIRE). It comes naturally to hand.
CLAIRE (*indicating drapes*). Shouldn't that be a bit higher?
PAUL. Probably. You want to try?
CLAIRE. I was asking.
PAUL. Jolly good.
MAURICE. She's a bloody authority, man.
KAY. Marshall. Over here.
FITZPATRICK. Watch it, Marshy. Watch it.
MARSHALL. Don't worry, now. I shall.

They laugh. KAY *and* MARSHALL *adjust the muslin.*

FITZPATRICK. And what's it like, then, to be the happy
couple? The blushing bride and the handsome groom?
MAURICE. All right, I suppose.
FITZPATRICK. I was never married myself.

MARSHALL *snorts.*

I could never find the time.

MARSHALL *snorts again.*

MAURICE. No. It is a bit of a problem.
FITZPATRICK (*to* CLAIRE). On the other hand, I could
never find a lady, as beautiful as yourself, who'd be glad
enough to have me.
BENNETT (*calling*). I'd take no notice of Fitzpatrick. He
has a tongue where his brains belong.
FITZPATRICK. I have. It's true. I suffer from over-
stimulation. (*To* MAURICE.) Have you got a fag?
MAURICE. I have. (*Brings out a case.*)
FITZPATRICK. Now. That makes a pleasant change. (*Takes*
one.) I won't smoke it at the present. I'm not allowed.

(*Indicates* KAY *with sly gestures*.) But I assure you: I'll
enjoy it all the same.

MARSHALL. All the greater, now, for saving it till after.

FITZPATRICK *laughs and goes back to work.*

GLENDENNING. Ha . . . Ha . . . Ha . . . Ha . . . Ha . . .
Ha . . . Have you seen . . . mmmmmmmmmm . . . Mister
Ewbank?

MAURICE. Wh . . . what?

CLAIRE (*to* MAURICE). My dad. (*To* GLENDENNING.)
No . . . We haven't.

GLENDENNING. I . . . I . . . I . . . I . . . I . . . I . . . I . . .

MARSHALL (*sings*). Ay, yi, yi, yi . . . Ay, yi, yi, yi . . .

GLENDENNING. I . . . I . . . I . . . I've got some . . .
mmmmmmm . . . tobacco for him.

CLAIRE. I'll give it to him if you like.

GLENDENNING. I . . . I . . . I . . .

MARSHALL (*sings*). Ay, yi, yi, yi . . . Ay, yi, yi, yi . . .

GLENDENNING. I . . . I . . . I'll give it to him.

PAUL. There's not much more now to do.

OLD EWBANK *has come in with a short piece of rope
and wanders round the back of the tent.*

CLAIRE. I don't know. There's a lot of stuff in the house.
He says he wants it bringing out. He's left it a bit late if
you ask me.

PAUL, *having gone back to his work after the last
exchange, has got up and crossed over again to* CLAIRE.

CLAIRE. Still. A bit of improvisation might go a long way
in here.

PAUL. That's right . . .

FITZPATRICK. I heard that. I heard that. A woman who
improvises is never to be trusted.

BENNETT (*calling*). And what sort of woman would you
trust, Fitzpatrick? (*Polishing the floor where he's kneeling
with a rag.*)

FITZPATRICK. Why, Benny, one very much, I think, like
you.

They all laugh, but for BENNETT.

OLD EWBANK. Am I in the way? What? Sitting about in the house. (*He looks vaguely about him, spots* MARSHALL *and goes over.*) Here. Now that's a bit of the rope I made.

MARSHALL. Oh. That's . . . (*Polishing.*)

OLD EWBANK. All by hand. Up and down a rope walk. You wind it up at one end and come up along it with a shuttle. Like this. You can walk up to twenty or thirty miles a day.

MARSHALL. That's a fine bit of rope.

OLD EWBANK. They don't make them like that no more. Machines. A hand-made rope is a bit of the past. (*Gestures up blindly.*) All these: machines.

MARSHALL. Still, they do their job.

MRS EWBANK *has come in.*

OLD EWBANK. Good God, man, I've had one all my life. It's my wife who got me to retire. I'd be in here I can tell you if I had a chance.

MRS EWBANK (*to* CLAIRE *and* MAURICE). I've been looking for him all over . . . Have you finished in here, Paul?

PAUL. Me personally? Or them in general?

MRS EWBANK. You personally, I think.

PAUL. I'm not sure. I'm standing here, I believe, waiting for instructions.

MRS EWBANK. As long as you're not in the way.

PAUL. I think I've been able to lend a little hand.

MRS EWBANK (*to* CLAIRE). Will he be all right in here? (*Gesturing at* OLD EWBANK.)

MAURICE. He'll be all right. Don't worry.

OLD EWBANK. Good God . . . Now what does she want?

EWBANK *has appeared, oblivious it seems to all of them, carrying two long boxes, five or six feet tall, which will be used to enclose the bottom of the poles. He walks to the centre and puts them down. Over his shoulder are three further lengths of muslin which he'll use to drape the poles, and in his coat pocket is a hammer. His mood is one of self-absorption.*

EWBANK. Get out of the bloody way . . . God Christ . . . Walking all over the bloody floor. God damn and blast. Just look at his bloody boots.

MRS EWBANK (*to* CLAIRE). I'll go in, and make some tea. Keep out of trouble. (*She goes.*)

EWBANK's *remarks are directed to no one person in particular.*

OLD EWBANK. Poor? Damn it all, I've never owed a penny to any man!

EWBANK. Put some bloody bags down. Bags. Kay. Get them off here and get it covered. Marshall. Fetch in that other box outside.

MARSHALL, *after a good look round at* FITZPATRICK, *does so. The others begin to cover the floor with the discarded muslin and tent bags.*

OLD EWBANK. When I was sixteen I was working eighteen hours a day.

FITZPATRICK, *softly, has begun to sing his drinking song.*

BENNETT. God, look. I've got a splinter in my foot. (*Examines it, sitting on the floor.*)

EWBANK (*to* KAY). If you've got it covered you can't do any harm. Where have I put it? (*Hunts round for his hammer, finding it in his pocket.*) What's he doing in here? (*Seeing* OLD EWBANK.)

CLAIRE. He's come to show them his rope.

EWBANK. Rope . . . There's a ladder out there, Fitzpatrick.

MARSHALL *has come in with the third box which he places by the third tent pole.* FITZPATRICK *goes to fetch the ladder.*

EWBANK (*calling after him*). And don't put it down until I tell you. (*To* KAY.) Have these been fastened off? (*Indicating poles.*)

KAY. Aye. We've just been doing that.

OLD EWBANK. What's he on about? I'll damn well clip his ear.

MARSHALL (*low to* BENNETT). I wish he bloody would.
EWBANK. What's that? (*Blindly.*)
MARSHALL. I say. It's very soft, this wood.
EWBANK. Keep your fingers off it!

> MARSHALL, *working on the floor, draws his hand away.*
> PAUL, BENNETT, MARSHALL, *and* GLENDENNING
> *are working on the floor.*

OLD EWBANK. When I was twenty-four I earned thirteen
  shillings a week.
CLAIRE. Come on, Grandad . . . (*Goes to take his arm.*)
OLD EWBANK. I was married when I was nineteen. Three
  died. Four survived.

> FITZPATRICK *has come in with the ladder.*

PAUL. Do you want a hand? (*To* CLAIRE.)
MAURICE. We'll manage.

> OLD EWBANK, CLAIRE, *and* MAURICE *go.*

FITZPATRICK. Now, then. Where would you want it?
EWBANK. Here, now. Put it down on that . . . Gently.

> *He has put a bag at the foot of the first pole and*
> FITZPATRICK *brings the ladder to rest against it.*

GLENDENNING. I . . . I . . . I . . . I . . . I . . . I . . . I . . .
MARSHALL (*sings*). Ay, yi, yi, yi . . . Ay, yi, yi, yi . . .

> GLENDENNING *has come up to* EWBANK *with the tin
> of tobacco.*

EWBANK (*to* FITZPATRICK *as he manoeuvres the ladder*).
  Gently, gently. God Christ, do you want to drive it
  through the floor! Gently!
GLENDENNING. I . . . I . . . I . . . I . . .
EWBANK. What? What? What? (*He's busy getting the
  muslin drapery ready to take up the ladder.*)
BENNETT. He's brought you your tobacco, Mr Ewbank.
EWBANK. What? . . . Oh. (*Pauses. Then takes it.*) Aye.
  You're a good lad.
GLENDENNING. I . . . I . . . I . . . I . . .

EWBANK. Did you buy yourself some chocolate?
GLENDENNING. Aye.

MARSHALL *whistles 'Down Mexico Way' refrain.*

EWBANK (*to* FITZPATRICK). Hold it. Hold it. Hold it.
Hold it. God damn and blast . . . (*He has turned to the
ladder and begun to mount it, hammer in one hand,
drapery in the other.*)

All the men now, but for GLENDENNING, *and*
FITZPATRICK, *who is holding the ladder, are working,
watching* EWBANK *at the same time.*

FITZPATRICK (*sings*).
Somebody has had a tipple . . .
Somebody has had a drop . . .
PAUL. I think we've had enough of that
FITZPATRICK. What . . . ?
PAUL. I think we've had enough of it.
FITZPATRICK. I was just . . . (*To* MARSHALL.) I have a
very melodious voice.

BENNETT *snorts.*

MARSHALL. He has. It's right.

FITZPATRICK *shrugs.*

PAUL *goes back to work.*

FITZPATRICK, *so the others can see, sings silently,
mouthing the words hugely.*

KAY. All right, Fitzpatrick. You've had your laugh.
EWBANK (*above*). Hold it. God damn and blast.
FITZPATRICK. No hands! (*Stands with his arms out, one
foot pressed against the foot of the ladder.*)
KAY. Get that bloody floor rubbed up. Glendenning, do you
hear?
GLENDENNING. Aye!

FITZPATRICK *looks up to where* EWBANK *is tacking
the muslin, draping it round the pole.*

MARSHALL. Go on. Go on. It'll be over in a flash.

They laugh.

EWBANK. I'm coming down . . . (*Finishing.*)
PAUL (*having crossed over*). Here. I'll hold it.

FITZPATRICK *hesitates.*

I'll hold it.

PAUL *takes the ladder from* FITZPATRICK *who shrugs.*

EWBANK *comes down the last rungs.*

FITZPATRICK *has gone off, picking up bags, clearing the mess.*

EWBANK (*to* PAUL). If you want summat to do you can fetch the flowers in from outside. Fitzpatrick, I thought I told you to hold this. Carry it over. (*Indicating the next pole.*)
FITZPATRICK (*to* PAUL, *taking it*). Do as the old lad says.
PAUL. I'll hold it. I don't mind. (*To* EWBANK.)
EWBANK. Do you think I don't know what goes on. I've got eyes in my backside I have . . .
FITZPATRICK. He has. I've seen them.
EWBANK. I miss nowt here. Don't worry. Bennett. Fasten the box round this last pole . . .

PAUL *watches him cross to the next pole where* FITZPATRICK *is setting up the ladder. Then he turns and goes.* BENNETT *has begun to fasten the box round the first pole, the end of the muslin, draped round the pole, hung inside. One side of the box is hinged, like a door, and round the top fits a kind of round collar or tray, hinged too so that it can fit round the pole.*

EWBANK (*mounting the ladder and beginning to hang the second drape*). Glendenning, help to bring in those flowers. Marshall . . .
MARSHALL. Yes, sir!
EWBANK. When you've got your boots off start at that end polishing the floor.
FITZPATRICK. Good God. It's come at last.
MARSHALL. My boots?

FITZPATRICK. He can't mean it.

EWBANK. Get on with it. Get on . . . (*To* FITZPATRICK.) Hold that ladder!

MARSHALL *takes off his boots and begins, at the farthest end, with a mop and duster, to polish the floor.*

Thousands on his education . . . Bloody flowers. Six bob an hour.

KAY *is finishing off the floor and then adjusts the drapes round the walls.*

PAUL *has begun to carry in the flowers, arranging them round the box that* BENNETT *has fastened.*

FITZPATRICK (*to* EWBANK). Can you see up there all right?

EWBANK. I can see, all right. Don't worry.

FITZPATRICK. Which pair, now, is it that you're using?

MARSHALL, BENNETT, *and* FITZPATRICK *laugh.*

EWBANK. Hold it, now. I'm coming down . . . Bennett. Let's have the other box round here. God damn and blast. I can see somebody's feet marks from up here. Kay, just watch it . . . Boots. Boots. Boots, man. Boots. (*As he reaches the ground.*) Here, Fitzpatrick. You take it. Hammer. Tacks. Drape. Have it up on that last pole.

FITZPATRICK. Me?

MARSHALL *has begun to laugh, giggling.*

EWBANK. I'm not talking to the bloody floor?

FITZPATRICK. No . . .

EWBANK. Right, then. Get on with it. (*To* KAY.) I'm not so bloody silly as I look.

MARSHALL. No, no. He's probably right, at that.

EWBANK. What's that?

MARSHALL (*indicating floor where he's polishing*). I say, there's a hell of a shine, on that.

EWBANK (*to* KAY). You'll find the tables out there. The chairs as well.

KAY (*going*). Glendenning. Here, give me a hand.
EWBANK (*looking up at the interior*). I shall never do it
again. I shan't. Never . . .

BENNETT *is fastening the box and its collar round the
second pole.*

FITZPATRICK *has carried the ladder over to the third
pole and begun to climb it, tacking up the drape.*

OLD MRS EWBANK *comes in carrying a pot plant with
a splendid flower.*

PAUL *is arranging the flowers now round the second pole
as* BENNETT *finishes the box.*

MARSHALL *polishes the floor, starting the farthest end
and now working towards the middle, leaving it clear
behind him. The whole interior now has slowly fallen into
shape, a gentle radiance coming through the drapes.*

KAY *and* GLENDENNING *have begun to bring in the
rest of the white, wrought-iron tables: they're small and
neat, with chairs to match. They set them round the edge
of the floor.*

OLD MRS EWBANK. Where shall I put it?
FITZPATRICK (*calling down*). The lady here . . . wants to
know where you'd like her to put it.
PAUL. Here. I'll take it.
OLD MRS EWBANK (*admiring the flowers*). It's very nice.
PAUL. Yes. Just about.
OLD MRS EWBANK. He has a great flair with flowers.
EWBANK. What?
OLD MRS EWBANK. Paul.
EWBANK. Aye. (*To* BENNETT.) I'll finish that. You can get
out now and start loading the truck.
MARSHALL (*calling*). He's going to put his boots on.
FITZPATRICK (*calling*). What?
MARSHALL. He's going to put his boots on.
FITZPATRICK. Thank God for that. (*Wafts his nose.*) The
atmosphere up here is damn near revolting.

EWBANK. Marshall, finish off that floor. I want you out of here now, as quick as you can.

MARSHALL. It'll be over in a jiffy . . . (*Polishing*.)

EWBANK *himself has taken the box over to the last post.*

EWBANK. Come on. Come on, Fitzpatrick. I could have fastened up half a dozen.

FITZPATRICK. I'm coming. I'm coming. Now clear the decks.

MARSHALL. Steady as she goes.

FITZPATRICK. Steady as she goes. You're right. (*He comes down, and starts to take the ladder out.*)

EWBANK *begins to fasten on the box.*

OLD MRS EWBANK (*to* PAUL). I'll give you a hand. If you like. (*She helps to arrange the flowers.*) Was your Grandad in here?

PAUL. With his bit of rope.

EWBANK. He'll bloody hang himself with it one of these days. (*To the men.*) Come on. Come on.

OLD MRS EWBANK *gestures in the direction of* EWBANK *and* PAUL *nods his head.*

OLD MRS EWBANK. There are some more in the house to come across I think.

PAUL (*still arranging*). It's all right. I'll fetch them. There's no hurry.

OLD MRS EWBANK. No, no. I'd like to help . . . (*She goes out.*)

FITZPATRICK *has come back after taking out the ladder. He begins to take out odds and ends, setting chairs, winking at* MARSHALL *who is still polishing, making him laugh.*

EWBANK (*to* KAY). You've fastened off them guys, I take it. (*Indicating outside.*)

KAY. Aye. Aye. They're all right. We're nearly ready for off.

EWBANK. You've got to watch every damn thing yourself in this place, Kay. If you don't, not one . . . not one do you ever get done . . . Who the hell's that shouting? (*To* FITZPATRICK.) Get out of here, now. Go on. Clear off.

KAY *collects bags from floor and goes.*

FITZPATRICK. Have we finished?

EWBANK. Finished? You were finished long ago. You want to think yourself damn lucky there's somebody here'll employ you.

FITZPATRICK. Oh, I do. I do. Those are lovely flowers.

EWBANK. Get out. Go on. Clear off. Marshall, you clear off with him.

MARSHALL. Thank the Lord for that. (*Going.*) It's been a hard day, now. It has.

The whole place now has been cleared: the floor shining, the men crossing it on tip-toe. The white tables and chairs have been set round the sides, bowls of flowers put on them, PAUL completing this and arranging flowers round the last of the three poles as EWBANK finishes fastening the box.

Gradually the whole place is cleared, leaving, finally, EWBANK and PAUL alone.

EWBANK. I said arrange them, lad. Not plant them.

PAUL. That's all right. Don't worry. None of these'll grow.

EWBANK (*looking up at awning*). It's not straight even now . . . I don't know. All that damn care and trouble.

PAUL. Don't worry.

EWBANK. What . . . ? (*Suddenly aware that he and PAUL are alone.*) Aye. Well . . .

They both fall silent.

For some little while PAUL works quietly at the flowers, EWBANK standing in the centre of the tent, still.

KAY *suddenly comes in.*

KAY. I've checked on all the guys. Slacked them off for the night . . . (*He glances at them both, he himself still standing in the door.*) The truck's loaded . . . I'll get them back down, then. To the yard.

EWBANK. Aye.

KAY. Well, then. I'll say good night.

EWBANK. That's right.

PAUL. See you.

KAY. Aye. Right, then . . . (KAY *nods and goes. Silence. Then:*)

EWBANK. Do you ever fancy this job?

PAUL *looks up.*

EWBANK *gestures at the tent.*

This.

PAUL *looks round. Then, after a moment, he shakes his head.*

Aye. Well . . . I'm not surprised. (*Briskly.*) Not much thanks you get for it.

PAUL. No.

EWBANK. Aye. Well . . . (*Pause. Then:*)

FITZPATRICK *pops his head in.* MARSHALL *is just behind him.*

FITZPATRICK. I'll say good night then. Looks a picture.

MARSHALL. Wouldn't mind living here meself.

FITZPATRICK. You should see his bloody room.

MARSHALL. An hovel.

FITZPATRICK. Pig-sty.

MARSHALL. It is. He's right.

BENNETT (*popping in behind*). We'll say good night, then, er . . . er.

EWBANK. Aye. Right-o.

FITZPATRICK. Right, then. Let's be off.

MARSHALL. Good luck tomorrow.

EWBANK. Aye.

FITZPATRICK (*going*). They'll need it, now, all right.

They go.

MARSHALL (*off*). Come on, now, Glenny . . .

GLENDENNING (*off*). Aye!

GLENDENNING *appears in doorway.*

G . . . g . . . g . . . g . . . g . . . g . . .

EWBANK. Aye. Good night, lad. I'll see you at the yard tomorrow.

GLENDENNING. I . . . I . . . I . . . I . . . I . . . I . . .

MARSHALL (*sings off*). Ay, yi, yi, yi . . . Ay, yi, yi, yi.

EWBANK. Aye. Thanks for the tobacco.

GLENDENNING. Mmmmmmmmmmm . . . (*Can't get it out.*)

PAUL. Bye, Glenny. (PAUL *gets up now from the flowers.*)

GLENDENNING. See you . . . mmmmmm . . . d-day after tomorrow!

PAUL. Aye. That's right.

GLENDENNING (*gesturing at tent*). I . . . I . . . I . . . I . . . I . . .

MARSHALL (*sings off*). Ay, yi, yi, yi . . . Ay, yi, yi, yi . . .

GLENDENNING. Lovely.

PAUL. Aye . . .

GLENDENNING. W . . . w . . . w . . . well . . . (*Nods and grins at them.*)

FITZPATRICK (*off*). Come on, Glenny. We're going to be here all night.

MARSHALL (*off*). Spends forty-eight hours, does Glenny, saying good morning.

EWBANK. Get off, lad. Or they'll be gone without you.

GLENDENNING. Aye! (*He smiles at them, then goes.*)

EWBANK *and* PAUL *stand silently in the tent. Vaguely they look around.*

EWBANK. You know. You mustn't mind them . . . (*Gestures off.*)

PAUL. Oh . . . (*Realizing.*) No.

EWBANK. They've a mind for nowt, you know.

PAUL. Yes . . . (*Nods.*)

EWBANK. It'll not happen again, you know . . .

PAUL *looks up at him.*

EWBANK *gestures round.*

This.

PAUL. There'll not be the chance.

EWBANK. Too bloody old to start again.

PAUL. Aye.
EWBANK. Ah . . . well, then . . .

Pause.

PAUL. Aye . . . Well . . . I'll go and fetch some flowers.

PAUL *goes.*

EWBANK *stands gazing at the tent. He leans up after a moment against one of the boxes, his arm stretched to it, contemplative.*

OLD MRS EWBANK *comes in quietly, unnoticed, carrying a plant. She puts it in place, regards it. Then, seeing EWBANK, she looks up.*

OLD MRS EWBANK. Oh . . . It's lovely.
EWBANK. Aye.

MRS EWBANK *has come in, admiring.*

OLD MRS EWBANK. It's finished, love. D'you like it?
MRS EWBANK (*nods, coming farther in*). Well, then . . .
They should be pleased. (*To EWBANK.*)
EWBANK. Aye.
OLD MRS EWBANK. I'll . . . There are one or two more to fetch in.

EWBANK *nods.*

OLD MRS EWBANK *goes.*

MRS EWBANK. Have the men gone?
EWBANK. That's right.

MRS EWBANK *comes farther in, looking round.*

MRS EWBANK. Is it what you were hoping for?
EWBANK. Hoping?
MRS EWBANK (*pause*). He's done the flowers well . . .
EWBANK (*looking up at the tent*). Come today. Gone tomorrow.
MRS EWBANK (*watches him. Then:*) Ah, well.
EWBANK. Aye . . .

CLAIRE *and* MAURICE *appear at the door after a moment, looking in together.*

MAURICE. Can we come in? Is it all right to enter?

EWBANK. Aye. That's what it's for.

MRS EWBANK. Come in . . .

CLAIRE. It's lovely. (*Slides across the floor in a vague dance.*) Super. (*To* MAURICE.) What do you think?

MAURICE (*standing in the centre, gazing up*). Lovely.

MRS EWBANK (*to both*). Well . . . I'm glad you like it.

CLAIRE. Course we do. Why not?

MRS EWBANK. Tell your Dad. Not me.

CLAIRE. 'Thanks, old man,' she said.

EWBANK. Aye.

MAURICE. Lovely.

PAUL *has come in quietly at the back with flowers.*

OLD EWBANK *comes in carrying a piece of rope, entering quite confidently, only then, as he reaches the centre, looking round, aware that it isn't as it was before.*

OLD MRS EWBANK *has come in after him.*

OLD EWBANK. Where are they? I've brought him another bit to look at.

MRS EWBANK. They've gone.

PAUL. On the lorry.

OLD EWBANK. I damn well would. It's not often you get the chance.

MAURICE. Wanna dance?

CLAIRE. Sure. (*Holds out her hands.*)

MRS EWBANK. Do you think you should . . .

CLAIRE. Why not? (*Laughing.*)

MRS EWBANK. I don't know . . . (*Laughs.*) I'm not sure.

MAURICE. 'S bad luck.

CLAIRE. Luck never came into it.

She laughs and dances tentatively with MAURICE *round the floor.*

CLAIRE. Aren't you going to give your mother a dance, Paul?

PAUL. I don't know . . . If she wants one.

MRS EWBANK *shrugs, pleased.*

MRS EWBANK. I don't mind. If you think you can manage . . . (*She laughs.*)

PAUL. Mind me hands. Black. (*Holds them up.*)

He holds her tentatively, and they dance round with some pleasure.

OLD EWBANK. I've never seen ought like it. Can you turn up the sound?

OLD MRS EWBANK (*crossing to him*). There isn't any. Here . . . Sit down.

They sit at one of the tables.

MAURICE. Ought to break out a few drinks. What? Celebrate.

MRS EWBANK. Oh, there's plenty enough time for that.

CLAIRE. In any case. We're not hitched.

MAURICE. Not yet.

MRS EWBANK. Oh, now. Don't let's start on that.

CLAIRE (*gestures at tent*). If only for this we have no option.

They laugh.

PAUL. Do you want to dance with my mother, Dad?

EWBANK. Aye. I'll give her a dance. Why not?

EWBANK takes MRS EWBANK firmly. They begin to dance, whirling round in an old-fashioned waltz.

MAURICE and CLAIRE have stopped dancing to watch.

EWBANK and MRS EWBANK dance round the whole tent. EWBANK's dancing is heavy, firm, and implacable, entirely characteristic of himself.

MRS EWBANK. Wow! Wow! Not so fast.

MAURICE. I'd say . . . He was a drop or two ahead of us.

CLAIRE (*puts her finger to her lips, shaking her head*). Aye, now. That's enough.

MAURICE. Go on, Dad. Let 'em have it.

EWBANK and MRS EWBANK dance on.

EWBANK (*stopping*). There now.

MRS EWBANK. Oh. Goodness. (*Holds her head, pulls back her hair.*) Am I still in one piece? (*To* CLAIRE. *She staggers, laughing.*) Oh, dear. I'm spinning.

OLD EWBANK. If I had my time o'er again, I'd burn the bloody lot.

PAUL. What's that?

OLD EWBANK. Machines. It's never too late. Bloody burn them, and that's that.

CLAIRE. If he's like this now, what's he going to be like tomorrow?

OLD EWBANK (*holding rope*). A bit of pressure, and they come to pieces in your hand.

OLD MRS EWBANK. I'll take him in and let him lie down.

EWBANK. Aye . . . He needs looking after.

EWBANK. I worked thirty or forty hours a day.

OLD MRS EWBANK. He means at week-ends.

OLD EWBANK (*going*). What? If I'd had any more I'd have given him a bit . . .

OLD MRS EWBANK. Oh, well. We might find a piece or two you've forgotten.

OLD EWBANK. By God. They are. One glance and they damn well come apart.

They go.

EWBANK *sits.*

Silence.

MRS EWBANK. Well, then . . .

Pause. Then:

PAUL. I'll go in and wash up. (*Looking at his hands.*)

MAURICE. Yes. Well, I better be getting home . . .

CLAIRE. I'll get your things.

MAURICE (*to* MRS EWBANK). I'll see you later. This evening.

MRS EWBANK. Yes. Later on.

They go.

CLAIRE. And tonight, try and stay . . .
MAURICE. What?
CLAIRE. Sober.

*EWBANK and MRS EWBANK are left alone. They are
silent. Then:*

MRS EWBANK. Well. All ready.
EWBANK. Aye.

They are silent. Then:

MRS EWBANK. Are you coming in?

EWBANK looks up.

Spend your last evening with your daughter.
EWBANK. Aye . . . (*He looks up at the finished tent.*)
MRS EWBANK. We'll manage.
EWBANK. Aye. We'll make a damn good job of it. (*Half-
laughs.*) . . . We will.
MRS EWBANK. Well, then. (*Going.*) Aren't you coming?
(*Goes.*)

*EWBANK gazes round, picks up the old piece of rope
OLD EWBANK has left. Gazes round. Rises. Goes.*

Slowly the light fades.

Curtain.

City College Norwich

Customer name: MR Nicholas Fretwell
Customer ID: 3731**

Title: Plays
ID: A205757
Due: 22 Mar 2012

Title: Plays 1: Shopping and F***ing, Faust is
Dead, Handbag, Some Explicit Polaroids
ID: A212126
Due: 08 Mar 2012

Total items: 2
Total fines: £1.80
01/03/2012 16:33
Checked out: 2
Overdue: 0
Hold requests: 0
Ready for pickup: 0

Thank you for using the
3M SelfCheck™ System.

ACT THREE

Early morning.

The tent has suffered a great deal. Part of the muslin drapery hangs loosely down. Similarly, parts of the lining round the walls hang down in loose folds, unhooked, or on the floor. Part of the dance floor itself has been removed, other parts uprooted and left in loose slabs: chairs have been upturned, tables left lying on their sides. Bottles lie here and there on the floor, along with discarded napkins, streamers, tablecloths, paper-wrapping. Most of the flowers have gone and the few that remain have been dragged out of position, ready to be disposed of.

GLENDENNING (*heard*). I . . . I . . . I . . . I . . . I . . .
MARSHALL (*heard, sings*). Ay, yi, yi, yi . . . Ay, yi, yi, yi.
FITZPATRICK (*heard*). Wakey-wakey!
BENNETT (*heard*). Not a word . . .

    FITZPATRICK *trips and falls into the door, regaining his balance as he stumbles into the tent.*

FITZPATRICK. Good grief and God help us . . . Et cetera and all that . . .

    BENNETT *has come in behind him after a few moments. He too stands dazed, looking round.*

GLENDENNING (*heard*). I . . . I . . . I . . . I . . .
MARSHALL (*heard, sings*). Ay, yi, yi, yi . . . Ay, yi, yi, yi.
FITZPATRICK. Somebody's been enjoying themselves. I'd say, at a very quick guess . . . (*Picks up a bottle, examines it, finds it empty, puts it down.*) At a very quick guess indeed, I'd say there was nothing left.
BENNETT. There's not a lot left here for us to do, Fitzie . . .
FITZPATRICK. There's not. There's not . . . Just look at that. (*Indicates some damage.*)

    KAY *has come in the other side, lifting the walling and stooping underneath.*

FITZPATRICK (*calling off*). Come in here, Marshy, old man. This should impress you all right.

KAY. Mind the floor . . . Don't step on any glass.

MARSHALL (*appearing*). Good God. And may the saints preserve us.

FITZPATRICK. More empty bottles, Marshy, than even you can count.

MARSHALL. And me not a drinking man, either.

FITZPATRICK (*laughs*). No. No. And you not a drinking man at all.

MARSHALL. That's a rare old sight indeed. (*Picks up a bottle.*)

FITZPATRICK. And not a drop to have.

MARSHALL. I wouldn't at all, now, like to be the one to foot the bill.

He puts the bottle down and, like FITZPATRICK, *drifts around the interior inspecting the bottles.*

GLENDENNING *has come in, eating a sandwich.*

GLENDENNING. Th . . . th . . . th . . . th . . . that's a good old . . . mmmmm . . . mmmmess.

KAY. You better start on the bottles, Fitzpatrick.

MARSHALL *roars with laughter.*

FITZPATRICK. And what's so funny about that?

MARSHALL (*to* KAY). Ah, now, if they'd sent him down to yonder . . . (*Thumbs down.*) That'd be just the job they'd find.

FITZPATRICK (*picking up bottles*). Empty . . . empty . . . every one.

KAY. Marshall. You help him. And with the mess as well.

FITZPATRICK *roars with laughter.*

Bennett . . . (*Indicates tables.*) Glendenning . . . (*Indicates chairs.*)

GLENDENNING. I . . . I . . . I . . . Aye!

MARSHALL. Don't you ever get tired of eatin', Glenny?

FITZPATRICK (*holding bottle to light*). And where now, do you think, is the happy bride? (*He drinks off the dregs, grimaces, holds his stomach.*)

BENNETT. Not here, for one. That's sure.

MARSHALL. I don't know. Might find half a dozen under the table, if this place is any indication to go by at all.

BENNETT. God. God. But it's freezing.

MARSHALL (*holding bottle up, gazing at it*). Ice.

GLENDENNING. I . . . I . . . I . . . I . . .

MARSHALL (*sings*).Ay, yi, yi, yi . . . Ay, yi, yi, yi . . .

GLENDENNING. I . . . I . . . I . . . I . . . Ice!

FITZPATRICK. In summer, Glenny.

BENNETT. It's damn near autumn now.

MARSHALL. What?

GLENDENNING. Aye!

MARSHALL (*drinking dregs*). To God! It's glass! (*Spits out.*)

FITZPATRICK *laughs.* GLENDENNING *and* BENNETT *laugh.*

FITZPATRICK. You mad Patrick. You'll never learn.

MARSHALL. It's glass. God damn it! I've nearly cut meself to death!

FITZPATRICK. A bloody booby-trap. (*Doubles up with laughter at* MARSHALL's *discomposure.*) Watch out!

KAY. I said take it outside.

BENNETT. That stuff'll poison you.

KAY. Glendenning, *chairs.*

GLENDENNING (*happy*). Aye!

FITZPATRICK. And what, now, do you think of that?

BENNETT. What is it?

FITZPATRICK. A lady's undergarment, or I'm a frog. (*Holds up a piece of muslin.*)

KAY. It is not. (*Looks up at lining.*)

BENNETT. It's off the lining. Some madman has torn it down.

MARSHALL. He'll go through the tent top. When he sees all this.

FITZPATRICK. God damn and blast.

KAY. What is it?

FITZPATRICK *looks frantically about him.*

FITZPATRICK. Me hammer. Me hammer . . . I've lost it.
(*To* GLENDENNING.) God damn it. Will you go find it
in the cab?
GLENDENNING. Aye! (*He immediately puts down the
chair he's carrying, nods, and goes quickly outside.*)
BENNETT. You want to leave him alone . . .
MARSHALL. What?
BENNETT. Glendenning.
MARSHALL. Ah, now. Go jump on your bloody head.
BENNETT (*backs down*). God. It's freezing. (*Shivers.*)

They continue working. KAY *has begun to take down the
muslin walls.*

KAY. Marshall, will you bring in the muslin bags.
MARSHALL. Aye. Aye. (*To* BENNETT.) It's me today.
Fitzpatrick, no doubt it'll be you tomorrow.
FITZPATRICK (*looking round again*). Good God, you
know, but this is a bloody mess.
BENNETT. Aye. Aye . . .

MARSHALL *comes back in with the bags.*

FITZPATRICK (*to* KAY). Have you seen Ewbank this
morning?
KAY. I have not. (*Still working.*)
MARSHALL. Steady. Steady. Might find him underneath all
that. (*Indicates floor.*)
FITZPATRICK. No. No. Up! He's not there at all.

GLENDENNING *has come back in.*

KAY. You better keep your boots off just the same.
Marshall . . .

Indicates MARSHALL *to help him with the muslin
walling: wrap it and put it in the bags.*

BENNETT *has started sweeping the paper streamers and
debris off the floor.*

GLENDENNING *has resumed work as though nothing
has happened, picking up the chairs, carrying them out,
expressionless, not looking up.*

MARSHALL. Ay, now. And where's that hammer? Here's
   Fitzpatrick waiting to have a smash.
FITZPATRICK. I am. I am. That's right.
BENNETT. You want to leave him alone, Fitzpatrick.
MARSHALL (*innocent*). Was I intending any harm?
   (*Indicating* GLENDENNING.) He wouldn't know what
   to do without us.
FITZPATRICK. Have you noticed how – of recent times,
   I'm speaking – Bennett has grown quite dictatorial in his
   habits? (*Starts taking up the floor.*)
MARSHALL. He has.
FITZPATRICK. Censorious, if I didn't know him better.
MARSHALL. Censorious is the word.
FITZPATRICK. And we all know, now, the reason for it.
MARSHALL. Reason? Is there a reason, too, for that?
   (*Gazing up.*)
FITZPATRICK. It's explained, Benny, is it not, easily
   enough?

   BENNETT *goes on working.* KAY *looks up briefly then
   continues.*

MARSHALL. Now, now. You'll have to tell us all the rest.
FITZPATRICK. Benny, here is the one you ought to ask.

   BENNETT *glances up at* FITZPATRICK, *then continues
   with his work.*

   GLENDENNING *comes and goes with the remaining
   chairs and tables and the odd bits of rubbish.*

MARSHALL. No, no. We're going to get nothing out of
   that.
KAY. Fitzpatrick . . . (*Indicates he get on with his work.*)

   FITZPATRICK *gets on, clearing the rest of the rubbish,
   bottles, etc., then starting on the floor.*

FITZPATRICK. It's quite easy to explain, nevertheless, and
   though I might well be wrong in detail, the whole mass, as
   it were, is treasonably correct.
MARSHALL. Go on. Go on, I'm listening. Kay, have you

opened up an ear? Would you mind, Glenny, now, if you left the room?

GLENDENNING. Aye!

FITZPATRICK. His wife left him for another man.

MARSHALL. She did!

FITZPATRICK. She did.

MARSHALL. As long as it wasn't for another woman.

MARSHALL *and* FITZPATRICK *laugh*.

To God. And whoever would have thought of that? A man with a face like that . . .

FITZPATRICK. And figure.

MARSHALL. And figure.

FITZPATRICK. And boots.

MARSHALL. And boots.

FITZPATRICK. Socks.

MARSHALL. Socks.

FITZPATRICK. Teeth. (*Showing his.*)

MARSHALL. Teeth. (*Showing his.*)

FITZPATRICK. Smiling . . . (*Smiles.*)

MARSHALL. Smiling . . .

BENNETT. Your mouth's going to open too wide one of these days, Fitzpatrick.

FITZPATRICK. It'll be all the easier to let the truth come flying out.

BENNETT. And for me to put my fist inside it.

FITZPATRICK. Since when has a man like me let a man like you put his fist inside my mouth?

MARSHALL *laughs*.

BENNETT *tenses but doesn't answer*.

KAY. Fitzpatrick, get out, and load the truck outside.

FITZPATRICK. On my own? God damn it. I'm only human.

MARSHALL. Almost.

FITZPATRICK. Almost. (*Going.*) It's a hard bloody life is this: walk the straight and narrow and you end up working by yourself. (*He goes.*)

MARSHALL. Well. Well. Now there's a thing. (*Tuts away to himself.*) Revelations.

BENNETT. And it's not only Fitzpatrick.

MARSHALL. Not only what?

BENNETT. Who'll feel the end of this. (*Holds up his fist.*)

MARSHALL. What? What? . . . You're not thinking . . .
  You can't mean it?

  BENNETT *gazes steadily at him, obviously unable to
  carry out his threat, then turns and goes back to his work.*

MARSHALL. Good God. He can.

  FITZPATRICK *can be heard singing outside. Silence for a
  moment inside the tent.*

MARSHALL. Do you think now . . .

  BENNETT *looks up threateningly.*

MARSHALL (*spreading his arms*). We'd get anything back
  on the bottles.

  They go back to work.

  FITZPATRICK *pops his head in.*

FITZPATRICK. I can hear Mr Ewbank singing.

KAY. Singing . . . ?

FITZPATRICK. Round the back side of the house . . . (*Pops
  out.*)

MARSHALL. There's a blue sky around the corner.

FITZPATRICK (*listens*). Beautiful.

MARSHALL. Like a bird . . .

FITZPATRICK. Like a bird.

KAY. Fitzpatrick . . .

FITZPATRICK (*indicating house*). Must be in a great good
  humour.

MARSHALL. Great good humour: I think you're right.

FITZPATRICK. Tucked up warm and cosy.

MARSHALL. Warm and cosy.

FITZPATRICK. Shaving.

MARSHALL. Mirror . . .

FITZPATRICK. Hot water.

MARSHALL. Fingers . . .

FITZPATRICK. Toes.

KAY. Fitzpatrick!

FITZPATRICK. All right. All right. (*He goes.*)

BENNETT *has started taking up the floor;*
GLENDENNING *takes the pieces out.*

KAY *is detaching the muslin roof from the walls, letting it fall to the centre of the tent, where it hangs like a sail.*

MARSHALL *himself now has started on the floor.*

MARSHALL. How many hours, now, Glenny, do you sleep at night?

GLENDENNING. Aye!

MARSHALL. And how many hours is that? (*To* KAY.) I don't think Glenny sleeps at all. Like a damn great owl, sitting there, his eyes wide open.

GLENDENNING. Aye! (*He watches them, pleased, then takes out floor.*)

BENNETT. I never need more than six or seven.

MARSHALL. Six or seven . . . ?

BENNETT. Hours.

MARSHALL. Hours . . . I thought . . . Ah, well. But then . . .

BENNETT. What's that? (*Genially.*)

MARSHALL. A separated man . . . You can never sleep long, on your own, in a single bed.

BENNETT *seems about to turn on him.*

MARSHALL (*to* KAY). It's true, then, Kay. They put a man like you inside.

FITZPATRICK (*popping back*). There's many a better man been put in with him.

MARSHALL. There has. There has . . . Still singing?

FITZPATRICK (*shakes head, picks up piece of flooring*). Having, I think, a little rest.

MARSHALL. Recuperation. No sound of breathing? No shouts? No cries.

FITZPATRICK. Not a bird. Not a twitter.

MARSHALL. Resting then. No doubt. A damn great house like that . . .

FITZPATRICK. He's worked hard now, Marshy, for every penny he's got.

MARSHALL. He has. You're right. And we as well, now, have worked a damn sight harder.

FITZPATRICK laughs, taking up more of the dance floor.

MARSHALL. It looks to me like a damn great orgy . . .

KAY. What's that?

FITZPATRICK. He pricked his ears at that.

MARSHALL. I shouldn't wonder. Just look at that. Scratches . . .

BENNETT. That's made with glass.

MARSHALL. Glass? I'd have sworn it was somebody's fingers . . . Dragged out. Protesting to the last.

They laugh. BENNETT and GLENDENNING carry out pieces. Then:

If you ask me, they're both heading hard for trouble.

FITZPATRICK. Who?

MARSHALL. The bridegroom and the bride.

They're both taking up the floor, waiting for BENNETT to return.

FITZPATRICK. Oh, now. What makes you feel like that?

MARSHALL (*as BENNETT returns*). Experience, man. Marriage, as an institution – in my opinion – is all washed out. Finished . . . Kaput.

FITZPATRICK (*towards BENNETT*). Ah, now. There speaks a knowledgeable man.

MARSHALL. I do. I am.

KAY. All right, now. Let's have it down.

KAY has now released the muslin roof from the sides of the tent and it hangs in a single drape down the centre of the tent.

FITZPATRICK goes on clearing the floor; the others go to the ropes to lower the muslin.

FITZPATRICK. Bus-conductor . . .

MARSHALL. Rose nearly to inspector, but for her sex, Fitzpatrick.

FITZPATRICK. But for our sex, Marshy, and we'd all rise to something else. Greengrocer's right-hand assistant. Nun . . .

MARSHALL. Baked apple-pie. (*Lowering.*)

FITZPATRICK. Is that a fact.

MARSHALL. So many apples in, they nearly tore the crust apart.

FITZPATRICK. Good God. Glenny! I hope you're listening.

GLENDENNING. Aye!

FITZPATRICK. I wonder if old Benny's was a cook? (*He goes, carrying the floor.*)

The muslin now is lowered. BENNETT *looks up wildly, then he goes on with the others untaping the muslin from the ridges and unlacing it at the seams.*

MARSHALL (*untaping*). I knew a man once. Came home from work one afternoon . . . Been let off early – an act of charity – by the boss . . .

BENNETT. Aye?

MARSHALL. Found his wife in bed with another man.

BENNETT looks across.

KAY. Be careful where you let it fall.

MARSHALL. Comes in. Finds no dinner. Goes upstairs. Commotion . . . Opens door . . .

FITZPATRICK (*returning*). And Bob's your uncle.

MARSHALL. No. No. You weren't the one I had in mind at all.

They laugh.

KAY (*to* FITZPATRICK). Side poles . . .

FITZPATRICK. Good God . . . I was getting used, now, to trotting off outside.

MARSHALL. Aren't you going to let me finish my story?

FITZPATRICK. Hung up a notice.

MARSHALL. What?

FITZPATRICK. Hung up a notice: DO NOT DISTURB, outside.

FITZPATRICK and MARSHALL laugh.

KAY. All right, now. All right. Let's have it in the bags.

The men start to pack the three separated pieces of muslin lining.

FITZPATRICK *has started to remove the side poles.*

MARSHALL. I've been badly suited, I have, in the matter of fidelity.
FITZPATRICK. Easy come . . .
MARSHALL. That's what they say.
KAY. Careful . . . gently.

MARSHALL *and* FITZPATRICK *laugh.*

BENNETT. I've told you, Fitzpatrick. That's the last chance you'll have.
FITZPATRICK. That's what I said . . .
MARSHALL. She didn't believe me.

MARSHALL *and* FITZPATRICK *laugh.*

GLENDENNING. I . . . I . . . I . . . I . . . I . . .
MARSHALL (*sings*). Ay, yi, yi, yi . . . Ay, yi, yi, yi . . .

GLENDENNING *takes out the bagged muslin.*

BENNETT *is now releasing the ropes from the muslin ridges.*

FITZPATRICK. A faithful wife . . .
MARSHALL. Is like a stone round your neck . . .
FITZPATRICK. No decent man would be seen without it.

FITZPATRICK *and* MARSHALL *laugh.*

KAY. Fitzpatrick. Shut your mouth.
FITZPATRICK. It's Bennett . . .
BENNETT. You've had your chance, Fitzpatrick.
MARSHALL. You've had your chance, Fitzpatrick.
FITZPATRICK. That's what she said.

MARSHALL *and* FITZPATRICK *laugh.*

KAY (*to* MARSHALL). If you call that work, you better get yourself another job.
MARSHALL (*horrified*). Another!
FITZPATRICK. God. That's the worst thing I've ever heard.

MARSHALL *shakes his head, clearing out either ear with his little finger.*

KAY. Marshall . . . Fitzpatrick . . . (*Indicates the floor.*) Bennett . . .

The men start taking up the rest of the floor.

MARSHALL. Trade unions.
FITZPATRICK. What?
MARSHALL. Trade unions.

BENNETT *looks up, then continues taking out the floor with* GLENDENNING *as* MARSHALL *and* FITZPATRICK *lift it.*

FITZPATRICK. That's an interesting proposition.
MARSHALL. It is.
FITZPATRICK. Why certain people . . .
MARSHALL. Who shall be nameless . . .
FITZPATRICK. Come seeking employment . . .
MARSHALL. Of all places . . .
FITZPATRICK. At Mr Ewbank's place itself.
MARSHALL. Aye.
FITZPATRICK. Tenting contractor . . .
MARSHALL. For all outside . . .
FITZPATRICK. And inside occasions.

They laugh.

(*Direct to* MARSHALL.) Some of course . . .
MARSHALL. Have no alternative . . . No. No. They haven't. That's right.
FITZPATRICK. In a manner of speaking, they have no choice.
MARSHALL. No, no. That's right. They can't be blamed.
FITZPATRICK. While on the other hand . . .
MARSHALL. You're right. You're right.
FITZPATRICK. Some of them . . .
MARSHALL. You're right.
FITZPATRICK. Come here because they're bone idle.
MARSHALL. Like myself you mean.

FITZPATRICK. Like yourself. On the other hand . . .

MARSHALL. Aye . . .

FITZPATRICK. There are those . . .

MARSHALL. Aye . . .

FITZPATRICK. Who have it in them to rise to higher things.

MARSHALL. Higher things. They have.

FITZPATRICK. Who have, within them, Marshy, the capacity to get on.

MARSHALL. They have. They have. You're right.

FITZPATRICK. But who, suddenly – through some calamity on the domestic front . . .

MARSHALL. The domestic front . . .

FITZPATRICK. In a manner of speaking . . .

MARSHALL. In a manner of speaking. That's right.

FITZPATRICK. Lose . . .

MARSHALL. Lose.

FITZPATRICK. All interest in carrying on.

MARSHALL. They do. They do. You're right.

FITZPATRICK. Some terrible calamity overwelms them . . .

MARSHALL. . . . on the domestic front . . .

FITZPATRICK. And up, into the wide blue yonder . . . all pride and initiative: gone.

MARSHALL. Aye . . . Vanished.

BENNETT. I'm not above using this, Fitzpatrick!

BENNETT *has come in and has wrapped one of the muslin ropes: now he threatens* FITZPATRICK *with the shackle end.*

FITZPATRICK. No, no. Each man to his tools I've always said.

MARSHALL (*to* FITZPATRICK). A tradesman from his tools should never be divided.

BENNETT. I'll kill you. I bloody will!

KAY. That's enough, Fitzpatrick.

FITZPATRICK. I was merely ascertainin' the truth of the matter, Kay.

MARSHALL (*to* FITZPATRICK). What's a man's life worth if it's comprised of nothing but untruths and lies?

FITZPATRICK. What is it now, indeed?

KAY. And what's so remarkable about your life,
Fitzpatrick?
FITZPATRICK. Remarkable?
KAY. That it gives you the right to go poking so often into
other people's.

GLENDENNING *has come in slowly.*

A loud-mouth. A wet-rag. That doesn't do a crumb of
work unless he's driven to it.

KAY *has crossed slowly over to* FITZPATRICK.

FITZPATRICK. Loud-mouth, now, I might be. And bone-
idle.

MARSHALL *snorts.*

But I'm the only one round here who hasn't anything to
hide.
KAY. Are you, now. Then you're very lucky. You're a very
lucky man, Fitzpatrick. If you don't mind me saying so.
FITZPATRICK. No. I don't mind. I probably am. You're
right.

MARSHALL *laughs.*

KAY (*unruffled*). And you think that, then, has some virtue.
FITZPATRICK. Aye. I think it probably has. Meaning no
disrespect whatsoever, (*Indicating* BENNETT.) it was
Bennett who pointed out the fact with which, until then,
we were unacquainted. Namely that you, Kay, yourself,
had been in clink. So what . . . ?
MARSHALL. Some of my best friends are criminals.
FITZPATRICK. What I can't abide is a man who can point
his finger at other people but can't bear the same one to
be pointed at himself.
KAY. Some people, Fitzpatrick, have injuries that go deeper
than you imagine.
MARSHALL. Oh, very nice. (*Applauds discreetly.*) He got
that from a book.
FITZPATRICK. I mean, glass houses, Kay. Glass houses.

There's not one now you can't see here. Just by turning round.

MARSHALL *turns round*.

KAY. That's very fine, Fitzpatrick.

MARSHALL. It is. I agree with that myself.

KAY. Do you put a price on anything. Fitzpatrick?

FITZPATRICK. I don't know. I put a price on the work I do here. Minimal it may be, but I do put a price on that.

MARSHALL. Come on now, then. Let's get back to work. (*Rubs his hands.*)

FITZPATRICK. And one other thing. A little more civility might have been more becoming.

MARSHALL. It would.

FITZPATRICK. We're not just here, now, to be pushed around.

KAY. It looks to me, Fitzpatrick, that you've come here – this morning like any other – to cause trouble wherever you can . . .

FITZPATRICK (*looking at* BENNETT). If a man puts his fist in my face I'll be damned if he doesn't get one back. Wherever that man might come from.

BENNETT. And you think that's something to admire, Fitzpatrick?

FITZPATRICK. No. No. It's not admiration at all I'm after.

MARSHALL *laughs*.

KAY. I think you better get home, Fitzpatrick.

FITZPATRICK. What?

KAY. I think you better get off. Come into the office at the end of the week and you'll get whatever you're owed.

Silence. Then:

FITZPATRICK. Huh. (*Looks round for his jacket.*) Do you mean that?

KAY. I do.

FITZPATRICK *goes to his jacket. He slowly pulls it on.*

FITZPATRICK (*to* MARSHALL). Are you coming?

MARSHALL. Well, now . . . If there's one of us to be out of work . . . better that the other sticks to what he can.

FITZPATRICK (*bitterly*). Aye. I suppose you're right. (*He goes to the door.*) It's amazing, you know . . . the way he surrounds himself with cripples. (*Gestures at the house.*)

KAY. Cripples?

FITZPATRICK. Yourself . . . Bennett . . . Glenny . . . Marshall . . .

MARSHALL. Fitzpatrick . . .

FITZPATRICK. And lastly, of course, myself. It qualifies, I suppose, the nature . . . of his warm and understanding heart. Ah, well. You can tell him one thing for nothing. The road up yonder is a harder climb than that. (*Thumbs upwards.*) I'll say goodbye. May God go with you, and treat you more kindly than Himself. (*Taps GLENDENNING on the shoulder as he goes.*) Watch it, Glenny. One day, mind . . . (*Gestures hammer with his hand.*)

GLENDENNING. Aye! (*Laughs.*)

As he goes to the door EWBANK comes in.

EWBANK. And where the hell do you think you're going to? God Christ. Just look at the time. Knocking off and they've only been here half an hour.

FITZPATRICK. I've been fired.

EWBANK. Don't be so bloody silly. Get on with this bloody walling . . . God damn and blast. Just look. Covered in bloody muck. *Marshall* . . . ! (*Gestures at MARSHALL to get on with the floor.*) Fitzpatrick . . . let's have it up. (*Indicates floor.*)

Slowly they go back to their tasks. KAY alone doesn't look up.

Kay, let's have these battens out . . . Good God. We're going to be here all night.

KAY. Bennett . . .

MARSHALL. The couple got off to a happy start, then, Mr Ewbank.

EWBANK. What? . . .

MARSHALL. The happy . . .

EWBANK. Mind your own bloody business. Bennett, I don't
    call that working. (*To* MARSHALL.) How the hell would
    you know that?
MARSHALL. I . . . Me . . . We . . .
FITZPATRICK. Ah, but a great day. Celebratin' . . .
EWBANK. I'll celebrate my boot up your bloody backside,
    Fitzpatrick. That's what I'll do . . . God Christ. God
    Christ. They come in here and start telling you what sort
    of night you've had . . .
KAY. Bennett, over here.

*They work, silent, taking out the battens and the last of
the floor. EWBANK grunts, groans, murmurs to himself.*

*They watch him, glancing at one another, as they work.
Then:*

MARSHALL. Married life. There's nothing like it. You can't
    beat it. Though I do say so myself.
EWBANK. Lift it. Lift it. God Christ, they think you live
    here, you know, like they do at home . . .
MARSHALL. They do. They do. That's right. A bloody
    pigsty. He knows.
EWBANK. Flat on their backs all night. And flat on their
    bellies all day long to go with it . . .
MARSHALL. He was sacked, nevertheless, Mr Ewbank.
    Demoted.
EWBANK. There's been nobody sacked from this firm since
    the day it first began. God Christ, Kay, I've heard some
    bloody tales in my time, but that one takes the can.
FITZPATRICK. Ah, it's a great life if you can afford it.
MARSHALL. And what, now, is that?
FITZPATRICK. A wife. Home . . . children.
GLENDENNING. I . . . I . . . I . . . I . . . I . . . I . . . I . . .
MARSHALL. Hot chocolate by the fire.
FITZPATRICK. Hot chocolate by the fire.
GLENDENNING. I . . . I . . . I . . . I . . . I . . . I . . .

*EWBANK mumbles and groans to himself, not noticing,
then*:

EWBANK. If you took my advice, Kay, you'd bloody well
get shut . . .

KAY. What . . .

EWBANK. Four lasses. Good God. You ought to have more
common sense . . . A man your age: you ought to have
more bloody common sense . . . God Christ.

GLENDENNING. I . . . I . . . I . . . I . . .

EWBANK. That's all right, then . . .

*The men take out the battens. KAY is working, loosening
them.*

God. Bloody orchestra. Kay, you should have seen it.
Dressed up like a cockatoo. There'll be some of them
stretched out still, out yonder. I shouldn't be surprised.
God Christ. You've seen nowt like it.

FITZPATRICK. Had a damn fine time, did you, an' all?

EWBANK. Who's asking you?

FITZPATRICK. I thought . . .

MARSHALL. Married life. You can't beat it.

EWBANK (*to* KAY). Made me speech standing on the
bridegroom's table . . . Just look at that. (*Gestures at the
ground.*)

MARSHALL. On the other hand, Mr Kay here has been
telling us how he's been to prison. Enjoyed the experience,
he said, no end . . . Regaling us you know with all the
sordid details.

EWBANK. Tipped half a bottle over some chap's head . . .
Bloody waiters. Chef . . . If you can't for one day in your
life enjoy it.

FITZPATRICK. And not left a drop of the damn good stuff
for us.

EWBANK. What's that?

FITZPATRICK. I say, Kay here isn't one to make a fuss.

EWBANK. By God, bloody embezzlement. That'd make 'em
shift, Kay. Four lasses.

MARSHALL. Embezzlement?

EWBANK. By God. There's nowt for him to embezzle here.
(*Laughs.*) Ay bloody hell. You need a firework up your
arse. Just look at that . . . Get on. Get on. Here, I'll give
you a lift myself.

FITZPATRICK. Embezzlement. Now there's a wonder.

MARSHALL. And all the time now . . .

FITZPATRICK. One of us.

MARSHALL. Hiding his light beneath a bushel.

FITZPATRICK. Along, that is, with the cash from someone else's tub.

MARSHALL *and* FITZPATRICK *laugh*.

EWBANK. What's that?

MARSHALL. I say, your son's not out to help us, then, this morning.

EWBANK. No. He's not.

FITZPATRICK. Ah. It's a great life if you can mix it.

EWBANK. He's off on his bloody travels.

MARSHALL. Travels?

FITZPATRICK. Abroad, is that?

EWBANK. I wouldn't know if you told me . . . He's never in one place two minutes running.

FITZPATRICK. Ah, travelling. A great broadener of the mind.

EWBANK. A great emptier of the pocket, if you ask me, more likely.

OLD EWBANK *has come in at the back*.

FITZPATRICK. Don't worry. One day he'll settle down.

EWBANK. Will he? That's your opinion, Fitzpatrick?

FITZPATRICK. Modern times, Mr Ewbank. The up-and-coming generation.

EWBANK. Aye, well. They can up and come all right . . . You can start loading that bloody lorry, Kay. Let's have 'em out.

FITZPATRICK. The world of the imagination . . .

EWBANK. Is that what it is, Fitzpatrick?

FITZPATRICK. The ferment of ideas.

EWBANK. If he'd ferment something out of it we shouldn't be so bad.

MARSHALL. Like a damn good liquor . . .

FITZPATRICK. Like a damn good Scotch. You're right.

They go, taking the last of the battens with them.
BENNETT *remains, starting to strip the ropes on the
centre poles.*

After a while, as OLD EWBANK *talks,* MARSHALL *and*
GLENDENNING *return to wrap the walling, laying it out
on the ground at the back of the tent and folding it, seam
on seam.*

OLD EWBANK (*to* BENNETT). Did I show you that rope
the other day?

BENNETT. What? I don't . . .

OLD EWBANK. In the house. I keep it there.

BENNETT. Aye. I think I saw it . . .

OLD EWBANK. Four hundred feet some days. By hand.

BENNETT. Aye . . .

OLD EWBANK. What? You saw nothing like it.

BENNETT. Aye. That's quite a lot.

OLD EWBANK. Horses? Damn it all. Sheep-nets . . .
Fishing boats . . . Dogger Bank. Iceland. Scapa Flow . . .
Greenland. You'll find bits of rope I made, you know,
floating under the North Pole. Good God. A piece of rope
in those days . . .

BENNETT (*still working*). Aye . . .

OLD EWBANK. Balloons? Do you know once they used it
on an airship. Bigger than a house. Damn it all. You could
go anywhere with a bit of rope. (*Suddenly confidential.*) I
know. Don't you let these people mislead you.

BENNETT. Ah, well. I better get on with this.

OLD EWBANK. They haven't the strength to stand up. A
bit of an ache and they're dashing for a pill and a sup
from a bottle. They haven't the appetite, you know, for
work . . . There's one sat out there now, on the back of
the lorry, eating a damn great cake. I've never seen so
many people sitting down, eating . . . Have I showed you
my rope?

BENNETT. Aye.

OLD EWBANK. Twelve? Eighteen. Sometimes twenty hours
a day. Good God, you'd no time to sit eating. When I
married my wife I never used to see her but one day in
four.

MARSHALL. Those were the days, Benny, right enough!

OLD EWBANK (*turning to* MARSHALL). Steam? By God, there was!

EWBANK *has returned, followed by* KAY.

FITZPATRICK *has already come back and is laying out the walling.*

EWBANK. Come on, now. Let's have it folded.

OLD EWBANK. I can't stop now. I'm just going for my walk.

OLD MRS EWBANK *has come in.*

Got used to it, you know. Used to walk twenty or thirty miles a day. It'd take ten miles walking to make a hundred foot of rope.

OLD MRS EWBANK. I've been looking for you all over. Do you realize you haven't got on any socks? (*To* EWBANK.) Has he been here long?

EWBANK. He's just arrived. He'll be all right.

OLD MRS EWBANK (*reprovingly*). He's been out walking. He'll catch his death of cold.

MARSHALL. He's a fine old man, missis.

OLD MRS EWBANK. He needs looking after. That's a fact.

OLD EWBANK (*to* BENNETT). One day in four. Five if I worked over.

OLD MRS EWBANK (*looking around*). It's amazing how soon they disappear . . . (*To* EWBANK.) We're off in half an hour.

EWBANK. I'll come and see you . . .

OLD MRS EWBANK. Aye . . . Well, I'll take him in. Get him dressed. (*Shouts in* OLD EWBANK's *ear.*) I'll take you in!

OLD EWBANK. What? We've only just started.

OLD MRS EWBANK (*going, her arm in* OLD EWBANK's). He still thinks we're having the party.

OLD EWBANK. God damn and blast. When you tied a knot it'd take you a fortnight to unravel it.

They go.

EWBANK. Get packing this walling up . . . Let's have it out.

They start to pack the walling. The others are removing the last side poles.

FITZPATRICK. The lucky couple are on their travels, then?

EWBANK. Aye. Aye, that's right . . . Shan't see them again for a damn long time.

FITZPATRICK. A doctor . . .

EWBANK. Aye.

FITZPATRICK. The medical profession. It's a fine thing, to have a vocation in life.

EWBANK. And what's one of them when you've got it at home?

FITZPATRICK. Why, I'd say Kay, here, was a vocated man.

MARSHALL. That's right.

FITZPATRICK. An air of dedication.

EWBANK. Dedication . . . He knows which side his bread's buttered on. Isn't that right, Kay? So's all the rest of them, an' all.

FITZPATRICK. Aye. We're all pragmatists at heart.

EWBANK. Pragmatists, is it? Bone bloody idle. There's nobody else round here'd employ any one of you as far as I can make out.

MARSHALL. Ah, now. That's a fact . . .

FITZPATRICK. The debris of society . . . That's us.

EWBANK. Watch that bloody lacing . . .

MARSHALL and GLENDENNING are lacing the bag of walling; BENNETT goes to relieve GLENDENNING.

BENNETT. Here, let me have it . . .

He and MARSHALL carry it out. FITZPATRICK follows them, taking side poles; GLENDENNING, after glancing round, goes out after them.

PAUL has come in as the last of the work is being done; now he comes down the tent, casual. He wears a coat.

PAUL. Well, then, I'm off.

EWBANK. By God, then . . . Look at this.

PAUL. All up . . . all finished.

KAY. Just about.

EWBANK. Crawled out of his bloody hole . . . (*To* KAY, *who's now taking off the quarter guys.*) Seen him last night . . . wouldn't believe it . . . Comes up here, you know, for the bloody booze . . . nowt else . . .

PAUL. That's it. Just about.

EWBANK. By God. Nomads, Kay, that's us . . . Tenting . . . First tent I ever had, you know, caught fire . . . went up . . . should have seen it . . . Went up . . . (*Pauses, abstracted.*) Off, then, are you?

PAUL. That's right.

EWBANK. Aye . . . (*Gazes at him.*) Back up, I suppose, when you need some money.

PAUL. Manage by meself.

EWBANK. Aye . . . Still to see it.

PAUL. Alus a first time.

EWBANK. Aye . . . can just imagine.

PAUL. Well, then . . .

Pause, gazing over at one another.

FITZPATRICK *comes in, followed by the others.*
GLENDENNING *carries a little sack with which he goes round, picking up litter from the grass.*

FITZPATRICK. So you're leaving us behind.

PAUL. Aye. That's right.

FITZPATRICK. A wandering spirit. I know the feeling well . . .

PAUL (*laughs*). I can imagine.

FITZPATRICK. Aye. I'm a born traveller. Circumstances alone conspire against it.

MARSHALL. On the Dublin to Liverpool express.

They laugh.

FITZPATRICK (*to* BENNETT). Being a single man, I know the temptations very well.

MARSHALL. You don't know where you're off to, then?

PAUL. Oh . . . (*Shrugs.*)

FITZPATRICK. I'll give you one piece of sound advice.

PAUL *looks up.*

For nothing now. If you're ever tempted, at any time, to marry . . .

MARSHALL. Don't.

FITZPATRICK. Not until you're far too old.

MARSHALL. Not until you're far too old.

PAUL. I'll try and remember that . . . Good-bye, Glenny.

GLENDENNING. I . . . I . . . I . . . Aye! (*Nods his head.*)

PAUL. See you some time.

GLENDENNING. Aye!

PAUL. Well, then . . . (*Looks over at* EWBANK.)

EWBANK. Aye. I'll walk with you to the house . . . (*To* KAY.) When you let it down keep it clean. No bits and pieces . . .

KAY. Right . . .

EWBANK goes with PAUL, *who waves to the others and they call out as he goes.*

FITZPATRICK. They had a great time then, last night.

MARSHALL. Aye. You can tell it by his manner.

They laugh.

FITZPATRICK. It's a great feeling. (*Stretches.*)

MARSHALL. What's that?

FITZPATRICK. To feel reinstated.

MARSHALL *laughs.*

KAY. You can get the rest of this out now . . . (*Indicating remaining flooring.*) And start loading the truck.

FITZPATRICK. Aye, aye, sir! (*To* MARSHALL.) See that?

MARSHALL. It's a great man who knows his place.

FITZPATRICK. You're right, Marshy. It is that.

They take out the last side poles, and any remaining pieces.

KAY and BENNETT work alone, untying the laced edges of the canvas, prior to taking it down. The edges of the canvas are supported now only by the four corner side poles.

BENNETT, *aware suddenly that he and KAY are alone, wanders over to the view of the valley.*

BENNETT. It's amazing, isn't it. The number of chimneys they can put into a place the size of that.

KAY (*unlacing canvas*). Aye.

BENNETT. They'll soon be gone.

KAY. What's that?

BENNETT. Central heating. They don't need chimneys, you know, for that.

KAY. Aye.

BENNETT. Just roofs you'll see.

KAY. And aerials.

BENNETT. Aerials?

KAY. Television.

BENNETT. Oh, aye You can just see a car. Going up the other side. Sun shining on its window . . . Look . . . Gone.

KAY. I shouldn't let Fitzpatrick worry you.

BENNETT. No.

KAY. Gets under your skin. (*Watching him.*)

BENNETT. Aye . . . Well, I suppose you have to laugh.

KAY. Aye. (*Nods.*)

BENNETT. The thing is . . . I suppose one day, I'll bloody kill him.

KAY. Aye.

They laugh.

The others start coming back.

KAY (*as FITZPATRICK and MARSHALL come in*). Right, then. Let's have it down.

They go to the poles, FITZPATRICK rubbing his hands, spitting on them.

FITZPATRICK. Nice to know, now, that we're speaking.

MARSHALL. Ah, Kay's not the one to hold a grudge . . . A spot in jail would do us all the world of good.

FITZPATRICK (*fingering canvas*). Damn fine stuff . . .

They take the ropes.

FITZPATRICK. Easy come. Easy go.

MARSHALL (*lowering rope*). Benny, now: his old man . . .

> FITZPATRICK *and* MARSHALL *laugh.*

ALL. Ready!

KAY. Right, then . . . Let's have it down.

> *They've taken the ropes holding the canvas, and take the
> ends outside the tent, at each of the 'quarters'. At KAY's
> signal they release the hitches holding the ropes at the foot
> of the poles and the canvas slowly descends. As it comes
> down they rip the lacing, working towards the centre
> poles, separating the three pieces of canvas.*

> *Then, as the men unshackle the canvas:*

GLENDENNING. I . . . I . . . I . . . If I had a . . . had a . . .
had a . . . had a son . . .

FITZPATRICK. Aye? Aye? What's that?

GLENDENNING. If I . . . I . . . I . . . I . . . had a lad I w
. . . w . . . w . . . wouldn't have him w . . . w . . . w . . .
wandering off.

BENNETT. What's that, Glenny?

GLENDENNING. I . . . I . . . I . . . I . . . I . . .

MARSHALL (*sings*). Ay, yi, yi, yi . . . Ay, yi, yi, yi . . .

GLENDENNING. I'd have him a . . . a . . . a . . . at home.

FITZPATRICK. At home, would you?

GLENDENNING. W . . . w . . . w . . . w . . . working.

FITZPATRICK. Aye, well, lad. That day might come.

MARSHALL. Son and daughter, Glenny.

GLENDENNING. Aye!

FITZPATRICK. Though there's one thing, Glenny.

GLENDENNING. Aye!

FITZPATRICK. You'll have to stop 'em eating.

MARSHALL. Meal-times, now, and nothing else.

GLENDENNING. Aye!

> *The men have unshackled the canvas and now begin to
> fold it.*

MARSHALL. A big fat cream bun, now . . .

FITZPATRICK. Once every Christmas.

GLENDENNING. Aye!

MARSHALL. And the odd kiss at bedtimes, Glenny, for the wife. (*Winking.*)

GLENDENNING. Aye! (*Laughs, pleased.*)

FITZPATRICK. He'd make somebody a good husband would Glenny.

GLENDENNING. Aye!

MARSHALL. Either that, now, or a damn fine wife.

They laugh.

FITZPATRICK. I read in the paper once about this place where all the women live together . . .

MARSHALL. I can just imagine that. I can . . .

FITZPATRICK. And all the men in another place entirely . . .

MARSHALL. And they pass over there . . .

FITZPATRICK. That's right . . .

MARSHALL. At night.

They laugh, wrapping the canvas.

FITZPATRICK. Had families like you have chickens . . .

MARSHALL. Broilers . . .

FITZPATRICK. Or those cows that never see the light.

MARSHALL. And all the man had to do was his day's work. The rest of the time was all his own.

KAY. Suit one or two people I could mention.

BENNETT. Suit one or two people here. You're right.

KAY and BENNETT laugh.

MARSHALL. Bennett, on the other hand, of course, is a different case entirely.

FITZPATRICK. 'Tirely.

BENNETT (*to* FITZPATRICK). Aye . . . They'd create a special post for you.

KAY. One to lean up against, I'm thinking.

BENNETT. Aye. One to lean up against . . . you're right.

KAY and BENNETT laugh.

FITZPATRICK. Hey . . .

MARSHALL. Hey, now . . .

FITZPATRICK. There's a provocation.

KAY. That's right . . . (*To* BENNETT.) Without a bloody doubt.

KAY and BENNETT *laugh.*

Behind them EWBANK *has come back with a bottle and several glasses on a tray, together with several small pieces of wedding cake.*

EWBANK. Here, now. You've not finished. Get it off, now, and we'll have a drop of this . . . Glenny. Fetch us in a table.

GLENDENNING. Aye! (*He goes off.*)

FITZPATRICK *and* MARSHALL *exchange looks; the men have begun to bag the canvas and lace it in the bags.*

KAY. What about the poles, now? (*Looking up.*)

EWBANK. Leave them now for the other truck. They'll never fit on this one . . . Now go damn careful with that. (*Indicating canvas.*) By God, that was bloody quick.

GLENDENNING *has gone out and come back in with a white metalwork table.*

EWBANK. Mention food and you can't see him for dust.

MARSHALL. He's smelled that cake.

FITZPATRICK. He has.

EWBANK. Now off, lad. Let's see you working. It won't run away, don't worry. (*He puts the tray on the table.*) It'll still be here when you've finished.

BENNETT. It's a lovely view you have here, Mr Ewbank.

EWBANK. Aye. And it costs a tidy drop, an' all.

BENNETT. I never thought of that . . . (*Looking towards the house.*)

EWBANK. There's no compensation, I can tell you, for being saddled with a lot of brass.

MARSHALL. Aye. Those of us without it have a great job remembering.

EWBANK. You're a damn sight better off without . . . Ask Kay. He'll tell you. (*They laugh.*)

FITZPATRICK. Aye. Aye. We could ask him that.

BENNETT. Your lad's gone then, Mr Ewbank, on his travels?

EWBANK. Aye . . . He has. His mother's wept bloody buckets. I don't know why. He'll be back again tomorrow.

FITZPATRICK. It's a great thing to have. The spirit of adventure.

EWBANK. There's only one spirit that I know of and you don't have to travel far for that.

They laugh. EWBANK *remains impassive.*

KAY. Come on, Fitzpatrick. Let's have a bit of carrying . . .

EWBANK. Aye. Let's tidy up the lawn.

They carry the canvas out.

GLENDENNING *returns with his bag and wanders round the lawn, picking up the pieces of paper streamers.*

KAY. Well, then. I think that should do it.

EWBANK. Aye . . . (*Looks round.*) Left a few damn marks.

KAY. I suppose it has to be reckoned.

EWBANK. Aye . . . You pay a price for everything, Kay. Best not to look, then you never know whether you've got it, or you've gone without . . . (*Calling off.*) Put it straight, for Christ's sake. All that lot'll bloody well fall off. (*To* KAY.) There's one thing, though . . .

KAY. Aye?

EWBANK. Ah, well . . . (*Uncertain for a moment. Then:*) I came out here, you know, this morning . . . Saw it all . . . Damn near broke my bloody heart . . . You saw it. God. What a bloody mess . . . Seen nowt like it. I haven't.

KAY. S'all made to be used.

EWBANK. Aye. You're right. Doesn't bear much reckoning. Best get on with it while you can.

KAY. Aye. (*Laughs.*)

EWBANK. Did you see much of my son?

KAY. No . . . Not much.

EWBANK. What do you reckon to it, then? Do you know, I've lived all this time – and I know nowt about anything.

Least ways, I've settled that. I've come to that conclusion. (*He laughs. Shakes his head.*) A bloody wanderer.

KAY (*watches him. Then*). Your lad?

EWBANK. I've no idea at all. None. Do you know? Where he's off to. I don't think he has himself. His mother sits at home . . . (*Shakes his head.*) The modern world, Kay. It's left you and me behind.

KAY. Aye. Well. It can't be helped.

They are silent a moment. Then:

EWBANK. Pathetic. (*He looks round.*) A lot of bloody misfits. You could put us all into a string bag, you know, and chuck us all away, and none'd be the wiser.

KAY (*laughs*). Aye. I think you're right.

EWBANK. Aye. (*Laughs.*) Sunk without trace.

MARSHALL *comes in, rubbing his hands.*

MARSHALL. Ay, now. That's just the stuff you want . . . (*To* GLENDENNING.) Tickle your bloody tonsils.

GLENDENNING. Aye!

Follows MARSHALL *over to the table.* BENNETT *also comes in.*

EWBANK. Never changes. Tell 'em there's summat here needs shifting and you'll be bloody hollering all day long. Show 'em half a bottle and they'll knock you over where you stand.

KAY. Aye! (*He nods and laughs.*)

MARSHALL. Had a drop of this before we started and we'd have been over in half the time.

EWBANK. Aye. I know. Over the lawn, more likely. Stretched out, flat on your back. (*He's pouring a liberal portion into each glass.*)

FITZPATRICK (*coming in*). A lot of holes you have in here . . . (*Looking round.*)

EWBANK. Aye. Well. It'll grow again. Come today. Gone tomorrow.

BENNETT. Everything in its season.

EWBANK. Aye. that's right . . .

BENNETT. This time next year . . .
MARSHALL. Bloody philosopher.
BENNETT. I had a lawn of my own once . . . (*Pauses.*)
EWBANK. Here you are, then. Hand it round . . .

They pass round the glasses and EWBANK *holds out the plate with the cake.*

FITZPATRICK. Nay, Glenny, lad . . . This isn't for you.
MARSHALL. Make your ears drop off.
FITZPATRICK. Your tongue drop out.
MARSHALL. Black hairs sprout up all over.
GLENDENNING. Aye! (*Takes his glass.*)

They laugh.

KAY. Here's to your good health, then.
MARSHALL. And the happy couple.
BENNETT. Aye, and the happy couple.
FITZPATRICK. And to ought else now that you have in
   mind. (*They laugh. Drink.*)
MARSHALL. By God. But that's a mighty drop of stuff.
FITZPATRICK. That'll curl your bloody whiskers.
BENNETT. Aye!
FITZPATRICK. Still all there, Glenny, are they?

They laugh.

GLENDENNING. Aye!
MARSHALL. You better count them. We don't want you
   leaving, now, without.
GLENDENNING. Aye!
FITZPATRICK. He's a damn fine lad. (*Arm round*
   GLENDENNING's *shoulder.*)
MARSHALL. He is. He is. You're right.
BENNETT. And that's a lovely drop of cake, too, to go with
   it.
KAY. It is. It's very good.
GLENDENNING. I . . . I . . . I . . . I . . . I . . .
FITZPATRICK. He's after another.

They laugh.

EWBANK. Nay, lad. That'll have to do you.

KAY (*putting down his glass*). Right, then. We better be getting off.

EWBANK. Aye. I'll be down to the yard later . . . Make sure you've packed that load right, Kay.

KAY. Aye . . . (*He goes.*)

EWBANK. Drive carefully. Drop nowt off.

FITZPATRICK (*setting down his glass with* BENNETT). Ah, that was a damn fine drop. I won't say that I couldn't stand another . . . But then, work's work.

EWBANK. Aye. And don't you forget it.

FITZPATRICK *goes.*

MARSHALL. See you at the yard . . . (*Sets down his glass.*)

EWBANK. Aye. Aye. That's right.

BENNETT. Thanks again, Mr Ewbank . . .

EWBANK. . . . nothing of it.

BENNETT *goes with a nod.*

Go on, Glenny. Get off, or they'll leave you here behind.

GLENDENNING. Aye!

EWBANK. Sithee. I've a bit extra for you. (*Takes a bit of cake from his pocket.*) E't it now when they're not looking, or they'll have it off you.

GLENDENNING. Aye!

EWBANK. Right, then. Off you go.

GLENDENNING *goes, eating.*

EWBANK *is left alone.*

FITZPATRICK (*off*). Come on. Come on, now. My turn in the cab.

KAY (*off*). On the back, Fitzpatrick.

FITZPATRICK (*off*). Good God.

MARSHALL (*off*). He'll be blown away.

BENNETT (*off*). Some hopes of that.

MARSHALL (*off*). Ay, now. There's no room for me up there.

KAY (*off*). Are you right, then, Glenny . . . ?

GLENDENNING (*off*). Aye!

FITZPATRICK (*off*). Here he is. He's here.

MARSHALL (*off: sings*). Ay, yi, yi, yi . . . Ay, yi, yi, yi . . .

Laughter. Dies away.

Silence.

EWBANK *stands alone, gazing out from between the poles. Fastens the ropes hanging from the pulleys, almost absent-mindedly, abstracted. He gazes at view again.*

After a while, MRS EWBANK *comes on. Silent a moment, looking round.*

MRS EWBANK. They've gone, then.

EWBANK (*doesn't look up*). Aye.

MRS EWBANK (*pause*). You get used to the noise around you after a while.

EWBANK. Aye. You do.

MRS EWBANK *gazes across at the view.*

MRS EWBANK. Your mother and dad are leaving in a few minutes.

EWBANK. I'll come and see them off.

MRS EWBANK. He's lost his bit of rope.

EWBANK. I'll cut him off a bit. He'll never know the difference.

MRS EWBANK. . . . All that smoke . . . Like a carpet . . . They had a drink, then.

EWBANK. Aye. Wet the baby's head . . . (*Looks up at her expression.*) Well, I don't know, do I? These days . . . one damn thing . . .

Pause. Then:

Set an example there'll be no stopping. They'll be wanting a sup on every job from now on . . . I don't know. (*Looks down at the view, standing beside her.*) You'd think you'd have something to show for it, wouldn't you. After all this time.

MRS EWBANK. Well, now . . . (*Abstracted.*)

EWBANK. I don't know . . . (*Looks round. Then down at the lawn.*) Made a few marks in that.

MRS EWBANK. One or two . . .

EWBANK (*shivers. Looks up*). Autumn . . .

MRS EWBANK (*abstracted*). Still . . . It's been a good summer.

EWBANK. Aye. Comes and goes.

MRS EWBANK. What . . . ?

Pause.

EWBANK. Do you know that Kay was had up once for embezzlement?

MRS EWBANK. They've been had up for a lot of things. The men that work for you.

EWBANK. Aye . . . Nobody else'll have 'em . . . I must be bloody daft. Well. I suppose we better see the old uns off.

MRS EWBANK. Yes . . .

EWBANK. I don't know . . . What's to become of us, you reckon?

MRS EWBANK looks at him, smiles, then shakes her head.

Never do this again, you know.

MRS EWBANK. No . . . (*She smiles.*)

EWBANK. Me heart wouldn't stand it.

MRS EWBANK. No . . . (*She laughs.*)

OLD MRS EWBANK (*off*). Frank . . . !

EWBANK. Aye, well. (*Half-laughs.*) That's summat.

They turn slowly, arm in arm.

OLD MRS EWBANK (*off*). Frank . . . !

EWBANK. S'all right. We're coming. (*To* MRS EWBANK.) Well, then. We better go.

They go.

The stage stands empty: bare poles, the ropes fastened off. The light fades slowly.

Curtain.

HOME

Home was first presented at the Royal Court Theatre, London, on 17 June 1970. The cast was as follows:

HARRY	John Gielgud
JACK	Ralph Richardson
MARJORIE	Dandy Nichols
KATHLEEN	Mona Washbourne
ALFRED	Warren Clarke

Directed by Lindsay Anderson

ACT ONE

Scene One

The stage is bare but for a round metalwork table, set slightly off-centre, stage left, and two metalwork chairs.

HARRY comes on, stage right, a middle-aged man in his forties. He wears a casual suit, perhaps tweed, with a suitable hat which, after glancing pleasurably around, he takes off and puts on the table beside him, along with a pair of well-used leather gloves and a folded newspaper.

Presses his shoulders back, eases neck, etc., making himself comfortable. Settles down. Glances at his watch, shakes it, makes sure it's going; winds it slowly, looking round.

Stretches neck again. Leans down, wafts cotton from his turn-ups. Examines shoes, without stooping.

Clears his throat. Clasps his hands in his lap, gazes out, abstracted, head nodding slightly, half-smiling.

JACK. Harry!

> *JACK has come on from the other side, stage left. He's dressed in a similar fashion, but with a slightly more dandyish flavour: handkerchief hanging from top pocket, a rakish trilby. Also has a simple though rather elegant cane.*

HARRY. Jack.
JACK. Been here long?
HARRY. No. No.
JACK. Mind?
HARRY. Not at all.

> *JACK sits down. He stretches, shows great relief at being off his feet, etc.*

JACK. Nice to see the sun again.
HARRY. Very.
JACK. Been laid up for a few days.
HARRY. Oh dear.
JACK. Chill. In bed.
HARRY. Oh dear. Still . . . Appreciate the comforts.

JACK. What? . . . You're right. Still . . . Nice to be out.
HARRY. 'Tis.
JACK. Mind?
HARRY. All yours.

JACK *picks up the paper; gazes at it without unfolding it.*

JACK. Damn bad news.
HARRY. Yes.
JACK. Not surprising.
HARRY. Gets worse before it gets better.
JACK. 'S right . . . Still . . . Not to grumble.
HARRY. No. No.
JACK. Put on a bold front. (*Turns paper over.*)
HARRY. That's right.
JACK. Pretty. (*Indicates paper.*)
HARRY. Very.
JACK. By Jove . . . (*Reads intently a moment.*) Oh, well.
HARRY. That the one? (*Glances over.*)
JACK (*nods*). Yes . . . (*Clicks his tongue.*)
HARRY (*shakes his head*). Ah, well.
JACK. Yes . . . Still . . .
HARRY. Clouds . . . Watch their different shapes.
JACK. Yes? (*Looks up at the sky at which* HARRY *is gazing.*)
HARRY. See how they drift over?
JACK. By Jove.
HARRY. First sight . . . nothing. Then . . . just watch the edges . . . See.
JACK. Amazing.
HARRY. Never notice when you're just walking.
JACK. No . . . Still . . . Best time of the year.
HARRY. What?
JACK. Always think this is the best time.
HARRY. Oh, yes.
JACK. Not too hot. Not too cold.
HARRY. Seen that? (*Points at the paper.*)
JACK (*reads. Then*). By Jove . . . (*Reads again briefly.*) Well . . . you get some surprises . . . Hello . . . (*Reads farther down, turning edge of paper over.*) Good God.
HARRY. What I felt.

JACK. The human mind. (*Shakes his head.*)

HARRY. Oh dear, yes.

JACK. One of these days . . .

HARRY. Ah, yes.

JACK. Then where will they be?

HARRY. Oh, yes.

JACK. Never give it a thought.

HARRY. No . . . Never.

JACK (*reads again*). By Jove . . . (*Shakes his head.*)

HARRY *leans over; removes something casually from Jack's sleeve.*

Oh . . .

HARRY. Cotton.

JACK. Oh . . . Picked it up . . . (*Glances round at his other sleeve, then down at his trousers.*)

HARRY. See you've come prepared.

JACK. What . . . ? Oh.

HARRY *indicates* JACK's *coat pocket.*

JACK *takes out a folded plastic mac, no larger, folded, than his hand.*

Best to make sure.

HARRY. Took a risk. Myself.

JACK. Oh, yes . . . What's life worth . . .

HARRY. Oh, yes.

JACK. I say. That was a shock.

HARRY. Yesterday . . . ?

JACK. Bolt from the blue, and no mistake.

HARRY. I'd been half-prepared . . . even then.

JACK. Still a shock.

HARRY. Absolutely.

JACK. My wife . . . you've met? . . . Was that last week?

HARRY. Ah, yes . . .

JACK. Well. A very delicate woman.

HARRY. Still. Very sturdy.

JACK. Oh, well. Physically, nothing to complain of.

HARRY. Oh, no.

JACK. Temperament, however . . . inclined to the sensitive side.

HARRY. Really.

JACK. Two years ago . . . (*Glances off.*) By Jove. Isn't that Saxton?

HARRY. Believe it is.

JACK. He's a sharp dresser, and no mistake.

HARRY. Very.

JACK. They tell me . . . Well, I never.

HARRY. Didn't see that, did he?

They laugh, looking off.

Eyes in the back of your head these days.

JACK. You have. That's right.

HARRY. Won't do that again in a hurry. What? (*Laughs.*)

JACK. I had an uncle once who bred horses.

HARRY. Really.

JACK. Used to go down there when I was a boy.

HARRY. The country.

JACK. Nothing like it. What? Fresh air.

HARRY. Clouds. (*Gestures up.*)

JACK. I'd say so.

HARRY. *My* wife was coming up this morning.

JACK. Really?

HARRY. Slight headache. Thought might be better . . .

JACK. Indoors. Well. Best make sure.

HARRY. When I was in the army . . .

JACK. Really? What regiment?

HARRY. Fusiliers.

JACK. Really? How extraordinary.

HARRY. You?

JACK. No. No. A cousin.

HARRY. Well . . .

JACK. Different time, of course.

HARRY. Ah.

JACK. Used to bring his rifle . . . No. That was Arthur. Got them muddled. (*Laughs.*)

HARRY. Still.

JACK. Never leaves you.

HARRY. No. No.

JACK. In good stead.

HARRY. Oh, yes.

JACK. All your life.

HARRY. Oh, yes.

JACK. I was – for a very short while – in the Royal Air Force.

HARRY. Really?

JACK. Nothing to boast about.

HARRY. Oh, now. Flying?

JACK. On the ground.

HARRY. Chrysanthemums is my wife's hobby.

JACK. Really.

HARRY. Thirty-seven species round the house.

JACK. Beautiful flower.

HARRY. Do you know there are over a hundred?

JACK. Really?

HARRY. Different species.

JACK. Suppose you can mix them up.

HARRY. Oh. Very.

JACK. He's coming back . . .

HARRY. . . . ?

JACK. Swanson.

HARRY. Saxton.

JACK. Saxton! Always did get those two mixed up. Two boys at school: one called Saxton, the other Swanson. Curious thing was, they both looked alike.

HARRY. Really?

JACK. Both had a curious skin disease. Here. Just at the side of the nose.

HARRY. Eczema.

JACK. Really?

HARRY. Could have been.

JACK. Never thought of that . . . When I was young I had an ambition to be a priest, you know.

HARRY. Really?

JACK. Thought about it a great deal.

HARRY. Ah, yes. A great decision.

JACK. Oh, yes.

HARRY. Catholic or Anglican?

JACK. Well . . . Couldn't really make up my mind.

HARRY. Both got a great deal to offer.

JACK. Great deal? My word.

HARRY. Advantages one way. And then . . . in another.

JACK. Oh, yes.

HARRY. One of my first ambitions . . .

JACK. Yes.

HARRY. Oh, now. You'll laugh.

JACK. No. No . . . No. Really.

HARRY. Well . . . I would have liked to have been a dancer.

JACK. Dancer . . . Tap or 'balley'?

HARRY. Oh, well. Probably a bit of both.

JACK. A fine thing. Grace.

HARRY. Ah, yes.

JACK. Physical momentum.

HARRY. Yes.

JACK. Swanson might have appreciated that! (*Laughs.*)

HARRY. Saxton.

JACK. Saxton! By Jove . . . At school we had a boy called Ramsbottom.

HARRY. Really.

JACK. Now I wouldn't have envied that boy's life.

HARRY. No.

JACK. The euphemisms to which a name . . . well. One doesn't have to think very far.

HARRY. No.

JACK. A name can be a great embarrassment in life.

HARRY. It can . . . We had – let me think – a boy called Fish.

JACK. Fish!

HARRY. And another called Parsons!

JACK. Parsons!

HARRY. Nicknamed 'Nosey'.

JACK. By Jove! (*Laughs; rises.*) Some of these nicknames are very clever.

HARRY. Yes.

JACK (*moves away stage right*). I remember, when I was young, I had a very tall friend . . . extremely tall as a matter of fact. He was called 'Lolly'.

HARRY. Lolly!

JACK. It fitted him very well. He . . . (*Abstracted. Pause.*) Yes. Had very large teeth as well.

HARRY. The past. It conjures up some images.

JACK. It does. You're right.

HARRY. You wonder how there was ever time for it all.

JACK. Time . . . Oh . . . Don't mention it.

HARRY. A fine cane.

JACK. What? Oh, that.

HARRY. Father had a cane. Walked for miles.

JACK. A habit that's fast dying out.

HARRY. Oh, yes.

JACK. Knew a man, related to a friend of mine, who used to walk twenty miles a day.

HARRY. Twenty!

JACK. Each morning.

HARRY. That really shows some spirit.

JACK. If you keep up a steady pace, you can manage four miles in the hour.

HARRY. Goodness.

JACK. Five hours. Set off at eight each morning. Back for lunch at one.

HARRY. Must have had a great appetite.

JACK. Oh. Absolutely. Ate like a horse.

HARRY. Stand him in good stead later on.

JACK. Ah, yes . . . Killed, you know. In the war.

HARRY. Oh dear.

JACK. Funny thing to work out.

HARRY. Oh, yes.

Pause.

JACK (*sits*). You do any fighting?

HARRY. What?

JACK. Army.

HARRY. Oh, well, then . . . modest amount.

JACK. Nasty business.

HARRY. Oh! Doesn't bear thinking about.

JACK. Two relatives of mine killed in the war.

HARRY. Oh dear.

JACK. You have to give thanks, I must say.

HARRY. Oh, yes.

JACK. Mother's father . . . a military man.

HARRY. Yes.

JACK. All his life.

HARRY. He must have seen some sights.

JACK. Oh, yes.

HARRY. Must have all had meaning then.

JACK. Oh, yes. India. Africa. He's buried as a matter of fact in Hong Kong.

HARRY. Really?

JACK. So they tell me. Never been there myself.

HARRY. No.

JACK. Hot climates, I think, can be the very devil if you haven't the temperament.

HARRY. Huh! You don't have to tell me.

JACK. Been there?

HARRY. No, no. Just what one reads.

JACK. Dysentery.

HARRY. Beriberi.

JACK. Yellow fever.

HARRY. Oh dear.

JACK. As well, of course, as all the other contingencies.

HARRY. Oh yes.

JACK. At times one's glad simply to live on an island.

HARRY. Yes.

JACK. Strange that.

HARRY. Yes.

JACK. Without the sea – all around – civilization would never have been the same.

HARRY. Oh, no.

JACK. The ideals of life, liberty, freedom, could never have been the same – democracy – well, if we'd been living on the Continent, for example.

HARRY. Absolutely.

JACK. Those your gloves?

HARRY. Yes.

JACK. Got a pair like that at home.

HARRY. Yes?

JACK. Very nearly. The seam goes the other way, I think. (*Picks one up to look*.) Yes. It does.

HARRY. A present.

JACK. Really?

HARRY. My wife. At Christmas.

JACK. Season of good cheer.

HARRY. Less and less, of course, these days.

JACK. Oh, my dear man. The whole thing has been ruined. The moment money intrudes . . . all feeling goes straight out of the window.

HARRY. Oh, yes.

JACK. I had an aunt once who owned a little shop.

HARRY. Yes?

JACK. Made almost her entire income during the few weeks before Christmas.

HARRY. Really.

JACK. Never seemed to occur to her that there might be some ethical consideration.

HARRY. Oh dear.

JACK. Ah, well.

HARRY. Still . . .

JACK. Apart from that, she was a very wonderful person.

HARRY. It's very hard to judge.

JACK. It is.

HARRY. I have a car, for instance.

JACK. Yes?

HARRY. One day, in December, I happened to knock a pedestrian over in the street.

JACK. Oh dear.

HARRY. It was extremely crowded.

JACK. You don't have to tell me. I've seen them.

HARRY. Happened to see something they wanted the other side. Dashed across. Before you know where you are . . .

JACK. Not serious, I hope?

HARRY. No. No. No. Fractured arm.

JACK. From that, you know, they might learn a certain lesson.

HARRY. Oh, yes.

JACK. Experience is a stern master.

HARRY. Ah, yes. But then . . .

JACK. Perhaps the only one.

HARRY. It is.

JACK. I had a cousin, on my mother's side, who once fell off a cliff.

HARRY. Really.

JACK. Quite a considerable height.

HARRY. Ah, yes.

JACK. Fell into the sea, fortunately. Dazed. Apart from that, quite quickly recovered.

HARRY. Very fortunate.

JACK. Did it for a dare. Only twelve years old at the time.

HARRY. I remember I fell off a cliff, one time.

JACK. Oh dear.

HARRY. Not very high. And there was someone there to catch me. (*Laughs.*)

JACK. They can be very exciting places.

HARRY. Oh, very.

JACK. I remember I once owned a little boat.

HARRY. Really.

JACK. For fishing. Nothing very grand.

HARRY. A fishing man.

JACK. Not really. More an occasional pursuit.

HARRY. I've always been curious about that.

JACK. Yes?

HARRY. 'A solitary figure crouched upon a bank.'

JACK. Never stirring.

HARRY. No. No.

JACK. Can be very tedious, I know.

HARRY. Still. A boat is more interesting.

JACK. Oh, yes. A sort of tradition, really.

HARRY. In the family.

JACK. No. No. More in the . . . island, you know.

HARRY. Ah, yes.

JACK. Drake.

HARRY. Yes!

JACK. Nelson.

HARRY. Beatty.

JACK. Sir Walter Raleigh.

HARRY. There was a very fine man . . . poet.

JACK. Lost his head, you know.

HARRY. It's surprising the amount of dust that collects in so short a space of time. (*Runs hand lightly over table.*)

JACK. It is. (*Looks round.*) Spot like this, perhaps, attracts it.

HARRY. Yes . . . (*Pause.*) You never became a priest, then?

JACK. No . . . No.

HARRY. Splendid to have a vocation.

JACK. 'Tis . . . Something you believe in.

HARRY. Oh, yes.

JACK. I could never . . . resolve certain difficulties, myself.

HARRY. Yes?

JACK. The hows and the wherefores I could understand.
How we came to be, and His presence, lurking
everywhere, you know. But as to the 'why' . . . I could
never understand. Seemed a terrible waste of time to me.

HARRY. Oh, yes.

JACK. Thought it better to leave it to those who didn't
mind.

HARRY. Ah, yes.

JACK. I suppose the same was true about dancing.

HARRY. Oh, yes. I remember turning up for instance, to my
first class, only to discover that all the rest of them were
girls.

JACK. Really?

HARRY. Well . . . there are men dancers, I know. Still . . .
Took up football after that.

JACK. To professional standard, I imagine.

HARRY. Oh, no. Just the odd kick around. Joined a team
that played in the park on Sunday mornings.

JACK. The athletic life has many attractions.

HARRY. It has. It has.

Pause.

JACK. How long have you been here, then?

HARRY. Oh, a couple of er.

JACK. Strange – meeting the other day.

HARRY. Yes.

JACK. On the way back, thought to myself, 'What a chance
encounter.'

HARRY. Yes.

JACK. So rare, these days, to meet someone to whom one
can actually talk.

HARRY. I know what you mean.

JACK. One works. One looks around. One meets people.
But very little communication actually takes place.

HARRY. Very.

JACK. None at all in most cases! (*Laughs.*)

HARRY. Oh, absolutely.

JACK. The agonies and frustrations. I can assure you. In the end one gives up in absolute despair.

HARRY. Oh, yes. (*Laughs, rising, looking off.*)

JACK. Isn't that Parker? (*Looking off.*)

HARRY. No . . . N-no . . . Believe his name is Fielding.

JACK. Could have sworn it was Parker.

HARRY. No. Don't think so . . . Parker walks with a limp. Very slight.

JACK. That's Marshall.

HARRY. Really. Then I've got Parker mixed up again. (*Laughs.*)

JACK. Did you see the one who came in yesterday?

HARRY. Hendricks.

JACK. Is that his name?

HARRY. I believe that's what I heard.

JACK. He looked a very suspicious character to me. And his wife . . .

HARRY. I would have thought his girl-friend.

JACK. Really? Then that makes far more sense . . . I mean, I have great faith in the institution of marriage as such.

HARRY. Oh, yes.

JACK. But one thing I've always noticed. When you find a married couple who display their affection in public, then that's an infallible sign that their marriage is breaking up.

HARRY. Really?

JACK. It's a very curious thing. I'm sure there must be some psychological explanation for it.

HARRY. Insecurity.

JACK. Oh, yes.

HARRY. Quite frequently one can judge people entirely by their behaviour.

JACK. You can. I believe you're right.

HARRY. Take my father, for instance.

JACK. Oh, yes.

HARRY. An extraordinary man by any standard. And yet, throughout his life, he could never put out a light.

JACK. Really.

HARRY. Superstition. If he had to turn off a switch, he'd ask someone else to do it.

JACK. How extraordinary.

HARRY. Quite casually. One never noticed. Over the years one got quite used to it, of course. As a man he was extremely polite.

JACK. Ah, yes.

HARRY (*sits*). Mother, now. She was quite the reverse.

JACK. Oh, yes.

HARRY. Great appetite for life.

JACK. Really?

HARRY. Three.

JACK. Three?

HARRY. Children.

JACK. Ah, yes.

HARRY. Youngest.

JACK. You were?

HARRY. Oh, yes.

JACK. One of seven.

HARRY. Seven!

JACK. Large families in those days.

HARRY. Oh, yes.

JACK. Family life.

HARRY. Oh, yes.

JACK. Society, well, without it, wouldn't be what it's like today.

HARRY. Oh, no.

JACK. Still.

HARRY. Ah, yes.

JACK. We have a wonderful example.

HARRY. Oh. My word.

JACK. At times I don't know where some of us would be without it.

HARRY. No. Not at all.

JACK. A friend of mine – actually, more of an acquaintance, really – was introduced to George VI at Waterloo.

HARRY. Waterloo?

JACK. The station.

HARRY. By Jove.

. He was an assistant to the station-master at the time,
a lowly capacity, of course. His Majesty was making a
weekend trip into the country.

HARRY. Probably to Windsor.

Pause.

JACK. Can you get to Windsor from Waterloo?

HARRY. I'm . . . No. I'm not sure.

JACK. Sandringham, of course, is in the country.

HARRY. The other way.

JACK. The other way.

HARRY. Balmoral in the Highlands.

JACK. I had an aunt once who, for a short while, lived near
Gloucester.

HARRY. That's a remarkable stretch of the country.

JACK. Vale of Evesham.

HARRY. Vale of Evesham.

JACK. Local legend has it that Adam and Eve originated
there.

HARRY. Really?

JACK. Has very wide currency, I believe, in the district. For
instance. You may have read that portion in the Bible . . .

HARRY. I have.

JACK. The profusion of vegetation, for example, would
indicate that it couldn't, for instance, be anywhere in the
Middle East.

HARRY. No. No.

JACK. On the other hand, the profusion of animals . . .
snakes, for example . . . would indicate that it might
easily be a more tropical environment, as opposed, that is,
to one which is merely temperate.

HARRY. Yes . . . I see.

JACK. Then again, there is ample evidence to suggest that
during the period in question equatorial conditions
prevailed in the very region in which we are now sitting.

HARRY. Really? (*Looks around.*)

JACK. Discoveries have been made that would indicate that
lions and tigers, elephants, wolves, rhinoceroses, and so
forth, actually inhabited these parts.

HARRY. My word.

JACK. In those circumstances, it wouldn't be unreasonable to suppose that the Vale of Evesham was such a place itself. The very cradle, as it were, of . . .

HARRY. Close to where your aunt lived.

JACK. That's right.

HARRY. Mind if I have a look?

JACK. Not at all.

> HARRY *takes the cane.*

HARRY. You seldom see canes of this quality these days.

JACK. No. No. That's right.

HARRY. I believe they've gone out of fashion.

JACK. They have.

HARRY. Like beards.

JACK. Beards!

HARRY. My father had a small moustache.

JACK. A moustache I've always thought became a man.

HARRY. Chamberlain.

JACK. Roosevelt.

HARRY. Schweitzer.

JACK. Chaplin.

HARRY. Hitler . . .

JACK. Travel, I've always felt, was a great broadener of the mind.

HARRY. My word.

JACK. Travelled a great deal – when I was young.

HARRY. Far?

JACK. Oh. All over.

HARRY. A great thing.

JACK. Sets its mark upon a man.

HARRY. Like the army.

JACK. Like the army. I suppose the fighting you do has very much the same effect.

HARRY. Oh, yes.

JACK. Bayonet?

HARRY. What?

JACK. The er.

HARRY. Oh bayonet . . . ball and flame. The old three, as we used to call them.

JACK. Ah, yes.

HARRY. A great welder of character.

JACK. By Jove.

HARRY. The youth of today: might have done some good.

JACK. Oh. My word, yes.

HARRY. In the Royal Air Force, of course . . .

JACK. Bombs.

HARRY. Really.

JACK. Cannon.

HARRY. Ah, yes . . . Couldn't have got far, in our job, I can tell you, without the Royal Air Force.

JACK. No. No.

HARRY. Britannia rules the waves . . . and rules the skies, too, I shouldn't wonder.

JACK. Oh, yes.

HARRY. Nowadays, of course . . .

JACK. Rockets.

HARRY. Ah, yes.

JACK. They say . . .

HARRY. Yes?

JACK. When the next catastrophe occurs . . .

HARRY. Oh, yes.

JACK. That the island itself might very well be flooded.

HARRY. Really.

JACK. Except for the more prominent peaks, of course.

HARRY. Oh, yes.

JACK. While we're sitting here waiting to be buried . . .

HARRY. Oh, yes.

JACK (laughing). We'll end up being drowned.

HARRY. Extraordinary! (Laughs.) No Vale of Evesham then.

JACK. Oh, no.

HARRY. Nor your aunt at Gloucester!

JACK. She died a little while ago, you know.

HARRY. Oh. I am sorry.

JACK. We weren't very attached.

HARRY. Oh, no.

JACK. Still. She was a very remarkable woman.

HARRY. Ah, yes.

JACK. In her own particular way. So few characters around these days. So few interesting people.

HARRY. Oh, yes.

JACK. Uniformity.

HARRY. Mrs Washington. (*Looking off.*)

JACK. Really? I've been keeping an eye open for her. (*Stands.*)

HARRY. Striking woman.

JACK. Her husband was related to a distant cousin of mine, on my father's side. (*Straightening tie, etc.*)

HARRY. My word.

JACK. I shouldn't be surprised if she recognizes me . . . No . . .

HARRY. Scarcely glanced. Her mind on other things.

JACK. Oh, yes. (*Sits.*)

HARRY. Parker. (*Looking off.*)

JACK. Oh, yes.

HARRY. You're right. He's not the man with the limp.

JACK. That's Marshall.

HARRY. That's right. Parker is the one who has something the matter with his arm. I knew it was something like that.

JACK. Polio.

HARRY. Yes?

JACK. I had a sister who contracted polio. Younger than me. Died within a matter of hours.

HARRY. Oh. Goodness.

JACK. Only a few months old at the time. Scarcely learnt to speak.

HARRY. What a terrible experience.

JACK. I had another sister die. She was how old? Eleven.

HARRY. Oh dear.

JACK. Large families do have their catastrophes.

HARRY. They do.

JACK. I remember a neighbour of ours, when we lived in the country, died one morning by falling down the stairs.

HARRY. Goodness.

JACK. The extraordinary thing was, the following day they were due to move into a bungalow.

HARRY. Goodness. (*Shakes his head.*)

JACK. One of the great things, of course, about my aunt's house.

HARRY. Yes?

JACK. In Gloucester. Was that it had an orchard.

HARRY. Now they *are* lovely things.

JACK. Particularly in the spring.

HARRY. In the spring especially.

JACK. And the autumn, of course.

HARRY. 'Boughs laden.'

JACK. Apple a day.

HARRY. Oh, yes.

JACK. I had a niece once who was a vegetarian.

HARRY. Really.

JACK. Ate nut rissoles.

HARRY. I tried once to give up meat.

JACK. Goes back, you know.

HARRY. Oh, yes.

JACK. Proctor. The young woman with him is Mrs Jefferies.

HARRY. Really.

JACK. Interesting people to talk to. He's been a missionary, you know.

HARRY. Yes?

JACK. Spent most of his time, he said, taking out people's teeth.

HARRY. Goodness.

JACK. Trained for it, of course. Mrs Jefferies, on the other hand.

HARRY. Yes.

JACK. Was a lady gymnast. Apparently very famous in her day.

HARRY. My word.

JACK. Developed arthritis in two of her er.

HARRY. Oh dear.

JACK. Did you know it was caused by a virus?

HARRY. No.

JACK. Apparently. I had a maiden aunt who suffered from it a great deal. She was a flautist. Played in an orchestra of some distinction. Never married. I thought that very strange.

HARRY. Yes.

JACK. Musicians, of course, are a strange breed altogether.

HARRY. Oh, yes.

JACK. Have you noticed how the best of them have very curly hair?

HARRY. Really.

JACK. My maiden aunt, of course, has died now.

HARRY. Ah, yes.

JACK. Spot of cloud there.

HARRY. Soon passes.

JACK. Ever seen this? (*Takes out a coin.*) There. Nothing up my sleeve. Ready? One, two, three . . . Gone.

HARRY. My word.

JACK. Here . . . (*Takes out three cards.*) Pick out the queen of hearts.

HARRY. This one.

JACK. No!

HARRY. Oh!

They laugh.

JACK. Try again . . . There she is. (*Shuffles them round on the table.*) Where is she?

HARRY. Er . . .

JACK. Take your time.

HARRY. This one . . . Oh!

They laugh.

JACK. That one!

HARRY. Well. I'll have to study those.

JACK. Easy when you know how. I have some more back there. One of my favourite tricks is to take the ace of spades out of someone's top pocket.

HARRY. Oh . . . (*Looks.*)

JACK. No. No. No. (*Laughs.*) It needs some preparation . . . Sometimes in a lady's handbag. That goes down very well.

HARRY. Goodness.

JACK. I knew a man at one time – a friend of the family, on my father's side – who could put a lighted cigarette into his mouth, take one half from one ear, and the other half from the other.

HARRY. Goodness.

JACK. Still lighted.

HARRY. How did he do that?

JACK. I don't know.

HARRY. I suppose – physiologically – it's possible, then.

JACK. Shouldn't think so.

HARRY. No.

JACK. One of the advantages, of course, of sitting here.

HARRY. Oh, yes.

JACK. You can see everyone walking past.

HARRY. Oh, yes.

JACK. Jennings isn't a man I'm awfully fond of.

HARRY. No.

JACK. You've probably noticed yourself.

HARRY. I have. In the army, I met a man . . . Private . . . er.

JACK. The equivalent rank, of course, in the air force, is air-craftsman.

HARRY. Or able seaman. In the navy.

JACK. Able seaman.

They laugh.

HARRY. Goodness.

JACK. Funny name. (*Laughs.*) Able seaman. I don't think I'd like to be called that.

HARRY. Yes! (*Laughs.*)

JACK. Able seaman! (*Snorts.*)

HARRY. Fraser. Have you noticed him?

JACK. Don't think I have.

HARRY. A thin moustache.

JACK. Black.

HARRY. That's right.

JACK. My word.

HARRY. Steer clear, probably, might be better.

JACK. Some people you can sum up at glance.

HARRY. Oh, yes.

JACK. My mother was like that. Delicate. Not unlike my wife.

HARRY. Nevertheless, very sturdy.

JACK. Oh, yes. Physically, nothing to complain about. My mother, on the other hand, was actually as delicate as she looked. Whereas my wife looks . . .

HARRY. Robust.

JACK. Robust. My mother actually looked extremely delicate.

HARRY. Still. Seven children.

JACK. Oh, yes.

HARRY. My father was a very . . . emotional man. Of great feeling.

JACK. Like mine.

HARRY. Oh, very much like yours.

JACK. But dominated somewhat.

HARRY. Yes?

JACK. By your mother.

HARRY. Oh. I suppose he was. Passionate but . . .

JACK. Dominated. One of the great things, of course, about the war was its feeling of camaraderie.

HARRY. Friendship.

JACK. You found that too? On the airfield where I was stationed it was really like one great big happy family. My word. The things one did for one another.

HARRY. Oh, yes.

JACK. The way one worked.

HARRY. Soon passed.

JACK. Oh, yes. It did. It did.

HARRY. Ah, yes.

JACK. No sooner was the fighting over than back it came. Back-biting. Complaints. Getting what you can. I sometimes think if the war had been prolonged another thirty years we'd have all felt the benefit.

HARRY. Oh, yes.

JACK. One's children would have grown up far different. That's for sure.

HARRY. Really? How many have you got?

JACK. Two.

HARRY. Oh, that's very nice.

JACK. Boy married. Girl likewise. They seem to rush into things so early these days.

HARRY. Oh, yes.

JACK. And you?

HARRY. Oh. No. No. Never had the privilege.

JACK. Ah, yes. Responsibility. At times you wonder if it's worth it. I had a cousin, on my father's side, who threw herself from a railway carriage.

HARRY. Oh dear. How awful.

JACK. Yes.

HARRY. Killed outright.

JACK. Well, fortunately, it had just pulled into a station.

HARRY. I see.

JACK. Daughter's married to a salesman. Refrigerators: he sells appliances of that nature.

HARRY. Oh. Opposite to me.

JACK. Yes?

HARRY. Heating engineer.

JACK. Really. I'd never have guessed. How extraordinary.

HARRY. And yourself.

JACK. Oh, I've tinkered with one or two things.

HARRY. Ah, yes.

JACK. What I like about my present job is the scope that it leaves you for initiative.

HARRY. Rather. Same with mine.

JACK. Distribution of food-stuffs in a wholesale store.

HARRY. Really.

JACK. Thinking out new ideas. Constant speculation.

HARRY. Oh, yes.

JACK. Did you know if you put jam into small cardboard containers it will sell far better than if you put it into large glass jars?

HARRY. Really?

JACK. Psychological. When you buy it in a jar you're wondering what on earth – subconsciously – you're going to do with the glass bottle. But with a cardboard box that anxiety is instantly removed. Result: improved sales; improved production; lower prices; improved distribution.

HARRY. That's a fascinating job.

JACK. Oh, yes. If you use your brains there's absolutely nothing there to stop you.

HARRY. I can see.

JACK. Heating must be a very similar problem.

HARRY. Oh, yes.

JACK. The different ways of warming up a house.

HARRY. Yes.

JACK. Or not warming it up, as the case may be.

HARRY. Yes!

They laugh.

JACK. I don't think I've met your wife.

HARRY. No. No . . . As a matter of fact. We've been separated for a little while.

JACK. Oh dear.

HARRY. One of those misfortunes.

JACK. Happens a great deal.

HARRY. Oh, yes.

JACK. Each have our cross.

HARRY. Oh, yes.

JACK. Well. Soon be time for lunch.

HARRY. Will. And I haven't had my walk.

JACK. No. Still.

HARRY. Probably do as much good.

JACK. Oh, yes.

HARRY. Well, then . . . (*Stretches. Gets up.*)

JACK. Yours or mine?

HARRY. Mine . . . I believe. (*Picks up the newspaper.*)

JACK. Ah, yes.

HARRY. Very fine gloves.

JACK. Yes.

HARRY. Pacamac.

JACK. All correct.

HARRY. Cane.

JACK. Cane.

HARRY. Well, then. Off we go.

JACK. Off we go.

HARRY breathes in deeply; breathes out.

HARRY. Beautiful corner.

JACK. 'Tis.

Pause; last look round.

HARRY. Work up an appetite.
JACK. Right, then. Best foot forward.
HARRY. Best foot forward.
JACK. Best foot forward, and off we go.

They stroll off, taking the air, stage left.

Scene Two

KATHLEEN *and* MARJORIE *come on, stage right.*

KATHLEEN *is a stout middle-aged lady; she wears a coat, which is unbuttoned, a headscarf and strap shoes. She is limping, her arm supported by* MARJORIE.

MARJORIE *is also middle-aged. She is dressed in a skirt and cardigan. She carries an umbrella and a large, well-used bag.*

KATHLEEN. Cor . . . blimey!
MARJORIE. Going to rain, ask me.
KATHLEEN. Rain all it wants, ask me. Cor . . . blimey!
   Going to kill me is this. (*Limps to a chair, sits down and holds her foot.*)
MARJORIE. Going to rain and catch us out here. That's what it's going to do. (*Puts umbrella up; worn, but not excessively so.*)
KATHLEEN. Going to rain all right, i'n't it? Going to rain all right . . . Put your umbrella up – sun's still shining. Cor blimey. Invite rain that will. Commonsense, girl . . . Cor *blimey* . . . My bleedin' feet . . . (*Rubs one foot without removing shoe.*)
MARJORIE. Out here and no shelter. Be all right if it starts. (*Moves umbrella one way then another, looking up.*)
KATHLEEN. Cor *blimey* . . . 'Surprise me they don't drop off . . . Cut clean through, these will.
MARJORIE (*looking skywards, however*). Clouds all over. Told you we shouldn't have come out.
KATHLEEN. Get nothing if you don't try, girl . . . Cor *blimey*! (*Winces.*)
MARJORIE. I don't know.
KATHLEEN. Here. You'll be all right, won't you?
MARJORIE. . . . ?

KATHLEEN. Holes there is. See right through, you can.

MARJORIE. What?

KATHLEEN. Here. Rain comes straight through that. Won't get much shelter under that. What d'I tell you? Might as well sit under a shower. (*Laughs.*) Cor blimey. You'll be all right, won't you?

MARJORIE. Be all right with you in any case. Walk no faster than a snail.

KATHLEEN. Not surprised. Don't want me to escape. That's my trouble, girl.

MARJORIE. Here . . . (*Sits.*)

JACK *and* HARRY *slowly pass upstage, taking the air, chatting.* MARJORIE *and* KATHLEEN *wait for them to pass.*

KATHLEEN. What've we got for lunch?

MARJORIE. Sprouts.

KATHLEEN (*massaging foot*). Seen them, have you?

MARJORIE. Smelled 'em!

KATHLEEN. What's today, then?

MARJORIE. Friday.

KATHLEEN. End of week.

MARJORIE. Corn' beef hash.

KATHLEEN. That's Wednesday.

MARJORIE. Sausage roll.

KATHLEEN. Think you're right . . . Cor *blimey*. (*Groans, holding her foot.*)

MARJORIE. Know what you ought to do, don't you?

KATHLEEN *groans, holding her foot.*

Ask for another pair of shoes, girl, you ask me.

KATHLEEN. Took me laced ones, haven't they? Only ones that fitted. Thought I'd hang myself, didn't they? Only five inches long.

MARJORIE. What they think you are?

KATHLEEN. Bleedin' mouse, more likely.

MARJORIE. Here. Not like the last one I was in.

KATHLEEN. No?

MARJORIE. Let you paint on the walls, they did. Do

anyfing. Just muck around . . . Here . . . I won't tell you
what some of them did.

KATHLEEN. What?

MARJORIE *leans over, whispers.*

Never.

MARJORIE. Cross me heart.

KATHLEEN. Glad I wasn't there. This place is bad enough.
You seen Henderson, have you?

MARJORIE. Ought to lock him up, you ask me.

KATHLEEN. What d'you do, then?

MARJORIE. Here?

KATHLEEN. At this other place.

MARJORIE. Noffing. Mucked around . . .

KATHLEEN. Here . . .

JACK *and* HARRY *stroll back again, slowly, upstage, in
conversation; head back, deep breathing, bracing arms
. . .* MARJORIE *and* KATHLEEN *wait till they pass.*

MARJORIE. My dentist comes from Pakistan.

KATHLEEN. Yours?

MARJORIE. Took out all me teeth.

KATHLEEN. Those not your own, then?

MARJORIE. All went rotten when I had my little girl. There
she is, waitress at the seaside.

KATHLEEN. And you stuck here . . .

MARJORIE. No teeth . . .

KATHLEEN. Don't appreciate it.

MARJORIE. They don't.

KATHLEEN. Never.

MARJORIE. Might take this down if it doesn't rain.

KATHLEEN. Cor blimey . . . take these off if I thought I
could get 'em on again . . . (*Groans.*) Tried catching a
serious disease.

MARJORIE. When was that?

KATHLEEN. Only had me in two days. Said, nothing the
matter with you, my girl.

MARJORIE. Don't believe you.

KATHLEEN. Next thing: got home; smashed everything in sight.

MARJORIE. No?

KATHLEEN. Winders. Cooker . . . Nearly broke me back . . . Thought I'd save the telly. Still owed eighteen months. Thought: 'Everything or nothing, girl.'

MARJORIE. Rotten programmes. (*Takes down umbrella.*)

KATHLEEN. Didn't half give it a good old conk.

MARJORIE (*looking round*). There's one thing. You get a good night's sleep.

KATHLEEN. Like being with a steam engine, where I come from. Cor blimey, that much whistling and groaning; think you're going to take off.

MARJORIE. More like a boa constrictor, ask me. Here . . .

JACK *and* HARRY *stroll back, still taking the air, upstage; bracing, head back . . .*

Started crying everywhere I went . . . Started off on Christmas Eve.

KATHLEEN. S'happy time, Christmas.

MARJORIE. Didn't stop till Boxing Day.

KATHLEEN. If He ever comes again I hope He comes on Whit Tuesday. For me that's the best time of the year.

MARJORIE. Why's that?

KATHLEEN. Dunno. Whit Tuesday's always been a lucky day for me. First party I ever went to was on a Whit Tuesday. First feller I went with. Can't be the date. Different every year.

MARJORIE. My lucky day's the last Friday in any month with an 'r' in it when the next month doesn't begin later than the following Monday.

KATHLEEN. How do you make that out?

MARJORIE. Dunno. I was telling the doctor that the other day . . . There's that man with the binoculars watching you.

KATHLEEN. Where?

MARJORIE. Lift your dress up.

KATHLEEN. No.

MARJORIE. Go on . . . (*Leans over; does it for her.*) Told
you . . .

KATHLEEN. Looks like he's got diarrhoea!

They laugh.

See the chap the other day? Showed his slides of a trip up
the Amazon River.

MARJORIE. See that one with no clothes on? Supposed to
be cooking his dinner.

KATHLEEN. Won't have him here again . . .

MARJORIE. Showing all his ps and qs.

KATHLEEN. Oooooh! (*Laughs, covering her mouth.*)

MARJORIE. Here . . .

JACK *and* HARRY *stroll back across, a little further
down stage, glancing over now at* MARJORIE *and*
KATHLEEN.

KATHLEEN. Lord and Lady used to live here at one time.

MARJORIE. Who's that?

KATHLEEN. Dunno.

MARJORIE. Probably still inside, ask me . . . (*Glances after*
JACK *and* HARRY *as they stroll off.*) See that woman
with dyed hair? Told me she'd been in films. 'What films?'
I said. 'Blue films?'

KATHLEEN. What she say?

MARJORIE. 'The ones I was in was not in colour.'

They laugh.

I s'll lose me teeth one of these days . . . oooh!

KATHLEEN. Better'n losing something else . . .

MARJORIE. Oooooh!

They laugh again.

KATHLEEN. Here . . .

JACK *and* HARRY *have strolled back on.*

JACK (*removing hat*). Good day, ladies.

KATHLEEN. Good day yourself, your lordships.

JACK. Oh, now. I wouldn't go as far as that. (*Laughs
politely and looks at* HARRY.)

HARRY. No. No. Still a bit of the common touch.

JACK. Least, so I'd hope.

HARRY. Oh, yes.

MARJORIE. And how have you been keeping, professor?

JACK. Professor? I can see we're a little elevated today.

MARJORIE. Don't know about elevated. But *we*'re sitting down.

KATHLEEN *and* MARJORIE *laugh.*

KATHLEEN. Been standing up, we have, for hours.

HARRY. Hours?

MARJORIE. When you were sitting down.

JACK. Oh dear . . . I wasn't aware . . .

KATHLEEN. 'Course you were. My bleedin' feet. Just look at them. (*Holds them again.*)

MARJORIE. Pull your skirt down, girl.

KATHLEEN. Oh Gawd . . .

JACK. My friend here, Harry, is a specialist in house-warming, and I myself am a retailer in preserves.

MARJORIE. Oooooh! (*Screeches; laughs – covering her mouth – to* KATHLEEN.) What did I tell you?

KATHLEEN. No atomic bombs today?

JACK (*looks up at the sky behind him. Then*). No, no. Shouldn't think so.

MARJORIE. And how's your mongol sister?

HARRY. Mongol . . . ? I'm afraid you must have the wrong person, Ma'm.

KATHLEEN. Ooooh! (*Screeches; laughs.*)

JACK. My friend, I'm afraid, is separated from his wife. As a consequence, I can assure you, of many hardships . . .

MARJORIE. Of course . . .

JACK. And I myself, though happily married in some respects, would not pretend that my situation is all it should be . . .

KATHLEEN. Ooooh!

JACK. One endeavours . . . but it is in the nature of things, I believe, that, on the whole, one fails.

KATHLEEN. Ooooh!

HARRY. My friend . . . Jack . . . has invented several new methods of retailing jam.

KATHLEEN. Ooooh!
MARJORIE. Jam. I like that.
JACK. Really?
MARJORIE (*to* KATHLEEN). Strawberry. My favourite.
KATHLEEN. Raspberry, mine.
MARJORIE. Ooooh!

KATHLEEN *and* MARJORIE *laugh.*

JACK. A friend of mine, on my father's side, once owned a
   small factory which was given over, exclusively, to its
   manufacture.
KATHLEEN. Ooooh!
JACK. In very large vats.
KATHLEEN. Ooooh!
MARJORIE. I like treacle myself.
JACK. Treacle, now, is a very differnt matter.
MARJORIE. Comes from Malaya.
HARRY. That's rubber, I believe.
MARJORIE. In tins.
HARRY. The rubber comes from Malaya, I believe.
MARJORIE. I eat it, don't I? I ought to know.
KATHLEEN. She has treacle on her bread.
JACK. I believe it comes, as a matter of fact, from the West
   Indies.
KATHLEEN. West Indies? Where's that?
MARJORIE. Near Hong Kong.
HARRY. That's the East Indies, I believe.
MARJORIE. You ever been to the North Indies?
HARRY. I don't believe . . .
MARJORIE. Well, that's where treacle comes from.
HARRY. I see . . .

Pause. The tone has suddenly become serious.

JACK. We were just remarking, as a matter of fact, that Mrs
   Glover isn't looking her usual self.
KATHLEEN. Who's she?
HARRY. She's . . .
JACK. The lady with the rather embarrassing
   disfigurement . . .
MARJORIE. Her with one ear?

KATHLEEN. The one who's only half a nose.

MARJORIE. She snores.

KATHLEEN. You'd snore as well, wouldn't you, if you only had half a nose.

MARJORIE. Eaten away.

KATHLEEN. What?

MARJORIE. Her husband ate it one night when she was sleeping.

KATHLEEN. Silly to fall asleep with any man, I say. These days they get up to anything. Read it in the papers an' next thing they want to try it themselves.

HARRY. The weather's been particularly mild today.

KATHLEEN. Not like my flaming feet. Oooh . . .

JACK. As one grows older these little things are sent to try us.

KATHLEEN. Little? Cor blimey; I take size seven.

HARRY. My word.

JACK. My friend, of course, in the heating business, has a wide knowledge of the ways and means whereby we may, as we go along, acquire these little additional comforts.

MARJORIE. He wishes he was sitting in this chair, doesn't he?

HARRY. What . . .

JACK. It's extraordinary that more facilities of this nature aren't supplied, in my view.

KATHLEEN. Only bit of garden with any flowers. Half a dozen daisies . . .

HARRY. Tulips . . .

JACK. Roses . . .

KATHLEEN. I know daisies, don't I? Those are daisies. Grow three feet tall.

HARRY. Really?

MARJORIE. Rest of it's all covered in muck.

JACK. Oh, now. Not as bad as that.

MARJORIE. What? I call that muck. What's it supposed to be?

HARRY. A rockery, I believe.

KATHLEEN. Rockery? More like a rubbish tip, ask me.

JACK. Probably the flowers haven't grown yet.

MARJORIE. Flowers? How do you grow flowers on old bricks and bits of plaster?

HARRY. Certain categories, of course . . .

JACK. Oh, yes.

HARRY. Can be trained to grow in these conditions.

KATHLEEN. You're round the bend, you are. Ought to have you up there, they did.

HARRY (*to* JACK). They tell me the flowers are just as bad at that end, too.

HARRY *and* JACK *laugh at their private joke.*

MARJORIE. If you ask me, all this is just typical.

JACK. Typical?

MARJORIE. One table. Two chairs . . . Between one thousand people.

KATHLEEN. Two, they tell me.

MARJORIE. Two thousand. One thousand for this chair, and one thousand for that.

HARRY. There are, of course, the various benches.

KATHLEEN. Benches? Seen better sold for firewood.

MARJORIE. Make red marks they do across your bum.

KATHLEEN. Ooooh! (*Screeches, covering her mouth.*)

HARRY. Clouding slightly.

JACK. Slightly. (*Looking up.*)

MARJORIE. Pull your skirt down, girl.

KATHLEEN. Ooooh!

HARRY. Of course, one alternative would be to bring, say, a couple of more chairs out with us.

JACK. Oh, yes. Now that would be a solution.

HARRY. Four chairs. One each. I don't believe, say, for an afternoon they'd be missed from the lecture hall.

MARJORIE. Here, you see *Up the Amazon* last night?

JACK. Tuesday . . .

HARRY. Tuesday.

JACK. Believe I did, now you mention it.

MARJORIE. See that feller with a loincloth?

KATHLEEN. Oooh! (*Laughs, covering her mouth.*)

JACK. I must admit, there are certain attractions in the primitive life.

KATHLEEN. Ooooh!

JACK. Air, space . . .

MARJORIE. Seen all he's got, that's all you seen.

JACK. I believe there was a moment when the eye . . .

KATHLEEN. Moment . . . Ooooh!

HARRY. I thought his pancakes looked rather nice.

KATHLEEN. Ooooh!

HARRY. On the little log . . .

KATHLEEN. Ooooh!

MARJORIE. Not his pancakes he's seen, my girl.

KATHLEEN. Ooooh!

JACK. The canoe, now, was not unlike my own little boat.

KATHLEEN. Ooooh!

HARRY. Fishing there somewhat more than a mere pastime.

JACK. Oh, yes.

HARRY. Life and death.

JACK. Oh, yes.

MARJORIE. Were you the feller they caught climbing out of a window here last week?

JACK. Me?

MARJORIE. Him.

HARRY. Don't think so . . . Don't recollect that.

JACK. Where, if you don't mind me asking, did you acquire that information?

MARJORIE. Where? (*To* KATHLEEN.) Here, I thought you told me it was him.

KATHLEEN. Not me. Mrs Heller.

MARJORIE. You sure?

KATHLEEN. Not me, anyway.

JACK. I had a relative – nephew, as a matter of fact – who started a window-cleaning business . . . let me see. Three years ago now.

HARRY. Really?

JACK. Great scope there for an adventurous man.

MARJORIE. In bathroom windows 'specially.

KATHLEEN. Ooooh!

JACK. Heights . . . distances . . .

HARRY. On very tall buildings, of course, they lower them from the roof.

JACK. Oh, yes.

HARRY. Don't have the ladders long enough, you know.

KATHLEEN. Ooooh!

JACK. Your friend seems in a very jovial frame of mind.

HARRY. Like to see that.

JACK. Oh, yes. Gloom: one sees it far too much in this place. Mr Metcalf, now: I don't think he's spoken to anyone since the day that he arrived.

MARJORIE. What's he, then?

HARRY. He's the gentleman who's constantly pacing up and down.

JACK. One says hello, of course. He scarcely seems to notice.

KATHLEEN. Hear you were asking if they'd let you out.

JACK. Who?

MARJORIE. Your friend.

HARRY. Oh. Nothing as dramatic . . . Made certain inquiries . . . temporary visit . . . Domestic problems, you know. Without a man very little, I'm afraid, gets done.

MARJORIE. It gets too much done, if you ask me. That's half the trouble.

KATHLEEN. Ooooh!

HARRY. However . . . It seems that certain aspects of it can be cleared up by correspondence. One doesn't wish, after all, to impose unduly . . .

JACK. Oh, no.

HARRY. Events have their own momentum. Take their time.

MARJORIE. You married to me, they would. I can tell you.

KATHLEEN. Ooooh!

HARRY. Oh, now . . . Miss . . . er . . .

MARJORIE. Madam.

KATHLEEN. Ooooh!

HARRY. Well . . . er . . . that might be a situation that could well be beneficial to us both, in different circumstances, in different places . . .

JACK. Quite . . .

MARJORIE. Listen to him!

HARRY. We all have our little foibles, our little failings.

JACK. Oh, indeed.

HARRY. Hardly be human without.

JACK. Oh, no.

HARRY. The essence of true friendship, in my view, is to make allowances for one another's little lapses.

MARJORIE. Heard all about your little lapses, haven't we?

KATHLEEN. Ooooooh!

JACK. All have our little falls from grace.

MARJORIE. Pull your skirt down, girl!

KATHLEEN. Ooooooh!

MARJORIE. Burn down the whole bleedin' building, he will. Given up smoking because they won't let him have any matches.

KATHLEEN. Oooh!

JACK. The rumours that drift around a place like this . . . hardly worth the trouble . . .

HARRY. Absolutely.

JACK. If one believed everything one heard . . .

HARRY. Oh, yes.

JACK. I was remarking to my friend earlier this morning: if one can't enjoy life as it takes one, what's the point of living it at all? One can't, after all, spend the whole of one's life inside a shell.

HARRY. Oh, no.

MARJORIE. Know what he'd spend it inside if he had half a chance.

KATHLEEN. Ooooooh!

MARJORIE. Tell my husband of you, I shall.

KATHLEEN. Bus-driver.

JACK. Really? I've taken a lifelong interest in public transport.

KATHLEEN. Oooh!

MARJORIE. Taken a lifelong interest in something else more 'n likely.

KATHLEEN. Ooooooh!

MARJORIE. Pull your skirt down, girl!

KATHLEEN. Ooooooh!

MARJORIE. Know his kind.

KATHLEEN. Ooooooh!

JACK. Respect for the gentler sex, I must say, is a fast-diminishing concept in the modern world.

HARRY. Oh, yes.

JACK. I recollect the time when one stood for a lady as a matter of course.

HARRY. Oh yes.

MARJORIE. Know the kind of standing he's on about.

KATHLEEN. Oooooh!

JACK. Each becomes hardened to his ways.

KATHLEEN. Ooooooh!

JACK. No regard for anyone else's.

MARJORIE. Be missing your dinner, you will.

JACK. Yes. So it seems.

HARRY. Late . . .

JACK. Nevertheless, one breaks occasionally one's usual . . . Normally it's of benefit to all concerned . . .

MARJORIE. Here. Are you all right?

JACK. Slight moment of discomposure . . .

JACK has begun to cry, vaguely. Takes out a handkerchief to wipe his eyes.

HARRY. My friend is a man – he won't mind me saying this . . .

JACK. No . . . No . . .

HARRY. Of great sensibility and feeling.

KATHLEEN. Here. You having us on?

JACK. I assure you, madam . . . I regret any anxiety or concern which I may, unwittingly, have caused. In fact – I'm sure my friend will concur – perhaps you'll allow us to accompany you to the dining-hall. I have noticed, in the past, that though one has to queue, to leave it any later is to run the risk of being served with a cold plate; the food cold, and the manners of the cook – at times, I must confess . . . appalling.

KATHLEEN (*to* MARJORIE). We'll have to go. There'll be nothing left.

MARJORIE. It's this seat he's after.

HARRY. I assure you, madam . . . we are on our way.

KATHLEEN. Here: you mind if I lean on your arm?

MARJORIE. Kathleen!

HARRY. Oh, now. That's a very pretty name.

KATHLEEN. Got straps: make your ankles swell. (*Rising.*)

HARRY. Allow me.

KATHLEEN. Oh. Thank you.

HARRY. Harry.

KATHLEEN. Harry.

HARRY. And this is my friend – Jack.

KATHLEEN. Jack . . . And this is my friend Marjorie.

JACK. Marjorie . . . Delightful.

MARJORIE (*to* KATHLEEN). Here. You all right?

KATHLEEN. You carrying it with you, or are you coming?

JACK. Allow me . . . Marjorie. (*Holds her seat.*)

MARJORIE. Here . . . (*Gets up, suspicious.*)

HARRY. Perhaps after lunch we might meet here again.

JACK. A little chat . . . Time passes very slowly.

MARJORIE. Here, where's my bag?

KATHLEEN. Need carrying out, I will.

HARRY has taken KATHLEEN's arm.

HARRY. Now then. All right?

KATHLEEN. Have you all the time, I shall.

HARRY. Ready? . . . All aboard then, are we?

MARJORIE. Well, then. All right . . . (*Takes JACK's arm.*)

JACK. Right, then . . . Dining-hall: here we come!

They start off, HARRY *and* KATHLEEN *in front; slowly.*

HARRY. Sausages today, if I'm not mistaken.

KATHLEEN. Oooh!

MARJORIE. Corned beef hash.

KATHLEEN. Oooh!

JACK. One as good as another, I always say.

KATHLEEN. Oooooh!

HARRY. Turned out better.

JACK. Turned out better.

HARRY. Altogether.

JACK. Altogether.

HARRY. Well, then. Here we go.

They go.

Fade.

ACT TWO

ALFRED *comes in: a well-made young man, about thirty.*
His jacket's unbuttoned; he has no tie. He sees the table;
walks past it, slowly, eyeing it. Pauses. Glances back at it.
Comes back, watching the table rather furtively, sideways.
He pauses, hands behind his back, regarding it. Suddenly he
moves it, grasps it; struggles with it as if it had a life of its
own. Groans. Struggles. Lifts the table finally above his
head. Struggles with it . . .

MARJORIE *comes on, as before, her umbrella furled.*

MARJORIE. Here. You all right?
ALFRED. What?
MARJORIE. Alfred i'n'it?
ALFRED. Yeh. (*Still holds the table above his head.*)
MARJORIE. You'll break that, you will.
ALFRED. Yeh . . . (*Looks up at it.*)

   MARJORIE, *however, isn't much interested; she's already*
   looking round.

MARJORIE. You seen my mate?
ALFRED. . . . ?
MARJORIE. Woman that limps.
ALFRED. No.

   ALFRED *pauses before all his answers.*

MARJORIE. One day you get seconds and they go off
   without you. You like treacle pud?
ALFRED. Yeh.
MARJORIE. Get seconds?
ALFRED. No.
MARJORIE. Shoulda waited.
ALFRED. Yeh.
MARJORIE. Said they'd be out here after 'Remedials'.
ALFRED. . . . ?
MARJORIE. You do remedials?
ALFRED. Yeh.
MARJORIE. What 'you do?
ALFRED. Baskets.

MARJORIE. Baskets. Shoulda known.
ALFRED. You got sixpence?
MARJORIE. No.

ALFRED lifts the table up and down ceremoniously above his head.

Better go find her. Let anybody turn them round her hand, she will.
ALFRED. Yeh.

She goes.

ALFRED lowers the table slowly, almost like a ritual. Crouches; picks up one chair by the foot of one leg and lifts it, slowly, exaggerating the effort, etc. Stands, slowly, as he gets it up. Bends arm slowly; lifts the chair above his head. Puts it down. Stands a moment, gazing down at the two chairs and the table, sideways. Walks round them. Walks round a little farther. Then: grabs the second chair and lifts it, one-handed, like the first chair, but more quickly. Lifts it above his head; begins to wrestle with it as if it too possessed a life of its own, his grip, however, still one-handed.

MARJORIE crosses upstage, pauses, looks, walks on. She goes off; ALFRED doesn't see her.

ALFRED struggles; overcomes the chair. Almost absent-mindedly lowers it, looks left, looks right, casually; puts the chair beneath his arm and goes.

KATHLEEN (*off*). Oh Gawd . . . Oh . . . Nah, this side's better . . . Oh.

Comes on limping, her arm in HARRY's. HARRY carries a wicker chair under his other arm.

HARRY. Oh. Look at that.
KATHLEEN. Where's the other one gone, then?
HARRY. Well, that's a damned nuisance.
KATHLEEN. Still only two. Don't know what they'll say.
HARRY. Oh dear.

KATHLEEN. Pinch anything round here. Can't turn your
back. Gawd . . . !

Sinks down in the metal chair as HARRY holds it for her.

HARRY. There, now.
KATHLEEN (*sighs*). Good to get off your feet . . .
HARRY. Yes, well . . .

Sets his own chair to get the sun, fussing.

KATHLEEN. Better sit on it. No good standing about.
Don't know where she's got to. Where's your friend
looking?
HARRY. Went to 'Remedials', I believe.
KATHLEEN. Get you in there won't let you out again.
Here . . .

HARRY looks across.

He really what he says he is?
HARRY. How do you mean?
KATHLEEN. Told us he was a doctor. Another time he said
he'd been a sanitary inspector.
HARRY. Really? Hadn't heard of that.
KATHLEEN. Go on. Know what inspecting he'll do. You
the same.
HARRY. Oh, now. Certain discriminations can be . . .
KATHLEEN. I've heard about you.
HARRY. Oh, well, you er.
KATHLEEN. Making up things.
HARRY. Oh, well. One . . . embodies . . . of course.
KATHLEEN. What's that, then?
HARRY. Fancies . . . What's life for if you can't . . .
(*Flutters his fingers.*)
KATHLEEN. We've heard about that an' all. (*Imitates his
action.*)
HARRY. Well. I'm sure you and I have, in reality, a great
deal in common. After all, one looks around; what does
one see?
KATHLEEN. Gawd . . . (*Groans, feeling her feet.*)
HARRY. A little this. A little that.
KATHLEEN. Here. Everything you know is little.

HARRY. Well . . . I er . . . Yes . . . No great role for this actor, I'm afraid. A little stage, a tiny part.

KATHLEEN. You an actor, then?

HARRY. Well, I did, as a matter of fact, at one time . . . actually, a little . . .

KATHLEEN. Here, little again. You notice?

HARRY. Oh . . . You're right.

KATHLEEN. What parts you play, then?

HARRY. Well, as a matter of fact . . . not your Hamlets, of course, your Ophelias; more the little bystander who passes by the . . .

KATHLEEN. Here. Little.

HARRY. Oh . . . yes! (*Laughs*.)

KATHLEEN. Play anything romantic?

HARRY. Oh, romance, now, was . . . never very far away.

KATHLEEN. Here . . .

HARRY. One was cast, of course . . .

KATHLEEN. Think I could have been romantic.

HARRY. Oh, yes.

KATHLEEN. Had the chance . . . Got it here.

HARRY. Oh, yes . . .

KATHLEEN. Had different shoes than this . . .

HARRY. Oh, yes . . . everything, of course, provided . . .

KATHLEEN. Going to be a commotion, you ask me . . .

HARRY. Commotion . . . ?

KATHLEEN. When they get here. (*Indicates chairs*.) Three chairs – if he brings one as well . . . He'll have to stand. (*Laughs*.)

HARRY. Could have been confiscated, you know.

KATHLEEN. Confiscated?

HARRY. Often happens. See a little pleasure and down they come.

KATHLEEN. Here . . . little.

HARRY. Goodness . . . Yes.

Pause.

One of the advantages of this spot, you know, is that it catches the sun so nicely.

KATHLEEN. What bit there is of it.

HARRY. Bit?

KATHLEEN. All that soot. Cuts it down. 'Stead of
browning you turns you black.

HARRY. Black?

KATHLEEN. All over.

HARRY. An industrial nation . . .

KATHLEEN. Gawd . . . (*Eases her feet.*)

HARRY. Can't have the benefit of both. Nature as well as er
. . . The one is incurred at the expense of the other.

KATHLEEN. Your friend come in for following little girls?

HARRY. What . . .

KATHLEEN. Go on. You can tell me. Cross my heart and
hope to die.

HARRY. Well . . . that's . . .

KATHLEEN. Well, then.

HARRY. I believe there were . . . er . . . certain proclivities,
shall we say?

KATHLEEN. Proclivities? What's them?

HARRY. Nothing criminal, of course.

KATHLEEN. Oh, no . . .

HARRY. No prosecution . . .

KATHLEEN. Oh, no . . .

HARRY. Certain presures, in the er . . . Revealed
themselves.

KATHLEEN. In public?

HARRY. No. No . . . I . . . Not what I meant.

KATHLEEN. I don't know what you're saying half the time.
You realize that?

HARRY. Communication is a difficult factor.

KATHLEEN. Say that again.

HARRY. I believe he was encouraged to come here for a
little er.

KATHLEEN. Here. Little.

HARRY. Oh, yes . . . As it is, very few places left now
where one can be at ease.

KATHLEEN. Could go on his holidays. Seaside.

HARRY. Beaches? . . . Crowded all the while.

KATHLEEN. Could go to the country.

HARRY. Spaces . . .

KATHLEEN. Sent me to the country once. All them trees.
Worse'n people . . . Gawd. Take them off if I thought I

could get them on again. Can't understand why they don't let me have me laces. Took me belt as well. Who they think I'm going to strangle? Improved my figure, it did, the belt. Drew it in a bit.

HARRY. Oh, now, I would say, myself, the proportions were in reasonable condition.

KATHLEEN. Oh, now . . .

HARRY. Without, of course, wishing to seem immodest . . .

KATHLEEN. Get little enough encouragement in my life. Gawd . . . My friend, you know, was always crying.

HARRY. Oh, now.

KATHLEEN. Everywhere she went . . . cigarettes . . . No sooner in the shop, opens her mouth, and out it comes. Same on buses.

HARRY. Oh dear, now.

KATHLEEN. Doesn't like sympathy.

HARRY. Ah, yes.

KATHLEEN. Get all I can, myself.

HARRY. Husband a bus-driver, I believe.

KATHLEEN. Hers. Not mine.

HARRY. Ah, yes.

KATHLEEN. Mine's a corporation employee.

HARRY. Ah, yes. One of the . . .

KATHLEEN. Cleans up muck. Whenever there's a pile of muck they send him to clean it up.

HARRY. I see.

KATHLEEN. You worked in a bank, then?

HARRY. Well, in a er.

KATHLEEN. Clean job. Don't know why he doesn't get a clean job. Doorman . . . Smells awful, he does. Gets bathed one night and the next day just the same.

HARRY. Ah, yes.

KATHLEEN. Puts you off your food.

HARRY. Yes.

KATHLEEN. 'They ought to fumigate you,' I said.

HARRY. Yes?

KATHLEEN. Know what he says?

HARRY. Yes?

KATHLEEN. 'Ought to fumigate you, my girl, and forget to switch it orf.'

HARRY. Goodness.

KATHLEEN. Going to be tea-time before they get here.

HARRY (*examines watch*). No, no. Still a little time.

KATHLEEN. Your wife alive?

HARRY. Er.

KATHLEEN. Separated?

HARRY. Well, I . . .

KATHLEEN. Unsympathetic.

HARRY. Yes?

KATHLEEN. Your wife.

HARRY. Well . . . One can ask too much these days, I
    believe, of er.

KATHLEEN. Met once a fortnight wouldn't be any divorce.
    Ridiculous, living together. 'S not human.

HARRY. No . . .

KATHLEEN. Like animals . . . Even they run off when
    they're not feeling like it.

HARRY. Oh, yes.

KATHLEEN. Not natural . . . One man. One woman.
    Who's He think He is?

HARRY *looks round.*

No . . . Him. (*Points up.*)

HARRY. Oh, yes . . .

KATHLEEN. Made Him a bachelor. Cor blimey: no wife
    for Him.

HARRY. No.

KATHLEEN. Saved somebody the trouble.

HARRY. Yes.

KATHLEEN. Does it all by telepathy.

HARRY. Yes.

KATHLEEN. Kids?

HARRY. What? . . . Oh . . . No.

KATHLEEN. Got married how old?

HARRY. Twenty er.

KATHLEEN. Man shouldn't marry till he's forty.
    Ridiculous. Don't know what they want till then. After
    that, too old to bother.

HARRY. Oh, yes.
KATHLEEN. Here . . .

ALFRED *comes in carrying the chair. Sees them, nods;
then goes back the way he's come.*

KATHLEEN. Here! (*Calls after.*) That's where it's gone.
HARRY. Don't believe . . .
KATHLEEN. That's Alfred.
HARRY. Yes?
KATHLEEN. Wrestler.
HARRY. Yes.
KATHLEEN. Up here. (*Taps her head.*)
HARRY. Oh.
KATHLEEN. Where you going when you leave here?
HARRY. Well . . . I . . . er.
KATHLEEN. Lost your job?
HARRY. Well, I . . .
KATHLEEN. Wife not have you?
HARRY. Well, I . . .
KATHLEEN. Another man.
HARRY. Oh, now . . .
KATHLEEN. Still . . . Could be worse.
HARRY. Oh, yes.

Pause.

KATHLEEN. What's he want with that, then? Here . . . you
were slow to ask.
HARRY. Yes . . .
KATHLEEN. You all right?
HARRY. Touch of the . . . (*Wipes his eys, nose.*)
KATHLEEN. Here, couple of old cry-babies you are. Bad as
my friend.
HARRY. Yes . . . Well . . .
KATHLEEN. Shoot my brains out if I had a chance. Gawd!
. . . (*Feels her feet.*) Tried to kill myself with gas.
HARRY. Yes . . . ?
KATHLEEN. Kiddies at my sister's. Head in oven. Knock
on door. Milkman. Two weeks behind, he said. Broke
everything, I did.
HARRY. Yes?

KATHLEEN. Nearly killed him. Would, too, if I could have got hold. Won't tap on our door, I can tell you. Not again.

HARRY. Goodness.

KATHLEEN. You all right?

HARRY. Yes . . . I . . . er

KATHLEEN. Here. Hold my hand if you like.

HARRY. Oh, now.

KATHLEEN. Go on.

Puts her hand on the table.

Not much to look at.

HARRY. Oh, now. I wouldn't say that.

KATHLEEN. Go on.

HARRY. Well, I . . . (*Takes her hand.*)

KATHLEEN. Our age: know what it's all about.

HARRY. Oh, well . . . A long road, you know.

KATHLEEN. Can't get to old age fast enough for me. Sooner they put me under . . .

HARRY. Oh, now . . .

KATHLEEN. Different for a man.

HARRY. Well, I . . .

KATHLEEN. I know. Have your troubles. Still. Woman's different.

HARRY. Oh, I . . .

KATHLEEN. Wouldn't be a woman. Not again . . . Here!

ALFRED has entered. He goes past, upstage, carrying the chair. Glances at them. Goes off.

Been here years, you know. Do the work of ten men if they set him to it.

HARRY. I say . . . (*Looking off.*)

KATHLEEN. Dunno where they've been . . . (*Calls.*) Oi! . . . Deaf as a post. Here, no need to let go . . . Think you're shy.

HARRY. Oh, well . . .

KATHLEEN. Never mind. Too old to be disappointed.

HARRY. Oh, now . . .

JACK and MARJORIE enter, the former carrying a wicker chair.

MARJORIE. Here you are, then. Been looking for you all over.

KATHLEEN. Been here, haven't we, all the time.

HARRY *stands*.

JACK. Sun still strong.

HARRY. Oh, yes.

MARJORIE. Here. Where's the other chair?

KATHLEEN. He's taken it over there.

MARJORIE. What's he doing?

KATHLEEN. Dunno. Here, sit on his knee if you want to!

MARJORIE. Catch me. Who do you think I am? (*Sits.*)

KATHLEEN. Well, no good you both standing.

JACK (*to* HARRY). No, no. After you, old man.

HARRY. No. no. After you . . .

KATHLEEN. Be here all day, you ask me. Here, I'll stand . . . Gawd . . .

JACK. Oh, no . . .

HARRY. Ridiculous.

MARJORIE. Take it in turns.

JACK. Right, I'll er.

HARRY. Do. Do. Go ahead.

JACK. Very decent. Very. (*Sits; sighs.*)

MARJORIE. Been carrying that around, looking for you, he has.

KATHLEEN. Been here, we have, all the time.

MARJORIE. What you been up to, then?

KATHLEEN. Nothing you might mind.

MARJORIE (*to* HARRY). Want to watch her. Men all the time.

KATHLEEN. One who knows.

MARJORIE. Seen it with my own eyes.

KATHLEEN. Lot more besides.

JACK. Think it might look up. Clearing . . . (*Gazing up.*)

HARRY. Oh. Very. (*Gazes up.*)

MARJORIE. Fallen in love, she has.

JACK. Damn nuisance about the chair, what?

HARRY. Oh. Very.

MARJORIE. Has to see the doctor about it, she has.

KATHLEEN. See the doctor about you, girl.

MARJORIE. Can't let no tradesman near the house. Five kids. Milkman, window-cleaner . . .

KATHLEEN. Know your trouble, don't you?

MARJORIE. Nothing's bad as yours.

KATHLEEN. Can't go down the street without her trousers wetting.

JACK. Spot more sun, see those flowers out. Shouldn't wonder.

HARRY. Oh, yes.

JACK. By Jove, Farrer, isn't it? (*Rises.*)

HARRY. Say he was a champion quarter-miler.

JACK. Shouldn't be surprised. Build of an athlete. Square shoulders.

HARRY. Deep chest.

JACK. Oh, yes.

KATHLEEN. You know what you should do with your mouth, girl.

MARJORIE. You know what you should do with something else.

KATHLEEN (*to* HARRY). Take a little stroll if you don't mind . . . Gawd strewth . . .

KATHLEEN *gets up*; HARRY *hastens to help.*

MARJORIE. Mind she doesn't stroll you to the bushes.

KATHLEEN. Mind she doesn't splash.

MARJORIE. See the doctor about you, my girl!

KATHLEEN. See him all the time: your trouble. Not right in the head.

KATHLEEN *has taken* HARRY's *arm. They go off.*

MARJORIE. Can't keep away from men.

JACK. Oh dear. (*Gazing after.*)

MARJORIE. Gardens.

JACK. Oh. (*Sits, uncomfortable.*)

MARJORIE. Parks especially.

JACK. I have heard of such er.

MARJORIE. Complaints. Used to send the police in threes. Can't trust two and one was never enough.

JACK. My word.

MARJORIE. Oh, yes.

JACK. Can never tell a leopard . . .

MARJORIE. What? Should see her. Spots all over.

JACK. Oh dear.

MARJORIE. Never washes.

JACK. One of the advantages of a late lunch, of course, is that it leaves a shorter space to tea.

MARJORIE. What's your friend's name?

JACK. Harry . . .

MARJORIE. What's he do, then?

JACK. Temporary er . . . Thought a slight . . .

MARJORIE. Get one with her all right. Have another.

JACK. Oh, yes . . .

MARJORIE. Don't know what we're coming to.

JACK. Life . . . mystery . . . (*Gazes up.*)

MARJORIE *watches him. Then:*

MARJORIE. What you put away for, then?

JACK. Oh . . . what?

MARJORIE. In here.

JACK. Oh . . . Little . . .

MARJORIE. Girl?

JACK. Girl?

MARJORIE. Girls.

JACK. Girls?

MARJORIE. In the street.

JACK. Really? (*Looks around.*)

MARJORIE. Here . . . What you in for?

JACK. A wholly voluntary basis, I assure you.

MARJORIE. Wife put you away?

JACK. Oh, no. No, no. Just a moment . . . needed . . . Thought I might . . .

MARJORIE. Ever been in the padded whatsit?

JACK. Don't believe . . . (*Looking around.*)

MARJORIE. Here . . . Don't tell my friend.

JACK. Oh, well . . .

MARJORIE. Lie there for hours, you can.

JACK. Oh, now.

MARJORIE. Been here twice before.

JACK. Really . . .

MARJORIE. Don't tell my friend.

JACK. Oh, no.

MARJORIE. Thinks it's my first.

JACK. Goodness . . .

MARJORIE. One of the regulars. Wouldn't know what to do without me.

JACK. Oh, yes. Familiar faces.

MARJORIE. Come for three months; out again. Back again at Christmas.

JACK. Oh, yes.

MARJORIE. Can't stand Christmas.

JACK. No. Well. Season of festivities . . . good cheer.

MARJORIE. Most people don't talk to you in here. You noticed?

JACK. Very rare. Well . . . find someone to communicate.

MARJORIE. 'Course. Privileged.

JACK. Yes?

MARJORIE. Being in the reception wing.

JACK. Oh, yes.

MARJORIE. Good as cured.

JACK. Oh, yes.

MARJORIE. Soon be out.

JACK. Oh, goodness . . . Hardly worth the trouble.

MARJORIE. No.

JACK. Home tomorrow!

MARJORIE. You been married long?

JACK. Oh, yes . . . What?

MARJORIE. You in love?

JACK. What?

MARJORIE. Your wife.

JACK. Clouds . . . This morning, my friend was remarking on the edges.

MARJORIE. Hardly worth the trouble.

JACK. Oh, yes.

MARJORIE. Going home.

JACK. Oh, well . . . one has one's . . . thought I might plant some seeds. Soil not too good, I notice . . .

MARJORIE. Tell you something?

JACK. Oh, yes.

MARJORIE. Set up here for good.

JACK. Oh, yes.

MARJORIE. Here, you listening? What you in for?

JACK. Oh . . .

MARJORIE. Here; you always crying.

JACK. Light . . . eye . . . (*Wipes his eye with his handkerchief.*)

MARJORIE. Tell you something.

JACK. Yes.

MARJORIE. Not leave here again.

JACK. Oh, no.

They are silent.

ALFRED *comes on. He stands at the back, leaning on the chair.*

MARJORIE. You going to sit on that or something?

ALFRED. What?

MARJORIE. Sit.

ALFRED. Dunno.

MARJORIE. Give it to somebody who can, you do.

ALFRED. What? (*Comes down.*)

MARJORIE. Give it to somebody who can.

ALFRED. Yeh.

MARJORIE. You know my friend?

ALFRED. No.

MARJORIE. This is Alfred.

JACK. Oh . . . Good . . . day. (*Stands formally.*)

ALFRED. Where you get your cane?

JACK. Oh . . . (*Looks down at it.*) Came with me.

ALFRED. I had a cane like that once.

JACK. Ah, yes.

ALFRED. Nicked it.

JACK. Oh, now.

MARJORIE. Had it when he came. Didn't you? Sit down.

JACK. Yes. (*Sits.*)

ALFRED. Wanna fight?

JACK. No . . .

ALFRED. You?

MARJORIE. No, thanks.

ALFRED. Got sixpence?

JACK. No.

MARJORIE. Here. You seen my friend?

ALFRED. No.

MARJORIE. What you in for?

ALFRED. In what?

MARJORIE. Thinks he's at home, he does. Doesn't know his own strength, do you?

ALFRED. No.

MARJORIE. Took a bit of his brain, haven't they?

ALFRED. Yeh.

MARJORIE. Feel better?

ALFRED. Yeh.

MARJORIE. His mother's eighty-four.

ALFRED. Seventy.

MARJORIE. Thought you said she was eighty-four.

ALFRED. Seventy.

MARJORIE. Won't know his own name soon.

ALFRED. You wanna fight?

MARJORIE. Knock you down one hand behind my back.

ALFRED. Garn.

MARJORIE. Half kill you, I will.

ALFRED. Go on.

MARJORIE. Wanna try? (*Stands.*)

ALFRED *backs off a couple of steps.* MARJORIE *sits.*

Take that chair off you, you don't look out.

JACK. Slight breeze. Takes the heat off the sun.

MARJORIE. Wanna jump on him if he bullies you.

JACK. Oh, yes.

MARJORIE (*to* ALFRED). What you looking at then?

ALFRED. Sky. (*Looks up.*)

MARJORIE. They'll lock you up if you don't look out. How old's your father?

ALFRED. Twenty-two.

MARJORIE. Older than him, are you?

ALFRED. Yeh.

MARJORIE. Older than his dad he is. Don't know where that leaves him.

JACK. Hasn't been born, I shouldn't wonder.

MARJORIE. No! (*Laughs.*) Hasn't been born, he shouldn't wonder. (*Pause.*) Painted rude letters in the road.

ALFRED. Didn't.

MARJORIE. Did.

ALFRED. Didn't.

MARJORIE. Did. Right in the town centre. Took them three weeks to scrub it off.

ALFRED. Two.

MARJORIE. Three.

ALFRED. Two.

MARJORIE. Three. Apprentice painter and decorator. Didn't know what he was going to decorate. (*To* ALFRED.) They'll apprentice you no more. (*To* JACK.) Doesn't know his own strength, he doesn't.

JACK (*looking round*). Wonder where . . .

MARJORIE. Send the police out for them, they will.

JACK. Clouds . . . (*Looking up.*)

MARJORIE. Seen it all, I have. Rape, intercourse. Physical pleasure.

JACK. I had a cousin once . . .

MARJORIE. Here, you got a big family, haven't you?

JACK. Seven brothers and sisters. Spreads around, you know.

MARJORIE. Here, you was an only child last week.

JACK. A niece of mine – I say niece . . . She was only . . .

MARJORIE. What you do it for?

JACK. Oh, now . . .

MARJORIE (*to* ALFRED). Wanna watch him. Trained as a doctor he has.

JACK. Wonder where . . . (*Gazing round.*)

MARJORIE (*to* ALFRED). What you paint in the road?

ALFRED. Nothing.

MARJORIE. Must have painted something. Can't paint nothing. Must have painted something or they couldn't have rubbed it off.

ALFRED. Paint you if you don't watch out.

MARJORIE. I'll knock your head off.

ALFRED. Won't.

MARJORIE. Will.

ALFRED. Won't.

MARJORIE. Will.

ALFRED. Won't.

MARJORIE. What you doing with that chair?
ALFRED. Nothing. (*Spins it beneath his hand.*)
MARJORIE. Faster than a rocket he is. Wanna watch him
. . . Where you going?

JACK *has got up.*

JACK. Thought I might . . . Oh . . .

HARRY *and* KATHLEEN *have come on from the other
side, the latter leaning on* HARRY'*s arm.*

KATHLEEN. Gawd . . . they're coming off. I'll have nothing
left . . . Oh . . .

HARRY *helps her to the chair.*

MARJORIE. Here, where you been?
KATHLEEN. There and back.
MARJORIE. Know where you been, my girl.
KATHLEEN. Don't.
HARRY. Canteen. We've . . .
KATHLEEN. Don't tell her. Nose ten miles long she has.
Trip over it one day she will. What's he doing? (*Indicating*
ALFRED.)
MARJORIE. Won't give up his chair, he won't.
HARRY. Still got three, what?
JACK. Yes . . . what. Clouds . . .
HARRY. Ah . . . Rain.
JACK. Shouldn't wonder.
MARJORIE. Here. Put that chair down.

ALFRED *still stands there.*

MARJORIE *stands.* ALFRED *releases the chair quickly.*

MARJORIE (*to* JACK). You get it.
JACK. Er . . . right.

Goes and gets the chair. ALFRED *doesn't move.*

MARJORIE. One each, then.
HARRY. Yes . . .
MARJORIE. Well . . . (*Indicates they sit.*)

KATHLEEN. Gawd . . . (*Holds her feet.*)

MARJORIE. Had a job once.

KATHLEEN. Gawd.

MARJORIE. Packing tins of food.

KATHLEEN (*to* ALFRED). What you looking at?

ALFRED. Nothing.

MARJORIE. Pull your skirt down, girl.

KATHLEEN. Got nothing up mine ain't got up yours.

MARJORIE. Put them in cardboard boxes.

JACK. Really? I had a . . .

MARJORIE. Done by machine now.

KATHLEEN. Nothing left for you to do, my girl. That's
   your trouble.

MARJORIE. 'Tis.

KATHLEEN. Cries everywhere, she does.

HARRY. Oh. One has one's . . .

KATHLEEN. 'Specially at Christmas. Cries at Christmas.
   Boxing Day. Sometimes to New Year.

JACK. Oh, well, one . . .

KATHLEEN (*indicating* ALFRED). What's he doing, then?

MARJORIE. Waiting to be born, he is.

KATHLEEN. What?

MARJORIE. Eight o'clock tomorrow morning. Better be
   there. (*Laughs. To* ALFRED.) You better be there.

ALFRED. Yeh.

MARJORIE. Late for his own birthday, he is. (*To*
   ALFRED.) Never catch up, you won't.

HARRY (*holding out hand; inspects it*). Thought I . . . No.

JACK. Could be. (*Looks up.*)

HARRY. Lucky so far.

JACK. Oh, yes.

HARRY. Possibility . . . (*Looking up.*)

JACK. By Jove . . .

MARJORIE. One thing you can say about this place . . .

KATHLEEN. Yes.

MARJORIE. 'S not like home.

KATHLEEN. Thank Gawd.

MARJORIE (*to* ALFRED). What you want?

ALFRED. Nothing.

KATHLEEN. Give you nothing if you come here . . . What you staring at?

ALFRED. Nothing.

MARJORIE. Taken off a bit of his brain they have.

KATHLEEN (*to* ALFRED). Where they put it then?

MARJORIE. Thrown it in the dustbin.

KATHLEEN. Could have done with that. (*Laughs.*) Didn't cut a bit of something else off, did they?

MARJORIE. You know what your trouble is, my girl.

JACK. Time for tea, I shouldn't wonder. (*Stands.*)

HARRY. Yes. Well . . . let me see. Very nearly.

JACK. Stretch the old legs . . .

HARRY. Oh, yes.

MARJORIE. Not your legs need stretching, ask me.

JACK. Ah, well . . . Trim. (*Bends arms; stretches.*)

MARJORIE. Fancies himself he does.

KATHLEEN. Don't blame him.

MARJORIE. Watch yourself, my girl.

KATHLEEN. No harm come from trying.

MARJORIE. Good job your feet like they are, ask me.

KATHLEEN. Have them off in the morning. Not stand this much longer.

MARJORIE. Slow her down; know what they're doing.

KATHLEEN. Know what she is?

JACK. Well, I . . .

KATHLEEN. PO.

JACK. PO.

KATHLEEN. Persistent Offender.

MARJORIE. Ain't no such thing.

KATHLEEN. Is.

MARJORIE. Isn't.

KATHLEEN. Heard it in the office. Off Doctor . . . what's his name.

MARJORIE. Never heard of that doctor, I haven't. Must be a new one must that. Doctor what's his name is a new one on me.

KATHLEEN. I know what I heard.

MARJORIE. Here. What's he crying about?

HARRY *is drying his eyes.*

KATHLEEN. Always crying one of these two.
MARJORIE. Call them the water babies, you ask me. (*To* ALFRED.) You seen this?

ALFRED *gazes woodenly towards them.*

KATHLEEN. He's another.
MARJORIE. Don't know what'll become of us, girl.
KATHLEEN. Thought you was the one to cry.
MARJORIE. So d'I.
KATHLEEN. My dad was always crying.
MARJORIE. Yeh?
KATHLEEN. Drank too much. Came out of his eyes.
MARJORIE. Ooh! (*Laughs, covering her mouth.*)
KATHLEEN. Here, what's the matter with you, Harry?
HARRY. Oh, just a er.
JACK. Could have sworn . . . (*Holds out hand; looks up.*)
KATHLEEN. 'S not rain. 'S him. Splashing it all over, he is.
JACK. There, now . . .
MARJORIE. Here. Look at him: thinks it's raining.
KATHLEEN (*to* JACK). Here. Your friend . . .

JACK *breathes deeply: fresh-air exercises.*

JACK. Freshening.
MARJORIE. I don't know. What they come out for?
KATHLEEN. Crying all over, they are.
MARJORIE (*to* JACK). You going to help your friend, then, are you?
JACK. Oh. Comes and goes . . .
KATHLEEN (*to* HARRY). Wanna hold my hand?

HARRY *doesn't answer.*

MARJORIE. Not seen so many tears. Haven't.
KATHLEEN. Not since Christmas.
MARJORIE. Not since Christmas, girl.
KATHLEEN. Ooooh!
MARJORIE (*to* JACK). You all right?

JACK *doesn't answer. Stands stiffly turned away, looking off.*

Think you and I better be on our way, girl.

KATHLEEN. Think we had.

MARJORIE. Try and make something. What you get for it?

KATHLEEN. Get nothing if you don't try, girl.

MARJORIE. No.

KATHLEEN. Get nothing if you do, either.

MARJORIE. Ooooh! (*Laughs, covering her mouth; stands.*) Don't slow you down, do they? (*Indicates shoes.*)

KATHLEEN. Get my laces back or else, girl . . . Oh! (*Winces, standing. To* ALFRED.) What you staring at?

ALFRED. Nothing.

KATHLEEN. Be dead this time tomorrow.

MARJORIE. No complaints then, my girl.

KATHLEEN. Not too soon for me.

MARJORIE. Going to say goodbye to your boy-friend?

KATHLEEN. Dunno that he wants to know . . .

MARJORIE. Give you a hand, girl?

KATHLEEN. Can't move without.

MARJORIE. There . . . on our way.

KATHLEEN. Gawd.

MARJORIE. Not stop here again.

KATHLEEN. Better get out of here, girl . . . Gawd! Go mad here you don't watch out.

Groaning, KATHLEEN *is led off by* MARJORIE.

Pause.

ALFRED *comes up. Holds table, waits, then lifts it. Raises it above his head. Turns. Walks off.*

JACK. By Jove.

HARRY *stirs.*

Freshening . . . Surprised if it doesn't blow over by tomorrow.

HARRY. Oh, yes . . .

JACK. Saw Harrison yesterday.

HARRY. Yes?

JACK. Congestion.

HARRY. Soot.

JACK. Really?

HARRY. Oh, yes. (*Dries his eyes.*)

JACK. Shouldn't wonder if wind veers. North-west.

HARRY. East.

JACK. Really? Higher ground, of course, one notices.

HARRY. Found the er. (*Gestures after* MARJORIE *and* KATHLEEN.)

JACK. Oh, yes.

HARRY. Extraordinary.

JACK. 'Straordinary.

HARRY. Get used to it after a while.

JACK. Oh, yes . . . I have a sister-in-law, for example, who wears dark glasses.

HARRY. Really.

JACK. Each evening before she goes to bed.

HARRY. Really.

JACK. Following morning: takes them off.

HARRY. Extraordinary.

JACK. Sunshine – never wears them.

HARRY. Well . . . I . . . (*Finally wipes his eyes and puts his handkerchief away.*) Extraordinary.

JACK. The older one grows, of course . . . the more one takes into account other people's foibles.

HARRY. Oh, yes.

JACK. If a person can't be what they are, what's the purpose of being anything at all?

HARRY. Oh, absolutely.

ALFRED *has returned. He picks up one of the metalwork chairs; turns it one way then another, gazes at* JACK *and* HARRY, *then slowly carries it off.*

JACK. I suppose in the army, of course, one becomes quite used to foibles.

HARRY. Oh, yes.

JACK. Navy, too, I shouldn't wonder.

HARRY. Oh, yes.

JACK. A relative of mine rose to lieutenant-commander in a seagoing corvette.

HARRY. My word.

JACK. In the blood.

HARRY. Bound to be.

JACK. Oh, yes. Without the sea; well, hate to think.

HARRY. Oh, yes.

JACK. At no point is one more than seventy-five miles from the sea.

HARRY. Really.

JACK. That is the nature of this little island.

HARRY. Extraordinary when you think.

JACK. When you think what came from it.

HARRY. Oh, yes.

JACK. Radar.

HARRY. Oh, yes.

JACK. Jet propulsion.

HARRY. My word.

JACK. Television.

HARRY. Oh . . .

JACK. Steam-engine.

HARRY. Goodness.

JACK. Empire the like of which no one has ever seen.

HARRY. No. My word.

JACK. Light of the world.

HARRY. Oh, yes.

JACK. Penicillin.

HARRY. Penicillin.

JACK. Darwin.

HARRY. Darwin.

JACK. Newton.

HARRY. Newton.

JACK. Milton.

HARRY. My word.

JACK. Sir Walter Raleigh.

HARRY. Goodness. Sir . . .

JACK. Lost his head.

HARRY. Oh, yes. (*Rises; comes downstage.*)

JACK. This little island.

HARRY. Shan't see its like.

JACK. Oh, no.

HARRY. The sun has set.

JACK. Couple of hours . . .

HARRY. What?

JACK. One of the strange things, of course, about this place.

HARRY. Oh, yes.
JACK. Is its size.
HARRY. Yes.
JACK. Never meet the same people two days running.
HARRY. No.
JACK. Can't find room, of course.
HARRY. No.
JACK. See them at the gates.
HARRY. Oh, my word.
JACK. Of an evening, looking in. Unfortunately the money
    isn't there.
HARRY. No.
JACK. Exchequer. Diverting wealth to the proper . . .
HARRY. Oh, yes.
JACK. Witness: one metalwork table, two metalwork chairs;
    two thousand people.
HARRY. My word, yes.
JACK. While overhead . . .
HARRY. Oh, yes . . .

    They both gaze up.

    ALFRED *comes in; he picks up the remaining white chair.*

ALFRED. You finished?
JACK. What . . . ?
ALFRED. Take them back. (*Indicates their two wicker
    chairs.*)
HARRY. Oh, yes . . .
ALFRED. Don't take them back: get into trouble.
JACK. Oh, my word.

    ALFRED, *watching them, lifts the metal chair with one
    hand, holding its leg; demonstrates his strength.*

    They watch in silence.

    ALFRED *lifts the chair above his head; then, still
    watching them, turns and goes.*

JACK. Shadows.
HARRY. Yes.
JACK. Another day.

HARRY. Ah, yes.

JACK. Brother-in-law I had was an artist.

HARRY. Really?

JACK. Would have appreciated those flowers. Light fading
. . . Clouds.

HARRY. Wonderful thing.

JACK. Oh, yes.

HARRY. Would have liked to have been an artist myself.
Musician.

JACK. Really?

HARRY. Flute.

JACK. Beautiful instrument.

HARRY. Oh, yes.

They gaze at the view.

HARRY. Shadows.

JACK. Choose any card . . . (*Holds pack out from his
pocket.*)

HARRY. Any?

JACK. Any one . . .

HARRY (*takes one*). . . . . Yes!

JACK. Eight of diamonds.

HARRY. My word!

JACK. Right?

HARRY. Absolutely.

JACK. Intended to show the ladies.

HARRY. Another day.

JACK. Oh, yes.

JACK re-shuffles cards; holds them out.

HARRY. Again?

JACK. Any one.

HARRY. Er . . .

JACK. Three of spades.

HARRY. Two of hearts.

JACK. What? (*Inspects the cards briefly; puts them away.*)

HARRY. Amazing thing, of course, is the er.

JACK. Oh, yes.

HARRY. Still prevails.

JACK. Oh, my goodness.

HARRY. Hendricks I find is a . . .
JACK. Oh, yes.
HARRY. Moustache . . . Eye-brows.
JACK. Divorced.
HARRY. Oh, yes.
JACK. Moral fibre. Set to a task, never complete it. Find some way to back out.
HARRY. Oh, yes.
JACK. The sea is an extraordinary . . .
HARRY. Oh, yes.
JACK. Cousin of mine . . .
HARRY. See the church.

They gaze off.

JACK. Shouldn't wonder He's disappointed. (*Looks up.*)
HARRY. Oh, yes.
JACK. Heart-break.
HARRY. Oh, yes.
JACK. Same mistake . . . Won't make it twice.
HARRY. Oh, no.
JACK. Once over. Never again.

ALFRED *has come on.*

ALFRED. You finished?
JACK. Well, I . . . er . . .
ALFRED. Take 'em back.
JACK. Oh, well. That's very . . .

ALFRED *grasps the two wicker chairs. Glances at* JACK *and* HARRY; *picks up both the chairs.*

Glances at JACK *and* HARRY *again, holding the chairs. Takes them off.*

JACK. What I . . . er . . . yes.

HARRY *has begun to weep.*

JACK *gazes off.*

A moment later JACK *also wipes his eyes.*

After a while the light slowly fades.

Curtain.

STAGES

Stages was first presented in the Cottesloe at the Royal National Theatre on 12 November 1992. The cast included Alan Bates, Joanna David and Rosemary Martin.

FENCHURCH
KAREN
BEA
MARION
REBECCA

Directed by Lindsay Anderson

The sound of knocking. The ringing of a bell.

FENCHURCH *enters: sits.*

Further knocking. The bell rings twice.

Pause.

KAREN (*heard, calling*). Father?

    Pause.

    (*Heard.*) I've been knocking.

    Pause.

    Thank you.

    Pause.

    I shall.

    Pause.

    Father?

    Pause.

KAREN *enters.*

    Pause.

The woman next door let me have the key.
FENCHURCH. Did she?
KAREN. 'Always locking himself out.'
FENCHURCH. That's right.
KAREN. Good-looking.
FENCHURCH. Is she.
KAREN. If you like that sort of thing.
FENCHURCH (*pause*). I might.

    Pause.

KAREN. I went first of all to Emma's.
FENCHURCH. How is she?
KAREN. Working from home.
FENCHURCH. What on?

KAREN. A book. (*Picks up book. Reads.*) 'The Fiction and Paintings of Richard Fenchurch.'
FENCHURCH. It came the other day.
KAREN. Read it?
FENCHURCH. Not yet.
KAREN. The first of many.
FENCHURCH. The only one.

Pause.

How's your work going?
KAREN. Well.
FENCHURCH. Children?
KAREN. Fine.
FENCHURCH. Charlie?
KAREN. Giving up his job.
FENCHURCH. What for?
KAREN. Wants to work on his own.

Pause.

FENCHURCH. I see.
KAREN. Not for his father.
FENCHURCH. A solicitor.
KAREN. A barrister.

Pause.

FENCHURCH. What is Emma writing?
KAREN. A book to do with working from home.
FENCHURCH. Not from her office.
KAREN. No.

Pause.

FENCHURCH. Two authors in the family.
KAREN. Three.
FENCHURCH. How is 'The Caravaggio File'?
KAREN. Selling.

Pause.

FENCHURCH. I never liked him.
KAREN. Nor 'the artist is more important than his work' routine.
FENCHURCH. I'm very proud of you, Karen. Those years

at the Courtauld. You ran rings round Viklund and his
'Landscape and the European Mind'. And Emma: her
own consultancy at twenty-five.

KAREN. I telephoned Macauley.

FENCHURCH. When?

KAREN. Before I left.

FENCHURCH. Where was she?

KAREN. In her office.

Pause.

I ought to take you home.

FENCHURCH. I am at home.

KAREN. To Ardsley.

FENCHURCH. That's your mother's home is that.

KAREN. It's our home now.

FENCHURCH. You've spoken to your mother?

KAREN. Yes.

FENCHURCH. I lived twelve miles away. At Onasett. A
sandstone bluff of rock projecting into the Onar valley,
the river dividing near its source, up in the Pennines, one
arm ending in the North Sea, via the Humber, the other in
the Irish, via the Ribble. Ona's Headland. His Place. A
viking warlord. Onasett. A corporation housing estate on
which my parents lived for forty-five years.

KAREN. You always liked it.

FENCHURCH. Onasett.

KAREN. Ardsley.

FENCHURCH. In the days of Isabella.

Pause.

She doesn't live there any more.

KAREN. It's Mummy's parents' dying that changed your
attitude to everything, I think. (*Sits.*)

FENCHURCH.
I liked it well enough.
Trains shunting across the village street.
Smoke. Steam. Grit.

Your mother's father, Corrigan, made his living selling
land, coal, property and insurance. He owned all the
lorries for miles around. Built his business up from a horse

and cart. There were still 'osses and carts, as he called them, at the house the first time I went. Taken by your mother when she wa' still at school. 'A pitman's lad', I heard him say. 'She's brought a bloody pitman's son'.

He took me out one day to his yard. A truck had broken down. 'Help me shift these sacks,' he said. We spent the next two hours shifting hundred-weight bags of coal from one lorry to another. After that he never complained. Except once, six years later, when Bea told him we were going to marry. 'Couldn't you marry,' he asked her, '*summat else? Summat not an artist*?'

I painted pictures by the bedroom window. Wrote novels in the dark. Became the rage for a couple of months when, eight years later, the first was published. Pictures in an exhibition. A slow climb up from that.

First visited there one night, with Bea. Kissed her at the garden gate. 'Not one of those who allow intimacies,' she said, 'on first acquaintance.'

Six years later we married.

KAREN. Macauley thinks you ought to come.

FENCHURCH. Longcroft Professor of Psychiatry and sub-Dean of the Medical School at the North London Royal. Said she'd read my novels in medical school and seen my pictures in an exhibition.

I prefer to live here than go back to your mother.

KAREN. My mother has re-married, Dad.

FENCHURCH. Why she left I've no idea.

It was my idea she should go back to research after bringing up you and Emma.

Did you know in the anti-coagulant properties of the moorland leech she has found a possible cure for cancer?

No sooner out of college than she was cutting up leeches faster than I could paint a picture. I'm talking of thirty-odd years ago. I was painting pictures and writing novels twenty-four hours a day, year in, year out.

We lived in a garret. In the evenings we collected
vegetables and fruit from a street market after the stalls
had been wheeled away and before the sweepers got to
work.
Bea was eighteen. I was twenty.

I was happy at Ardsley. It was like living in a castle. A big
stone house, set in a park, above a village which is nobbut
a commuter's paradise today. In those days colliery
engines crossed the street. At night you could hear the
sound of trains, panting, as they swept off to the south.

Nowadays, you live there as a lawyer's wife.

Your mother met her current husband at the Medical
Research Centre at Horton. The Parliamentary Private
Secretary to the Minister of Health. Asked him for a grant
to do research.

KAREN. You're too much on your own in here.

FENCHURCH. There's her next door. The wife of a doctor.
We're halfway between Kings Cross where your mother
and I first started and Hampstead Heath where we ended
up with you and Emma.

I left school at seventeen and went into art. Forty years
later I end up at the North London Royal full of a drug
which even now I can't pronounce.

It's all too much. (*Holds his head.*)

The woman next door has got two sons. One's fourteen.
The other twelve. Her husband comes at the weekend to
take them out. He's married again. Like Bea. She'd only
left me fifteen months when I saw her photograph in the
paper with a round-featured little sod who'd made his
reputation by singing, to popular tunes, at each year's
party conference, lyrics of his own invention.

O singer beware,
O lover be true:
If you touch my wife
I'm coming for you.

KAREN. Do you spend much time in here?

FENCHURCH. These houses were built in the middle of the nineteenth century. Taravara Road. Taravara Crescent. Taravara Street.

KAREN. We can be back in Yorkshire by tea-time if we set off now.

FENCHURCH. We could.

The last time I was in Yorkshire I couldn't wait to leave.

Marion Macauley is famous for her treatment of depressives. 'I have over a dozen creative artists on my books', she said, 'and have files on one hundred and sixty whom I have treated in the past.'

Ghosts. I see ghosts here, Karen, every night.

Pause.

KAREN. I remember coming to your studio after school.

FENCHURCH. That's right.

KAREN. You'd do my homework.

FENCHURCH. 'Pilgrim's Progress.'

KAREN. 'Faith is not a matter of choice but temperament.'

FENCHURCH. 'Faith is a matter of duty', your teacher replied.

KAREN. In red.

FENCHURCH. I'm working all that out. Why some of us go mad and others don't.

I scarcely sleep at night.
Sometimes I sleep all afternoon.

I appreciate you coming.

This is a conspiracy by my former wife. I courted her at school. I courted her at college. I married her when her fortunes and mine were at an all-time low.

She came home one day – your mother – from the labs. She said, 'Can we have a talk about something important?' 'Not the moorland leech?' I said. There were leeches, by that time, all over the house. Ink drawings in the hall. Photos in the kitchen. Like the surface of the moon. The contours of each cell. Orange. Cinnamon. Ochre. Lemon.

'I've fallen in love,' she said, 'for the very first time.'

She had watched this politician adjust her microscope on a visit to the labs. His head bowed, his eye to the eye-piece, his hair fallen to one side. She realised, as she watched him, that she had, as she described it, 'fallen in love'.

At fifty-one she left. After twenty-eight years of married life.

She ups and leaves for the Parliamentary Private Secretary to the Minister of Health.

KAREN. We used to go up at Christmas. And when you and Mum were away in the summer. I loved riding Grandpa's horses. Those old shires he kept in the yard. And the servant.

FENCHURCH. Rosie.

KAREN. With her wrinkled stockings.

FENCHURCH. Picnics on the lawn.

KAREN. Parties in Ardsley Wood.

And Grandma.

FENCHURCH. Red hair.

KAREN. Moroccan.

FENCHURCH. Lebanese.

Your grandfather Corrigan met her on holiday in France.

The first time Bea took me home we came up the drive. The sun had set. A light shone in a ground-floor window. A woman – hearing our feet on the gravel – glanced up. Her eyes had a greenish glow, her cheekbones sharply raised, her hair piled up in plaits. She smiled.

A moment later she came to the door.
She was fifty-one. I was eighteen.
Bea one year and six months younger.

KAREN. You fell in love.

FENCHURCH. With her?

KAREN. With Mum.

FENCHURCH. Yes.

Rises.

I fell in love.

KAREN. She loves you still, as a matter of fact.

FENCHURCH. She came to see me at the NLR. 'Couldn't
you let me go?' she said. I was demented at the time. 'I
love you, too,' I told her. 'That's not love,' she said. 'In
that case, Bea,' I said, 'what is it?' 'That,' she said, 'is
obsession.'

KAREN. We could put together all you need. Tonight we'd
be in Ardsley.

FENCHURCH. Twelve miles from there to Onasett. A
council estate housing fifteen thousand people. Built just
after the First World War: a volute of avenues, roads and
crescents. Red brick and tile. Like a scree of rock.

I used to walk from Onasett to Ardsley: twelve miles of
country lanes and roads, past steaming heaps of colliery
slag until, coming to the summit of a hill – hedged fields
and copses on either side, the distant glimmer of Ardsley
Dam – I'd see the silhouetted balustrade and chimneys
and think, 'Beneath that roof lies the woman I love'.

KAREN (*moves away*). There's central heating now, of
course. The old brewery and stables have been taken
down. The floors are sanded. The panelling has gone. The
garden's changed. At the back of the house we've put a
walk to the top of Sugden's Bank. You can see across to
Onasfield. Most of the pits have gone. Ardsley slag heap is
a uniform slope, grassed to the summit and planted with a
crest of conifer and silver birch.

FENCHURCH. I've never got on with the middle class. The
working class disown me. The upper class, along with
some of their servants, were my principal companions at
the NLR. They're closing it down. Putting people like me
where we belong. In the community. (*Moves.*) Not sure
we've got one of those round here. A health visitor came

one afternoon. I showed her some of my drawings. I did
them when you and Emma were born. Did I show you
that series on life and death?

KAREN. The bridge is still there over Ardsley Dam.

FENCHURCH. I used to complain to Bea's father. 'Your
lorries are destroying that bridge.' Put up two hundred
and fifty years ago. 'Here's me digging the bloody stuff
out for next to nowt,' my father would say, 'and there's
your girl-friend's father meking a fortune from carrying
it.'

KAREN. Charlie approves.

FENCHURCH. What does he think of his step-father-in-law
being not much older than himself?

KAREN. He thinks Mummy did quite right.

FENCHURCH. My family hated me when I turned to art.
My father, back home from the coal-face at sixty-five to
find me painting "Osses! Clouds! – Bloody abstracts!" It
was only when I made a fortune from a novel, six times
his annual wage, that he changed his mind. 'There must
be more in this than meets the eye', scratching his head
with a coal-bitten hand. 'All that brass wi'out selling your
health.'

'Selling his health' was how he described it.

KAREN. You don't have to disparage all you've done.

FENCHURCH. You haven't been through all I've been
through: pursuing a vocation in the face of all that bloody
coal, all that blackness, all that death.

I passed the eleven-plus at the age of nine: an exam
intended to be taken by every child at the age of eleven.
Five years later I was sitting at a desk listening to a
teacher read aloud *A Song of Autumn* by Paul Verlaine.
'The violin sobs of the Autumn wound my heart with a
monotonous languor', when I had a vision: a house, a
wife, a job, a car: a set of rails above which was inscribed
the one word: 'Death'. 'Of course,' I said, 'I must do what
no one else can do. I must write what no one else can
write. Paint what no one else can paint.'

I left school at the end of the following year and got a job at a tent firm, setting up marquees at agricultural shows across the north of England. I painted on their canvas. I wrote in ledgers stolen from their office. At no time was I still. I wrote with swollen fingers, once with a broken arm. I met your mother while still at school. I pursued her for the next two years. When she got a scholarship to London I came down with her. We lived in an attic in Camden Town. Six years later I got an exhibition.

The melancholia I'd been prone to as a youth returned. The darkness thickened. How do you reconcile writing novels and painting pictures to working down a mine? How do you reconcile my father's silicosis to the schooling I'd rejected? My life to his? His death to mine?

Gets up.

I shan't come back. Give my love to Charlie.

Bell rings.

I'd leave it.
KAREN. I'll get it.

Goes.

Light focuses on FENCHURCH.

Pause.

FENCHURCH. Bea.

Pause.

BEA. How are you, Richard?
FENCHURCH. Marion Macauley said my indulgence in monologue was symptomatic.
BEA. What of?
FENCHURCH. Isolation.
BEA. I respect her opinion very much.
FENCHURCH. She's writing a book.

When on holiday in Egypt she was sold a copy of Rimbaud's diary, purchased off an Arab whose father's father had known him in Khartoum — a copy of which is sold to every gullible literary tourist. It explains, she says,

how a genius can go off into the desert at the age of
nineteen never to be seen again.

Know what her solution to that enigma is?

Depression.

BEA. I've read her paper. 'Lithium and the Creative Arts.'
Marion is a specialist.

FENCHURCH. She'd have treated Christ with anti-
depressants.

She'd have given him Atavan for his night on the Mount
of Olives.

BEA *comes into the light.*

How's Ken?

BEA. He's in the north of England.

FENCHURCH. For good?

BEA. Inspecting hospitals.

FENCHURCH. Lunatic?

BEA. General.

FENCHURCH. Funny to fall in love.

BEA. It is.

FENCHURCH. At fifty-one.

A facsimile of Crippen.

BEA. He has his impediments, Richard, just like you.

FENCHURCH. I didn't run off with his wife.

BEA. He didn't run off with yours.

FENCHURCH. The self disintegrates at night. When I wake
in the morning my state of mind is indistinguishable from
that of a man falling off a cliff.

The psyche has five cells.

The primal self,
comprised of the primal appetites.

The intrinsic self,
comprised of the unique blending
of the two genetic systems.

The construct self,
being the structure
that arises out of

the encounter of the two
previous selves
with everything around them.

The preceptorial self,
which is the governing structure
which evolves
out of the previous encounter.

The super-preceptorial self,
which is the ultimate structure
which oversees
the previous four.

The five, in conjunction,
comprise the composite self.

I've analysed each one.

During sleep they come apart. In cases like mine, sensory
perception, on waking, is incapable of bringing them
together.

Except at the end of a very long day when, in the evening,
something like normality returns. Sleep inevitably follows
and, on waking, the cycle of disassembly begins again.
The discovery of the five parts of the psyche will
revolutionise psychiatry. I haven't told Marion Macauley.
She plagiarises everything. I found her, on one occasion,
quoting one of my novels.

Pause.

We all find God
if only to declare
that, Jesus Christ,
he isn't there.

How are your leeches?
BEA. I've found a new way of sectioning cells. It speeds
things up no end.
FENCHURCH. Adequately funded?
BEA. Yes.
FENCHURCH. Despite the cuts?

BEA. That's right.

FENCHURCH. The cut from our divorce must have gone down well. Made a good investment, marrying me. Twenty-eight years then up and off, taking half the proceeds.

You've sold your parents' home, I hear, to Karen.

BEA. My inherited wealth, for what it's worth, is invested in our children.

FENCHURCH. Your children.

BEA. Ours.

FENCHURCH. They'll have bugger all to do with me.

BEA. Karen is here to take you back.

FENCHURCH. If you'll come with me.

Pause.

BEA. No thanks.

Pause.

FENCHURCH. Saw your picture in the press.

BEA. Yes.

FENCHURCH. More famous than me by all accounts.

BEA. Not yet.

FENCHURCH. I put you up to going back.

BEA. You did.

FENCHURCH. 'Always be grateful.'

BEA. I shall.

FENCHURCH. Since Vivien died I've felt quite happy.

I've a doctor's wife next door. Lets me in when I get locked out. Would do a bit more if I gave her a chance.

BEA. She rang me.

She thought, from what she'd seen of you, you were suffering a relapse.

FENCHURCH. How would she know?

BEA. She'd seen you in the street.

FENCHURCH. I see lots of people in the street. I don't ring up their wives.

BEA. She saw a reference in the paper – to my work at the MRC – and rang me there.

Over the past few months she's seen you pacing up and down. When she's spoken to you you've said you're lost.

FENCHURCH. The woman keeps my keys. I made one advance, of an entirely tentative nature, to which she didn't respond. She took it as a gesture of neighbourly affection. The fact of the matter is, she has a liaison with someone else. A businessman she hopes to marry.

BEA. I've spoken to Karen. There's plenty of room at Ardsley. It's a place you've always liked.

Pause.

Professor Macauley, when I rang her, thought it the best thing you could do.

FENCHURCH. The time you had me sectioned was the worst time of my life.

BEA. You were spending all our money.

FENCHURCH. Your money.

BEA. Our money.

Pause.

It was all too painful to bear.

Pause.

I can't tell you what it was like when I took you in.

I kept seeing a youth come swinging up the drive, a bag slung over his shoulder. Or sitting, drawing, under the trees. Sharp. Inquisitive. Vindictive, when he saw the chance. But, overall, determined. All that casualness that came once we were in that attic flat in London. The endless stews.

FENCHURCH. Cabbage.

BEA. Bones from the butcher which he'd left out for the dogs.

FENCHURCH. Bread from the baker.

BEA. Which you swapped for a picture.

FENCHURCH. Made his fortune, I should think, by now.

BEA. Why don't you go? If everyone who cares about you thinks you should.

FENCHURCH. What would I do?

BEA. Work.

FENCHURCH. Karen has two kiddies.

BEA. They're both at school. Charlie's at the office. Karen is thinking of writing a book.

FENCHURCH. She ought to pick on me.

BEA. She might.

FENCHURCH. Has she suggested it?

BEA. Not yet.

FENCHURCH. Is this a bribe?

BEA. It would do a great deal for her.

FENCHURCH. What would it do for me?

BEA. A lot.

FENCHURCH.
'All forr'ad-drive', as my foreman used to say.
At Alderton's, the tent firm.
'On'y forr'ad-drive on this un, Dick.'
He called me Dick to rhyme with prick.
'A college-boy,' he said, 'among us.'
Fitters, otherwise, who had lost a finger.
Colliers with pneumoconiosis.
No connection, you would think, with art.
They should have called me Paul.
Saul of Tarsus's father was a tent-man.

This neighbour rang you up.

BEA. She asked me not to tell you.

FENCHURCH. These houses have party-walls so thin you can hear every word the other side.

BEA. Self-immolation.

FENCHURCH. That's what it is?

BEA. As Marion once described it.

FENCHURCH. The best thing you did was leaving me.

BEA. That's right.

FENCHURCH. My father, just before he died, hearing I'd been at the NLR, told me he'd been afflicted by blacknesses himself. 'Well, you would,' I said, 'with all that bloody coal.' 'Mental blacknesses,' he said. And then, quite quaintly, lying in his bed, said, 'I've been up to here in blackness all my life,' holding his hand above his head.

Pause.

I shan't say a word to Mrs Brennan. She's hoping to re-marry. I was hoping, at one time, it might be me.

Rang you, I suppose, as 'the former wife of Richard Fenchurch'. I read it in the paper. 'And the present wife', it went on, 'of Kenneth Chapman, the Parliamentary Private Secretary to the Minister of Health, the mother of two children. Beats all the full-time boffins at their job.' A possible cure for cancer in the non-coagulant properties of the moorland leech.

The bloody leech.

Drawings on the wall, blow-ups in the kitchen. Insertion of the dye.

'Such lovely blooms!'

Looking down your microscope.

I shan't complain.

There's a moral there for me: 'When your wife runs off with another man there'll alus be another.'

I handed her the keys. Previous to that the police were called. A constable got in through the bathroom window. 'Leave your keys with a neighbour', he said. '*Someone you can trust.*'

I've intervened in two muggings since I came down here. On both occasions the youths ran off. I interceded in a domestic conflagration between a husband and a wife. And escorted a lady to her home whom I found one evening lying in the gutter. Like Onasett in the old days. Kids in bare feet. Smoke as thick as fog. Soot a hundred tons per acre. Male expectancy of life a hundred years before, at Onasett, was twenty-one. My father's father's father's . . . father.

Where's Karen gone?

BEA. Your living here, Richard, won't do you any good.

Emma has agreed to sell it. Charlie will see you get a good price.

FENCHURCH. I'm broke.

BEA. You have your Public Lending Rights.
FENCHURCH. I never joined.

I've been a maverick all my life.

Affiliation to the State is something I never went in for, Bea.

Unwanted by the workers,
Rejected by the bourgeoisie:
The upper class, my darling wife,
Has – meanwhile – all gone nuts like me.

The drive that characterised the first half of the century in pictures, plays and books has gone.

(*Calls.*) Karen!

I shouldn't be left alone with you.

Pause.

Light changes.

Pause.

KAREN. Made no progress, Mummy?
BEA. None.

Strange how being here brings it back.
KAREN. Have you been to the house before?
BEA. When Vivien died.

It's the only time I saw it.
KAREN. Poor bastard.
BEA. It's unlike you to feel sorry, Karen.
KAREN. Do you ever regret you left him?
BEA. Kenneth thinks I do. 'Aren't I dull,' he says, 'compared to Richard?' 'Not at all,' I tell him.
KAREN. Can get on with your work.
BEA. I do.
KAREN. Going well?
BEA. It is.
KAREN. I should start on something else.
BEA. Ever thought of Richard?
KAREN. No thanks.

BEA. Could turn the tide.
KAREN. No thank you, Mummy.

I've never known anyone so odd.
BEA. Make him a subject.
KAREN. Too close.

I could never understand why you up and went. After twenty-eight years of married life.
BEA. Things move on.
FENCHURCH. Like what?
BEA. Life. Circumstance.

What did you think of Gran?
KAREN. Gran?
BEA. What did you think of Isabella?
KAREN. He mentioned her today.

The first occasion you took him home.

Light focuses.

BEA. My parents said if I wanted to see him again – I was seventeen at the time – I'd have to bring him back. 'Daddy will have a look,' my mother said. When we got back my father was out. I took him up the drive. We came out on the terrace.

The sun had set. Shadows ran off across the grass. The air was chill. A light shone in the drawing-room window. My mother was sewing. I saw the effect on Richard at a glance. She looked more beautiful than I'd ever seen her: her coppery hair done up in plaits, the boning of her cheeks. I adored her. I always did.

When we went inside she was waiting in the hall: the wife of a transport contractor, landowner, coal-merchant, insurance agent.

Light changes.

Half Lebanese. Half Celt.
FENCHURCH. Her father was Irish.
BEA. Kells.
FENCHURCH. Invented Kell-Cakes. Made of coal-dust,

senna-pods, and vitamin D. Ate many a thousand during the war. Came in a greaseproof packet. A yellow powder you mixed with milk.

BEA. 'The working-man's Yorkshire Pudding.'

FENCHURCH. You fried it in a pan.

BEA. Came out like rubber mats.

Light changing.

FENCHURCH. Her mother's father thought of that. H J Kells, a one-time syndicalist and fellow-traveller. Became a dietician during the Second World War. Got to Cambridge as a youth and wrote 'The Life of the African Locust: the history of a central nervous system', in which, digressing from his principal theme – that there is in each cell an imprint of its previous existence – he offered the suggestion that golf was the one activity in life that would unite the middle and the working classes. 'On the links and in the clubhouse', he wrote, 'are where true spirits meet.'

BEA. He was mad on golf.

FENCHURCH. 'Run off wid her', says he one day, when Corrigan had given me a shallacking about 'the improvidence of art': '*Nowt but a bag o' wind*' – referring to my latest picture – an abstract – he'd hung up sideways on the wall.

The greatest influence on Bea's life – Kells! Took after him, she did.

Kells had magic in his fingers,
Kells had magic in his toes:
Kells had magic up his arsehole,
As every arsehole knows.

BEA. His idea about golf was to do with the limitation on the numbers who could play it, the space required, and the simplicity of the game itself.

FENCHURCH. Never got on with Corrigan's mother.

BEA. Nan.

FENCHURCH. A local woman with a ravaged face who lived to nearly a hundred.

BEA. The two of them shared a bathroom and used to call to each other through the door.

FENCHURCH. '*Are you going to be in there all day, woman?*'

BEA. She'd shout back.

FENCHURCH. '*Go eat your bloody Kell-Cakes!*'

Pause.

BEA. She never swore.

FENCHURCH. No. No. She never swore.

Pause.

KAREN. How did the Lebanese meet up with the Celt?

FENCHURCH. She was one of three sisters sent to Europe before the First World War. She met young Kells at college. In no time they were married – Kells went to the Middle East to plead his case. He ended up in Egypt. Hence his thesis.

His daughter – Bea's mother – met Corrigan on a Riviera holiday.

BEA. The sands of the desert and the bogs of Connemara!

FENCHURCH. Isabella!

BEA. Right!

Pause: light changes.

FENCHURCH. I'm not to be sectioned again, I take it?

BEA. I want to get you settled.

FENCHURCH. I am.

BEA. Somewhere you like.

FENCHURCH. I like it here.

BEA. With someone you know.

FENCHURCH. I know her next door.

Pause.

Despair, tha knows, is not my line.

BEA. This afternoon I'll come again.

Charlie and Karen will be glad to have you.

You'll like the improvements to the house.

It's not as inhospitable as it was before.

FENCHURCH. I never thought it was.

BEA. Those draughts. You could never get rid of the cold in winter.

FENCHURCH. I always think of it as summer.

We had some good summers there.

BEA. The ponds and streams. The pits and woods.

Lots of pictures, Richard. Lots.

We'll get your neighbour to let us in.

You'll be here, will you?

Light changing.

FENCHURCH. I have this little pit. I dig it every night.

In the old days a horse would travel round a windlass, winding up the coal. Nowadays all you see is a pile of slag amongst the fields – grey ash and waste. Silver birch and sycamore grow on top.

They stand amongst the houses at Onasett – incongruous piles of muck, the gardens running up on every side.

We played on them for hours – like pyramids of buried treasure: the spoil-heaps from the gin-pits of two hundred years before.

BEA. It's a morning's walk to Onasett. You can draw it once again.

FENCHURCH. I think it's all worked out. Then, without reckoning, I find another seam. A different coal entirely, less friable, more compact.

Breaks less easily under pressure.

BEA. Those Christmases at Ardsley.

Those summers on Ardsley Dam.

We can have them once again.

FENCHURCH. When I first came here with you it was the anonymity that I liked. *The not being known by anyone.*

Funny bloody life.

BEA. It is.

FENCHURCH. I started off with certainty. And end up here with doubt.

BEA. Will you see me to the door?

FENCHURCH. I'll sit here for a while.

Light refocusing.

I do nowt else at present.

Pause.

Light changing.

How are they going to manage at the North London Royal without their principal consultant?

MARION. I'm attached to the medical school, not the department.

FENCHURCH. Longcroft Professor of Psychiatry.

Set great store by that Chair, Professor.

Used to look exhausted.

MARION. Still do from time to time.

FENCHURCH. Full o' mad 'uns, are you?

MARION. We're overful, at present. Which is why I haven't much time.

FENCHURCH. Must be something special.

MARION. It is.

FENCHURCH. Four children.

MARION. Five.

FENCHURCH. I've two. Girls. One in business, the other an academic. Wrote a book debunking the myth of the artist. Her husband's a practitioner of law. 'Charlie,' she said, when she introduced him, 'is one of those sentimentalists without whom socialism couldn't exist.'

You were summat of a socialist yourself. All those arguments we used to have.

Father still alive?

MARION. Dead.

FENCHURCH. Mother?

MARION. Also.

FENCHURCH. On the night before my father's funeral I was sitting over there. The door was standing open. I'd last seen my father in a hospital bed, his eyes as large as saucers, dark-shadowed, half-fearful, looking round. Suddenly he was there. As real as you are now.

I said to him, 'If it is you,' holding up my hand, 'make yourself as real as that.'

'Why should I make myself as real as that,' he said, 'when you can see me here already?'

A feeling of great peace came over me.

We sat there for an hour.

He comes when I least expect him. As old – at first – as when he died. Then – later – as old as when I was a boy.

Finally, I saw him as a child: a snotty nose. A bruise on his knee. A cut on his brow. A boot that needed mending.

One night there was a cradle lying there, sea-green, with an ogee-shaped headboard and, inset, a thin pink line. His voice declared: 'This is me on the first Christmas of the century.'

He was born on Christmas Eve.

For much of the time I was with you I was preoccupied by the thought that if this struggle – typified by the people at the NLR – goes on in the way it does, then it must be nothing less than the expression of God's passion to exist.

If his image is embodied in ours, this massacre of the innocents must be his struggle too.

Otherwise creativity becomes a childish appetite in which all the miseries and misfortunes we are heir to count as – nothing.

MARION. Have you spoken to Bea about her mother?

FENCHURCH. No.

MARION. Have you mentioned it to your daughter?

FENCHURCH. You didn't think going into causes would do me any good.

I think of Isabella a lot.

I was on the point of telling Karen.

It happened without warning.

I'd known Beatrice for several months. She was studying for exams. Waiting for her, I'd go out in the grounds. Or find a corner in the house to read. One afternoon Bea's mother came to the door. Half Lebanese. Half Celt. A tennis-player and gardener. Dark-skinned. Red-haired.

'Come and look at the Swansons', she said. This was a testament to the latest style in architecture that was being built over a ridge at the back of the house. Bea was upstairs. Her mother called, 'I'm taking Richard to look at the Swansons!'

The path she took me to at the back of the house was encroached by shrubs on one side, on the other by a dell. I took her hand. When I glanced back I saw her face, dark, her red hair couched against the collar of her coat – a loose-fitting garment, drawn in at the waist – dark green – and trimmed at the cuffs and collar by dark brown fur. Her hand was delicate and thin. I was conscious of the coolness of its palm. 'The hand,' I thought, 'of another man's wife, pregnant with the intimacy of their twenty-odd year marriage.'

I was nineteen. She was fifty-one.

We reached a bank. With a final scramble I went in front, stooped, took both her hands, and drew her to me.

How long we stood there I've no idea.

We stared at the house. A concrete edifice with oval windows. It had a swimming-pool laid out in the garden, the site, at the foot of the slope, separated from the grounds in which we were standing by a half-completed wall.

My thoughts were obsessed with her entirely: her hands, her hair, her mouth, her throat.

We returned to the house without a word. I didn't see her again for several days. Each night I fell asleep with her imagined shape beside me. One evening she came to a meeting in town. I arranged to be waiting outside when she came out. I walked with her to her bus. I suggested a route which took us by a cul-de-sac. We paused beneath a tree.

It was something in her spirit. Something in both of us, for which there's no account. No woman before or since has affected me in the way that Bea's mother did.

That winter I rented a room above a barber's. She came up to town, each Thursday, shopping. After the first few weeks I persuaded her to pose.

The reason, you say, why Bea left. She never knew.

On all other occasions Isabella was as circumspect as any parent with a son-in-law might be: a jocular remark, an enquiry about my work, advice to Bea on what time that evening she might be in, what clothes she ought to wear – a warning about spending too much time in the dark: 'Think of your schoolwork. Think of your exams. Don't go leaving your homework uncompleted.'

My relationship with Bea was defined by circumspection. I was 'the dark tornado' – a nickname derived from school – who, when I was alone with her, drew a line at holding hands: me, whose reputation with girls had initially, when reported to her by a schoolfriend, filled her with alarm.

I agreed to be seduced by her in order to conceal the fact that I'd been seduced already by her mother.

Once the room above the barber's had gone – the barber curious to know who Isabella was – we'd spend our afternoons in the fields and woods between Onasfield and Ardsley.

We were never discovered.

We haunted the countryside which, before and after, I have always loved and which, years later, as a writer and an artist, made my reputation.

I live – and still live – for her alone.

On buses, in cafes, I would take her hand. 'I've got your son's fare,' the conductor would say. 'Your son has paid the bill,' the waitress would announce.

She provided me, finally, at Ardsley, with a room in which to paint. She would bring me something she had baked – a piece of bread, a bun, a cake – and, Corrigan busy in the yard, Bea in her room, the housekeeper in the kitchen, the grandparents invariably asleep – invite me to her bed.

'This is madness,' she'd declare as if, in identifying her passion, she might subdue it.

MARION. Mad.

FENCHURCH. One night, at the height of our romance, we visited a dam. We lay amongst the bushes, on a grassy slope.

A moon shone through the leaves above our heads. A woman of fifty-three. A youth of twenty-one.

Her face was scarcely that of anyone I knew. As if she'd come from another planet.

Years later, whenever she came to London, after Bea and I were married, I'd take a stroll in the evenings and we'd meet, minutes later, at her hotel.

When we went to pay a visit to Ardsley, within minutes of our arrival Isabella would say, 'Come and look at the nest I've found', or 'flower', or 'shrub', or 'tree', or 'plant'. Even at Christmas, when Emma and Karen were there, Corrigan and his mother, Kells.

I still loved Bea. I thought it would defile her. It didn't. Mother and daughter. Sun and moon. Night and day.

The year before she died I'd gone up on a visit. She'd bought herself new clothes. She went in her room to try them on.

I went to the door.
She was stooping by the bed.

She was seventy-nine.
I was forty-seven.

They say she died of a broken heart. I'd say more nearly
from the advent of our children – whom, like Bea, she
couldn't bear to harm.

The day she died I went quite mad.

In a curious way, until today, I've scarcely even mentioned
her. Except, of course, to you.

MARION. Beatrice never knew.

FENCHURCH. There was never any cause.

I'd marvel at Isabella. She was a different person when
Bea was there. Equally involved. Equally absorbed.
Equally engaging.

I'd notice the smoothness of her blouse, the tautness of her
skirt – properties, I always thought, peculiar to another
woman: someone whom, away from that place, I scarcely
knew at all.

Time for you to go.

MARION. Not quite.

FENCHURCH. Hoping to persuade me.

MARION. I might.

FENCHURCH. Remember those talks we used to have?
Consulting me about your patients.

'What would you do with her?'

'What would you do with this one?'

At the door would come a knock.
'Can I speak to you now, Professor?'
'I'm busy with a patient.'
'Come to the door and look at me!'
'Shortly.'
'Now!'
'*Shortly!*'

You'd open the door and explain, with great compassion, that you were busy with another patient.

Then let me carry on.

I saw through your trick.

Like now, Professor.

MARION. Your future lies in Ardsley.

FENCHURCH. Ardsley's past.

MARION.
Not with your daughter there.
Get away from here.
Get away from London.

FENCHURCH. Vivien came to see you.

MARION. She did.

FENCHURCH. Impressed you, so she said, no end.

MARION. That's right.

FENCHURCH. 'Nothing the matter.'

MARION. She took me in.

FENCHURCH.
She took us both in.
That's right.

MARION. How did you meet her?

FENCHURCH. One of my books was about to be filmed. She auditioned for a part. We met in an office in Wardour Street. Her marriage by that time had broken down. She wore dark glasses. Beneath them she wore a second pair. Beneath the second pair, a third.

'I'm afraid,' she said, 'I don't audition.' 'I came,' she said, 'to interview you.' She had a good figure. She was forty-five. She'd made a reputation over here, gone to California and made an even bigger one.

Red hair.
Rouged cheeks.
A thin-lipped mouth.

'Who are you?' she asked me.

I was two weeks out of the NLR.

She invited me to dinner.

'I hate hotels,' she said.

I brought her here. She took a bottle from a paper bag. She drank. She talked about her husband. She talked about Dundee, where she'd been born, and Aberdeen, where she'd been brought up, and London, where she'd started in the theatre. She came for the evening and stayed a year.

She went away once to a Park Lane hotel. The police were called to throw her out.

It was at that time she came to see you.

She came back here with a bottle of booze.

I realised then what I hadn't before.

Ever since her husband left she'd been looking for a place to die.

One day I came in and found a note. 'Gone to L.A. Thanks. Vi.' Her cases were gone. The only thing I found was her wedding ring.

Three days later I went out to the yard. The shed door was off its catch. When I tried to fasten it I found it jammed. Inside, her cases were neatly stacked. Beside them, turned to the door, curled up, lay Vi. Beside her lay a bottle of household bleach. Her lips were charred. Her eyes were glazed. Her teeth bared in a grimace.

My daughters came. Ever since, with their mother's backing, they've suggested I should leave.

Your lithium, Doc, didn't do the trick.

MARION. It's time you lived at Ardsley. It's where your life as an artist began. What nourished you at the start will nourish you again.

FENCHURCH. The night you sectioned me I had a dream. I was walking down a street in Onasfield. A hole had been dug. In it, I could see, were many pipes, bent and twisted at every angle. Beneath the pipes were massive engines, wet with steam. Sombre in their heat and power. Each of them in motion. Throbbing. 'All this is hidden,' I declared.

'An energy as immense as the planet itself.' My body shook.

It was the morning Bea rang you.

You'll find my daughter waiting outside. My former wife is persuading her to put me in a book. 'The Fenchurch File.' Revive my flagging fortune.

I feel better than I did before. The underground tubes and pipes have gone. Everything's on the surface. Gleaming.

Bea made a good settlement from our marriage. I've no complaints. This is all I need. A couple of rooms. If anything, something smaller.

MARION. Stay there for a month. Consider your position. Supervision of that sort can be a help. Something to connect to.

FENCHURCH. Phone Bea. Phone my daughter. Tell them what you think.

Light refocusing.

You called her up.

REBECCA. I had to.

FENCHURCH. At the lab.

REBECCA. I got the address from the paper.

FENCHURCH. You're supposed to be my neighbour.

REBECCA. I am.

FENCHURCH. Despite your bloody husband.

REBECCA. My husband is of no consequence at all.

FENCHURCH.

I see it in his eyes.
I see it when he comes.
He gets out from his car.

He pads over to your door.

He knocks.
He waits.

He cries.

I can hear him through the wall.

'Rebecca!'

Pause.

REBECCA. Is your daughter taking you or not?
FENCHURCH. You heard that through the wall.
REBECCA.
    I'd seen you walking in the street.
    Other neighbours notice.
    They'll section you again.
FENCHURCH.
    I can't stay at my daughter's.
    I can't stay where it all began.
    They want me taken out of here.
    Away from where it happened.
    Vivien.
    My living on my own.

    When you offered her the keys did she look you in the
    eye? Did she ask, 'Is this the woman who will take my
    place – the place of all the women who have loved him
    and, but for me, have let him down?'

    Children at school?
REBECCA. They are.
FENCHURCH. Nothing else to do.
REBECCA. I have.
FENCHURCH. Counselling.
REBECCA. What I can.

    None of us is perfect.
FENCHURCH. Alarmed, was she? Or disappointed?
REBECCA. She thanked me.
FENCHURCH. For what?
REBECCA. For keeping her informed.
FENCHURCH. Of everything?
REBECCA. Of how you are.
FENCHURCH. You had to be back at work this morning.
REBECCA. I have been.
FENCHURCH. Damn good job.
REBECCA. Like yours.
FENCHURCH. Flexibility.

REBECCA. It has.

FENCHURCH. At the height of my illness I went to a shelf in the local library and, for no reason I can think of, pulled out the first book that I came to. I read, in black print on the red-bound cover, 'The English Social Novel from Sir Walter Scott to Richard Fenchurch'.

Or was it, 'Sir Richard Fenchurch to Walter Scott'?

At that moment I began to get well.

REBECCA. Your daughter came a long way to take you back.

FENCHURCH. A product of the Courtauld Institute. An historian of art. 'This essay,' her professor wrote of one of hers, 'is the product of a mind in which imagination outpaces commonsense'.

You're looking well.

Don't let anyone tell you that a woman of thirty loses her looks. Creases. Fat. Furrows – maturity and bruises – improve a woman all the time. Add layer to layer, depth to depth, resonance to resonance. She never stops. The supreme achievement she must aim for.

I don't know why you let her in.

I shall never hear the end of it.
I shall never hear the end.

Isn't that what you want from the man next door?

REBECCA. I prefer to do what's best for you.

FENCHURCH. The mother of two sturdy boys.
No sooner are they off than out she comes.
'Shall it be the neighbours at the back today or the neighbours at the front who have a view of her arrival?'

The days in bed.
The days, of course, we only talk:
your marriage, my marriage. My past. Your present.
The prospect which you couldn't face.

'All men are wrecks and those who aren't are little less
than bastards!'

Light changes.

I hadn't expected you to come.

Not yet.

I had this woman here in mind.
A doctor's wife from the house next door.
Professes to keep an eye on me.
I eye.
She eyes.
We eye together.
Since I became one of the statistical ten in every
hundred.
Who is no longer safe in front of a bus.
Who is no longer.

In the evening she invites me in.
'To break the ice', as she describes it.
Watch television as, in days of yore, I did with you and
Bea.
The boys, on one occasion, calling me, 'Dad'.
Glancing up as I came in.
'Dad!'
Their father's hours in heaven.
Hallowed by thy next door neighbour.
'Come in on an evening, Mr Fenchurch. The boys will
welcome you,' she said.
Rebecca.
Past her prime.
Her marriage a disaster.
'On the shelf', she said.
Invited, after that, to stay.
One summer afternoon.
Not long. 'The boys come home at five.'
The problem was I couldn't respond.
REBECCA. Not all adversity comes from working down a
  mine.
FENCHURCH. It doesn't.

REBECCA. The wife who spelt disaster.

FENCHURCH. The husband poor in bed.

REBECCA. The children who came after.

FENCHURCH. 'In public school,' you said.

REBECCA. Paid for by their father.

FENCHURCH.

I'd recommend him as a father.
Not a hug.
Seldom a kiss.
Not even, I suspect, a lascivious glance.

I gave my daughters other things instead.
Passion. Pride.
What every girl should ask for.

REBECCA. Those evenings over dinner.

FENCHURCH. The sound of your boys in the house next door.

REBECCA. Weekends with their father.

FENCHURCH. I take it they're all right.

REBECCA. All right?

FENCHURCH. Not one of us in loving stands a chance.

Isabella was the same.
'Only the best in you I love. The rest,' she said,
'I never see.'

REBECCA. She made a wise decision.

FENCHURCH. She was fifty-one. I not that age by the time she died.

It all goes on.
The unacceptable.
The unforgivable.

I'm surprised you had two sons.
Red hair.
That look of apprehension.
A curious name. Rebecca. Not like you at all.
The way you paint your mouth.
Kissing on the bed.
'The imaging,' you said.
As if you'd never touched a man and I, in fifty years, had never touched a woman.

REBECCA. There's all the time in the world, you said.

FENCHURCH. Long list of my credentials.

REBECCA. Things came better in the end.

FENCHURCH. Not only the colour but the texture of your hair.

The way it's done.

And then, of course, her scent.

Above all else, her eyes.

The first time that it worked I saw, not her, but you.

You let me – what?

REBECCA. Transpose.

FENCHURCH. Dread.

REBECCA. Terror.

FENCHURCH. It's with me now, as a matter of fact.

Pause.

REBECCA. Now you have to leave.

FENCHURCH. I can't.

The story of his life.

He cries.

She hears him in the night.

She rings his bell.

'Are you all right?'

'Come in,' he said.

'At this time of the morning?'

Seven.

Five.

Sitting on his knee.

'Dreaming.'

'Oh!' they said. And, 'Oh!'

Upholstered bed, a table lamp on either side where both, or either, might have read.

The light.

Burning.

'Christ's ambassadress,' he said.

Baring palms before his son's erection.

He wrote all day.

He wrote all night.

He wrote, he told her,

Out of sight:
Wrote upstairs and into bed.
'Some of my best words,' he said.

Inscribed on her vagina.

Light refocuses.

REBECCA. They told me you were ill.
FENCHURCH. Never better.
REBECCA. How are all your children?
FENCHURCH. Well.

Bea is your age now. The age we came together. That time at Sugden's Bank. Looking down at the Swansons' house.

I liked your coat. Its brown fur collar. And then your hair. Done up in plaits. More beautiful, my dear, than anything I painted.

Mornings in the winter walking in the grounds, one ungloved hand pushed in my pocket, the crackle of the twigs as you raced ahead, showing me the nest you'd failed to find all summer – stooping to the hedge, your hair caught on a twig, and me – your cheek flushed – leaning to release it.

Love!

Skating on the ice at Ardsley Dam, taking my hand as you glided to the bank.
The weight and touch of your coated body.

Those afternoons when you came to town.

Lying on my coat beneath the trees.
'What will I say,' you said, 'when I get back?
What will I say,' you said, 'to Freddie?'

That day at Ardsley Crag, couched by the anemones, saying, 'My life is in your hands.'
Yet Freddie said, 'Been looking for birds at Ardsley Edge?'
Turning to me to add, 'Don't have her scrumping trees, tha knows. Even if she has a nest to show you.'

His blindness drove you mad.

'Doesn't he suspect at all?' I'd ask.
'Not a bit,' you'd tell me.
Even when Rosie caught us, beneath the mistletoe at
Christmas, and said, 'I'll not be safe, mesen!'
To the extent I had to give her one such kiss herself.
'Crikey, Mrs Corrigan! Yon Richard packs a wallop!'

Those walks in Ardsley Wood when we talked of the
reality of God's existence.
'We are born to destroy and to be destroyed,' I said.
'Where does love come from?' you enquired.
'The pain,' I said, 'of our destruction.'
'Love nothing but a salve,' you said.
*'Not salve, my love, but our salvation. In all that happens
God is there.'*

For your daughter, I recall, you stood aside.
Seeing her love for me and my love for her disassociated
from the vividness of our own encounters.
'She has precedence,' you said.
Our pilgrimage, which is how I saw it, in Ardsley's fields
and woods and copses.

I had Japanese brushes to paint with, Bell.
The colour of your hair. Red squirrel hair.

Eyes shielded from the rain, head bowed.
'I haven't seen you, Rick, all week.'
Your hand inside my pocket.
The terror that greets me when I rise.
That's why I'll stay.

Beyond the door, the street.
Beneath the street the contours of an ancient river,
running between obliterated fields, copses, hedgerows.

His incorrigible question, 'How?'
And after 'How?' of course, came, 'Why?'

And after 'Why?' came, 'When?'
And – once 'When?' had been explained – came
'Where?'

And then when Karen comes, and then?
Bea might.
Rebecca will.

'No mercy on the saints,' the octogenarian Kells
announced, 'so why on us?'
Boasting to his daughter Isabella.

'Mother *and* daughter,' the housekeeper Rosie from the
village said. 'He'll be after a kiss from me.'
And then.
What will I do when Vivien comes?
When Isabella comes.

Sleeping on his hill, Ona, in his viking horns, bare-armed
and gaiter-legged. And, before him, too, a tessellated
pavement discovered in the grounds of Onasett Hall two
centuries before the estate was built, a Roman road
running west from Watling Street – over the Pennine hills
to Manchester and Chester.

The vision that his past had now become.

Not least his love of Isabella.

Constraint the secret of his life. And then.

BEA. The first occasion I took you back. Crossing in front
of the uncurtained window of the sitting-room into
which we looked – my mother sewing, her hair caught up
in a plaited bun above each ear – an envelope, or so it
seemed, of coppery light, her green eyes raised, enquiring,
at the sound of our feet outside on the gravel. I saw her
face. I see it now. I see her eyes. They haven't changed. It
was all contained in that single look. '*That woman I shall
love for ever.*'

FENCHURCH. You want me out of here.

REBECCA. It's time you settled down.

FENCHURCH. Pick up a brush.

REBECCA. Pick up a pen.

FENCHURCH. 'The bitumen,' a critic wrote, 'of
Fenchurch's early pictures.'

REBECCA. Pits and slag-heaps.

FENCHURCH. Mills and quarries.

REBECCA. Lakes and pastures.

FENCHURCH. Hills and follies.

REBECCA. An eruption that engulfed him.

FENCHURCH. Whole.

REBECCA.
Never painted.
Never wrote.
Never married.
Never spoke.

FENCHURCH. Never saw poor Vivien die.

REBECCA. Arc-lights in the street at night.

FENCHURCH. Neighbours renting out their rooms to
photographers and reporters.

REBECCA. The long-shot of the shed.

FENCHURCH. The stone-flagged walk to our back door,
still scarred from war-time bombing.

REBECCA. Those early years in Camden Town.

FENCHURCH. Parties in our garret.

REBECCA. 'I am your Isabella!'

FENCHURCH. A muse to me throughout my life. From the
moment I first saw her.

I put her into pictures.

REBECCA. Clothes.

FENCHURCH. 'I don't need you at all.'

REBECCA.
The detergent in the shed,
The bottle by her bed:
The message that she left behind,
The things she left unsaid.

FENCHURCH. His wife had left.

REBECCA. His children gone.

FENCHURCH. Their dogs and cats.

REBECCA. Their coats. Their hats.

FENCHURCH. Enquiring.

REBECCA. Wheretofore? Et cetera.

FENCHURCH. Such wealth.

Pause.

REBECCA. You've settled on this woman, then?
FENCHURCH. I have.

I take her hand.

I kiss her mouth.

I can't see any difference between Vivien and
yourself.
Between Isabella-Bella-Bell and you.
Between the former doctor's wife, the counsellor,
and you.

The crowd at the Tate, at the retrospective,
around the nude of Isabella.

Her body glowed.

The smoothness of her thigh
which took the eye
to the copper-coloured
pubic hair.

Cara-vara-vaggio.

The actress whom he never knew,
the mistress whom he always drew —

who came in at the door to end
what Hollywood,
Kirkcaldy,
the Scottish Church,
Dumfries, Aberdeen,
Dundee
had started.

He took up a stance.

He started to dance.

Lightly at first.

He danced.

Dancing.

How he danced.

REBECCA. Dancing . . .

FENCHURCH. Dancing.

REBECCA. For the dead.

FENCHURCH. Dancing.

REBECCA. Dancing.

FENCHURCH. In his head.

REBECCA. Dancing now.

FENCHURCH. Or so he said.

REBECCA. For those who had departed.

FENCHURCH. He made a covenant at the start.

REBECCA. Made over life and love to art.

FENCHURCH. Sold family, lover . . .

REBECCA. Friends as well.

FENCHURCH. And, dancing, dances now to hell.

REBECCA. Richard!

FENCHURCH. Dances . . .

His dancing figure: moving. Freezes.

Light fades.

CARING

Characters

ZENA
CLARKE

ZENA. Dressed to kill.
CLARKE. I am.
ZENA. You spoke to me directly.
CLARKE. I am talking to the wall.

Pause.

Thirty-eight years.
ZENA. I was nineteen when I married.
CLARKE. You were nearly twenty-six.

Your mother hated my guts.
ZENA. Your father hated mine.
CLARKE. He thought I was bound for the top.
ZENA. You were.
CLARKE. 'The melody of song is at your fingertips,' he told
   me.
ZENA. A funny place to have it.

Pause.

I had star-billing.
CLARKE. In a night-club.
ZENA. In a club that entertained the highest in the land.
CLARKE. Whores.
ZENA. An Arabian prince. I lived in the desert for fourteen
   months. Every night he had me. He or someone else.
CLARKE. Who?
ZENA. His cousins. His brothers. I could never tell one from
   the other in the dark.
CLARKE. Now she tells me.

Pause.

We promised to keep nothing from one another. Marion.
ZENA. Olivia.
CLARKE. Juanilda.
ZENA. Claudette.
CLARKE. Claudette!
ZENA. The one who made love with a hat on.
CLARKE. A hat.

ZENA. Now you forget. You spent half a day describing it.
CLARKE. I was twenty-one. A different venue every night.

Pause.

ZENA. Now you're going out.
CLARKE. An hour.
ZENA. Dressed like that.
CLARKE. I always dress like this.
ZENA. Only when you're going out.

An insurance clerk.
CLARKE. A manager.
ZENA. What a firm.
CLARKE. It might employ you, if you gave it a chance.
ZENA. Selling insurance!

Pause.

CLARKE. In that case, I'll stay in.

Pause.

I shall talk to the wall.

Pause.

I married you for love.
ZENA. You married me for money!
CLARKE. You hadn't a penny! Not a cent!
ZENA. I'd been happy! I was alive! I'd lived!
CLARKE. Your bank account was closed. The first letter I wrote after we were married was a disclaimer on the debts you owed.

I saved you, Zen, from prison.
ZENA. Three months in Holloway washing floors. Washing toilets. I ruined my nails. I ruined my back. My spirit was unbroken!
CLARKE. It was!

It was.
ZENA. No thanks to you.
CLARKE. I worked. I slaved. I gave you money.

ZENA. You did. You did. Selling insurance. So grand. Your bowler hat. Your cane. Your determination to look like no one else. Your eyes. Your cheeks!

CLARKE. I loved you, too, of course.

Pause.

ZENA. You did.

Pause.

CLARKE. You were in the Connolly Arms with that man who used to wrestle.

ZENA. I was already falling in love.

CLARKE. With him?

ZENA. With you!

CLARKE. He broke my back.

ZENA. Your arm.

CLARKE. He threw me fourteen feet.

ZENA. Five.

CLARKE. I cherished every one.

I was already, Zena, falling in love.

Pause.

ZENA. Now you're off to the pub.

CLARKE. For an hour.

ZENA. To sing your songs.

CLARKE. For love.

ZENA. You do everything for love.

CLARKE. I do.

Pause.

ZENA. I've been feeling very low.

CLARKE. You never said.

ZENA. The child, my dear, we never had.

CLARKE. If we'd had a child, you'd have carried it, Zena, lower down.

ZENA. I am talking now of love.

CLARKE. Children, in this world, are not a lot to lose. The noise. The smell. The constant drain.

ZENA. He might have had my talent.
CLARKE. He might have had my voice.
ZENA. He might have had my grace.
CLARKE. He might have been a drunk.

Pause.

ZENA. Did Etty sleep with you or not?
CLARKE. Etty?
ZENA. My dearest and my closest friend.
CLARKE. She with me, not I with her.
ZENA. Impossible.
CLARKE. She called me to her room.
ZENA. 'Meet me in Vienna.'
CLARKE. It was.
ZENA. Such lovely tunes.
CLARKE. They were.
ZENA. When I heard you'd been unfaithful I opened up my
    heart. I sobbed on Etty's breast. On both her breasts. The
    breasts you must have sobbed on, too!
CLARKE. She wasn't feeling well. 'If only I could lie,' she
    said, 'with you. I'm sure I'd feel much better. With anyone
    other than my husband my body would recoil.'

Pause.

She was over thirteen stone. I was never very strong. With
Ditty on top I couldn't move.
ZENA. We were almost newly wed.
CLARKE. You'd had that affair with Ted.
ZENA. He was looking for a brooch.
CLARKE. His arm was down your dress.
ZENA. Your charm, my dear, without which, on stage, I
    would have felt undressed.
CLARKE. You practically were.
ZENA. I don't remember.
CLARKE. All he did was smile.
ZENA. And Etty! (*Handkerchief.*)
CLARKE. She's dead.
ZENA. But only eighteen months! (*Weeps.*)

All I feel, my dear, is grief. Grief at the child I never had.

The loved one running to my knee.
The tiny hands.
The pretty mouth.

How was she as a lover?
CLARKE. I don't recall.

I was always full of good intentions. I had good intentions
when I married you. I had good intentions when I ruined
my health, singing in rubbish beneath contempt to keep
the two of us together.

I even bought a yacht.
ZENA. A rowing-boat with sails on.
CLARKE. I named it after you.
ZENA. I remember Norman Sheridan coming to our
dressing-room and saying, 'Your husband has invited me
aboard your yacht.' I didn't know whether to laugh or
cry.
I loved that man.
CLARKE. You hated him.
ZENA. I loved him! (*Weeps.*)

It cost us the next two tours. He didn't speak to me for
the rest of the run. It was like Eve being banned from
Paradise. He fell in the sea when he came on board.
CLARKE. All we need now is your soliloquy on Sunday
afternoons. 'The long, drear call of distant bells, pealing
above homes I shall never know.' Now we have a home
you're scarcely in it.
ZENA. I've been in it, Clarke, for fifteen years.
CLARKE. Seven.
ZENA. I'm talking about the one we had before.
CLARKE. Before.
ZENA. You defaulted on the mortgage.
CLARKE. I dedicated myself to art. Not to acquiring wealth.
ZENA. Claudette was married twice.
CLARKE. She lived with seven men.
ZENA. She lived with five.

Teddy I don't know about.
CLARKE. I'm surprised, when you had that abortion, you
didn't confess it was his.

ZENA. I was scarcely more than a child. (*Cries.*)

CLARKE. You were almost twenty-seven.

ZENA. I was nearly twenty-five.

CLARKE. He brought a woman home one night and carried her on his back to that attic place he had for next to nothing. The landlady always came out if she heard two pairs of footsteps going up. Four flights. They had to call a doctor. He was off for over a year. He always took hall-rooms after that.

ZENA. Lies.

CLARKE. Your Romeo, my darling, could roam no more.

ZENA. At least he gave me a child.

Pause.

It wasn't him at all.

CLARKE. I was there at the time. I saw what happened.

Pause.

ZENA. Lady Luck made the fortune of everyone I know. I don't know anyone who didn't come good with luck.

CLARKE. Luck and talent.

ZENA. I had talent. I had no luck. All I had was you.

CLARKE. A has-been, love, that never was.

ZENA. I had one chance. They asked me to audition. I played it to a 't'. The backers said I hadn't the class. Sing? I could sing! Dance? I could dance!

I cut my wrists.

CLARKE. It should have been your throat.

ZENA. Burnt out at fifty!

CLARKE. Burnt out, my darling, long before.

Pause.

ZENA. You know your problem, Clarkie?

CLARKE. Too soft. Too kind. Devoted to a woman who gave me nothing. Not even her abortion could I put down to myself.

ZENA. Mood.

CLARKE. Mood?

ZENA. Mood!

CLARKE. I had a voice!
ZENA. What happened?
CLARKE. Nothing.

My name went down in an office file and ended up with a
hundred thousand others.

ZENA. Moods.
CLARKE. I always sang. I always laughed. I was always last
man in the bar at night. Shall I tell you why? I sang the
whole night through and hardly touched a drop of liquor.
ZENA. Moods.
CLARKE (*sings*).
'A voice across a room.
A name among so many:
A love I lost too soon.'

It was plagiarised by Billy Clinton. Made the mistake of
sending him the song. Never heard from him again.

ZENA. Write and tell him.
CLARKE. Who am I?

Pause.

They sit silent for a while: abstracted.

Sings.

'I long for you,
I wait for you:
I live for you,
I die for you . . . '

That was another.

ZENA (*abstracted*). I never heard it.
CLARKE. I wrote half a dozen. A generation later I'd have
been a household word.
ZENA. You almost were.
CLARKE. I was.

Pause.

ZENA. How was Etty on the night in question?
CLARKE. I don't recall.
ZENA. A woman like her.

CLARKE. Claudette was nothing special.

ZENA. How do you know if you don't recall?

CLARKE. If it had been something special, how would I forget?

ZENA. You never said a word.

CLARKE. We were on the road ten weeks. It was the end of the second month. I was tired. I was dying for a break.

ZENA. She gave you one.

Pause.

CLARKE. It was nothing very special.

Pause.

Not like you gave Eddie Makepiece.
I never made her pregnant.
Not in all those years.

ZENA. I suffered a misconception.
I miscarried another man's child.

Pause.

I might have called it Harold.

CLARKE. Harold.

ZENA. My father's name was Harold.

CLARKE. A bank-clerk.

ZENA. A mechanic.

The Depression killed him off.

CLARKE. I might have married someone else.
I had plenty-plenty offers.

ZENA. So had I.

CLARKE. Who?

ZENA. Knights. Earls. Princes.

CLARKE. Princes.

ZENA. Massimov.

CLARKE. I never heard of Massimov.

ZENA. A Russian.

CLARKE. Everybody in Russia is a Prince. That's why they had a revolution. They shot the bastards. In a cellar.

ZENA. He had a large moustache and coiffured hair.

CLARKE. I had coiffured hair.

ZENA. A fur collar to his coat.
CLARKE. So had I.
ZENA. Skunk.
CLARKE. Squirrel.
ZENA. You grow more childish by the hour.

Pause.

CLARKE. It was your hair, as well, I liked.
ZENA. To my waist in 'Chorus Girl'. To my scalp in 'Girls at War'.
CLARKE (*sings*).
  'My girl is in the chorus.
  My heart is in the sky:
  The sun is in its heaven,
  And so, my love, am I'.

  Clinton stole it.

Pause.

  Made a big hit.
ZENA. 'Girls at Peace' was a terrible flop.

  I told them at the time.
CLARKE. Your worst.
ZENA. The story of my life.

Pause.

  Sleep has always been a problem. (*Stretches.*)
CLARKE. Could try it now.
ZENA. I often dream of heaven.
  Everyone so happy. A concert every night. Everyone in love!
CLARKE. Who with?
ZENA. Mohamet. Whoever they have in charge. Someone they can trust. A dream like that is special.

Pause: contented, ZENA *lies back.*

CLARKE. I have nightmares. I see a world of molten glass.
ZENA.
  'O come, dear God, and be my friend,
  and bring our torment to an end:

let us declare
that our despair
is only there
to bless the light.'
CLARKE. 'Return to Sodom.'
ZENA. Right.

Pause.

A comedian, Clarkie, all your life.
CLARKE. Halliday, the director, saw me in a play.
ZENA. You've told me, dear, a thousand times.
CLARKE. 'I could use a man like that,' he said.
ZENA. 'Someone with that style.'
CLARKE. 'Talent.'

Felix Pemberton told me.
ZENA. Pemberton could never stay sober long enough to
hear a single cue.
CLARKE. His timing was a legend.
ZENA. The only time he knew was opening time.
CLARKE. He turned you down.
ZENA. In thirty-five years he and I exchanged two words.
CLARKE. You admired his coat. It came to his feet. A dark
brown tartan with yellow lines. He also had that woman.
Blonde.
ZENA. I don't recall.

Rearranges her dress, her shawl.

Pause.

CLARKE. Are you going out?
ZENA. I might.
CLARKE. Your one night off.
ZENA. You play there, too, if you get the chance.
CLARKE. They're short of comics.
ZENA. You're not a comic.
CLARKE. I can be if I try. (*Pause.*) In any case, we need the
money.
ZENA. Money.
CLARKE. Someone has to earn the cash.
ZENA. Household insurance.

CLARKE. Security!

ZENA. Household insurance.

CLARKE. I was lucky to get the job. Without it we'd be lost.

ZENA. Clarkie: you're pathetic.

Pause: abstracted.

My time will come.

CLARKIE. So will mine.

Pause.

I always dream of hell.

ZENA. You always sleep so well.

CLARKE. Deeply.

ZENA. I'm up half the night.

CLARKE. Not half.

ZENA. Almost.

Pause.

I often see you lying there. I would never have thought you dreamt at all.

CLARKE. You always dream of heaven.

ZENA. I do.

Pause.

Life has always seemed like that. Paradise around the corner. 'We saw you in "Girls at War" and have loved you ever since.'

Lots of letters came like that. 'You are my second heaven.'

CLARKE. Who wrote that?

ZENA. Massimov.

CLARKE. If you were his second heaven, what was his first?

ZENA. His father's estate where he spent his childhood before the Revolution.

CLARKE. He must be over eighty.

ZENA. He was thirty-nine.

A mountain in the distance.
A silver-coloured lake.
Cossacks in the village.

CLARKE. He couldn't have been a child at the time of the Revolution and be standing outside the door of 'Girls at War' at the age of thirty-nine.

ZENA. He was.

CLARKE. Another bloody actor.

We had them all the time.

ZENA. Then there was Patrick.

CLARKE. Patrick.

ZENA. The son of an Irish peer.

CLARKE. I never heard of him.

ZENA. You might have. (*Straightens her skirt.*) If I'd gone along with what he asked.

CLARKE. What did he ask?

ZENA. To marry him.

CLARKE. And live in a Celtic bog.

ZENA. He had a bullet-proof car. A Mercedes-Benz with an open roof.

CLARKE. How could it be bullet-proof with an open roof?

ZENA. The bodywork was protected.

CLARKE. Mad.

ZENA. Such lovely hair.

CLARKE. Hair.

ZENA. Like down.

CLARKE. Down.

ZENA. Quite mad.

Pause.

I thought you were going out.

CLARKE. I'll stay.

Pause.

It was a long day at the office.

ZENA. I thought you spent your day on visits.

CLARKE. I do my books. I check my accounts.

I can't wait, each night, for your performance.

ZENA. None of this is real.

Pause.

CLARKE. My mother never loved me.
ZENA. No.
CLARKE. Without you I'd be lost.
ZENA. You would.

Pause.

CLARKE.
To my wife I am a loser.
To the world I am a clown.
A malcontent. A failure.

The only light is Zee herself.

Try it once again?
ZENA. You awful promenader.
CLARKE. I am.
ZENA. You awful, awful swank!

Pause.

CLARKE *moves away: repositions himself.*

CLARKE. I had a job, at the beginning of the war. Running
errands for a local grocer. One of the houses I took
groceries to was occupied by a widow. She would take me
on her knee. I would lean my head against her breast. She
gave me sweets.

One evening, having made an excuse to walk past her
door, I saw her curtains drawn and, a moment later, a
man came out. 'Do come early next time,' she said, 'and
not leave me waiting half the night.'

I gave up running errands after that. If I had to walk past
her house I chose a different route.
ZENA. I was caught by a man behind a hedge.
CLARKE. My precious.
ZENA. I never had a chance.
CLARKE. My love.
ZENA. All I dream of now is heaven. My mother. My
father. My brothers. My sisters.
CLARKE. You haven't any sisters.
ZENA. If I had.

CLARKE. Nor brothers.

ZENA. Pedant.

Pause.

A life of passion. Spent!

Pause.

CLARKE *repositions himself.*

ZENA, *likewise, on her couch.*

Light refocuses.

CLARKE: Then . . .
I went —

Singing.

'*back*wards,
and *for*wards,
and *side*ways . . .
And . . .
*back*wards
and *for*wards
again . . .'

ZENA. Then there was Steven.

CLARKE. Steven!

ZENA. Confidant.

CLARKE. Pilgrim.

ZENA. Friend.

CLARKE. He idolised the Russian Revolution. Sixty million people disposed of for the delectation of that comic genius Marx.

ZENA. When he was a child his mother and father killed themselves.

CLARKE. Sigmund was another.

ZENA. He was brought up in a Home. He ran away at ten.

CLARKE. To propagate a definitive view of human nature is, at heart, a comic intention.

ZENA. He lived in a shed. He was thrown into prison for stealing a cabbage.

A cabbage!

He stayed in fifteen months. Ice-cold cells and the bodily
abuse by other prisoners.

CLARKE. Lies.

ZENA. True!

CLARKE. His father owned a mill. I saw him in the bar of
'The Beautiful Madonna'. 'He was an utter bloody fool at
home,' he said.

ZENA. Not true.

CLARKE. Steve Macready. Steven Unready he was called
after that.

ZENA. He had red hair.

CLARKE. Dyed.

ZENA. On his chest.

CLARKE. Painted.

Pause.

He took you for a ride.

ZENA. At Bognor, Bridlington, Rhyl and Blackpool. What a
tour!

CLARKE. Red Macready!

ZENA. A wonderful man!

CLARKE. His father came in a chauffeured limousine. Said
he was leaving all his money to the church. 'The Catholic
Church,' he said. 'The only true bulwark against the
Commie revolution.'

ZENA. You are shattering a dream.

CLARKE. I am, my darling, asserting a truth.

ZENA. I loved him very much. (*Blows nose.*) The hands of
an artist. As were his features. So delicate. So thin. Like
porcelain. From his years of privation.

CLARKE. Eating cabbage.

ZENA. Eating anything he could get.

CLARKE. No wonder his breath smelled like it did.

ZENA. His breath was sweet. Like the mountain air. His
thoughts translucent. (*Blows nose.*) I don't believe he had
a father.

CLARKE. He had a photograph of Steve. On a lawn in front
of a house the size of Buckingham Palace. Turrets,
balustrading, steps, a plinth. He took to the stage to
embarrass his family. Same with the Russian Revolution.

Wrote letters to Molotov and Stalin, to Beria and to a woman whom he believed was a relative of Marx. It turned out to be a great-great niece who owned a shop in Greenwich. Asking him for money. 'Just like a bloody Marx,' he said. 'Cadging all his life.'

ZENA. I loved him.

CLARKE. He loved you.

ZENA. So much of a woman's life is spent in being deceived. So much.

CLARKE. He even went to college.

ZENA. 'Prison was my university,' he said. 'Hardship my profession.'

CLARKE. His mother sent him money. It was why he could rest for fourteen weeks while we went out on tour. Back streets. Dark houses. Cobbled alleys.

ZENA.
I felt transcendent. I felt transformed.
He recited Robbie Burns.
'If I should die, think only this of me.'

CLARKE. All his material he stole. Songs. Jokes. Poems. Stories. He borrowed one of mine. Changed 'Thinking of You' to 'Thinking of Joe and Vladimir Ilyich'.

When Steve Macready went on the stage he intended to be a recitateur. 'I am here on behalf of the working-class.' A class he had viewed for over half his life from behind the brick walls of his father's estate.

ZENA. He took me to a dance. Above the beach at Bournemouth.

'Revolution,' he said, 'is in my blood.' He had an antipathy to the status quo. All he liked, he said, was change. Change for the better. Change for the good.

CLARKE. There are pines above the beach at Bournemouth.

ZENA. This, my dear, was the Belmont Hotel. You could dance all night to the music of Eleanor Mason and the Masonettes. They wore purple gowns and had delicate arms. Such eager faces. Such wonderful hands. A credit, my dear, to our profession. Then, of course, there was Rosanna.

CLARKE. Rose!

ZENA. The 'husky-hues of the Southern Seas' were put on with a brush.

CLARKE. Sicilian.

ZENA. Welsh.

CLARKE. She couldn't speak a word of English. Not until I taught her.

ZENA. She came from Cardiff. Her father was a docker. If Teddy Makepiece was promiscuous I'd hate to think of a word that would sum up Rosanna Maserelli.

CLARKE. She was a very beautiful woman.

ZENA. Legs like a blacksmith.

CLARKE. She was famous for her elevations.

ZENA. So were you by all accounts.

Pause.

CLARKE. Makepiece. Massimov. Maserelli. Mason and the Masonettes. All m's.

ZENA. Mystery. Mimicry. Memory . . . Mother.

CLARKE. Mother.

Pause.

ZENA. Why don't you dance?

CLARKE. My dancing mood has gone.

ZENA. Meriel thinks I'm grand. 'Too grand,' she says, 'for our boutique. You belong, my dear, to Regent Street, to Hampstead Heath and Piccadilly. You fill the shop,' she says, 'with love.' Like the love, my dear, I feel for you.

I have so much to show the world!

I was a victim. Makepiece took me for a ride. Steven. Massy. All the rest.

'Another woman: another crime.
Another man: another swine!'

CLARKE. It had more tenderness the last time.

ZENA. It had?

CLARKE. More warmth.

ZENA. When a part is going well I feel an inner voice. Not lines I've learnt but something else.

CLARKE. On the train, this morning, going to work, I saw

a man and woman holding hands, their eyes on one
another, their thoughts on no one else. Such tenderness.
Such bliss.

ZENA. The world is built on love.

CLARKE. It is.

ZENA. Your man-made prophylactics: what do they do?
Nothing.

Pause.

'The Roebuck' has an open fire. The flames roar merrily
along. No wonder they listen to you sing. All beer and
skittles. That braying guffaw that goes up the moment
you arrive.

CLARKE. Then, of course, there's Sammy.

ZENA. Sampson was the one I liked!

CLARKE. He was met by the husband of the woman he was
currently seducing in an alleyway at the back of the
Empire Theatre, Wolverhampton, who did to him what
many a husband, brother, father, son had tried to do
before.

ZENA. He died in a seaman's home in Brighton.

CLARKE. Wolverhampton.

ZENA. He was a seaman in his youth.

CLARKE. A strongman.

ZENA. A ventriloquist.

CLARKE. He could talk out of the back of his head, it's
true.

ZENA. Sammy gave me every support.

CLARKE. He was old enough to be your father.

ZENA. Some thought he was.

Sex is not essential. Not as in a man.

He was like you are, Clarke. My friend.

We did so many things together.

CLARKE. I bet.

ZENA. We walked. We talked. We read. We travelled.

I showed him once or twice how much I cared.

It was the very least a girl could do.

I first went on the stage at twelve.

CLARKE. Fifteen.

ZENA. Twelve. In 'Puss in Boots'. After that my parents
sent me off to school. I hated every minute. I swore they'd
have to kill me if they sent me there again. Sammy didn't
treat me as a child. For the first time in my life I felt
myself. I've never known a gentler man. 'If only,' he'd say,
'I'd had an education. Not travelled the world when I
should have been in class.' He covered his face at times
and cried. He talked about his mother. By the time he got
to know her she looked, he said, immensely old. She was
only forty-seven, the mother of eight children. Sammy
went to sea at twelve. In Valparaiso, two years later, he
got a message. 'Mother dead. No need to come back
home.'

'No need to come back home', he said, had been the
motto of his life.

'Wherever you are, Zena,' he said, 'is always home for
me.'

I only understood how much I loved him after he had left.
'You need the love of a younger man,' he said.

He went off with an older woman. 'This,' he said, one
night, when I met him with her in a pub, 'is my natural
level.'

I've lived for Sammy ever since.

Somewhere out there his spirit roams – in that dank, dark
world of cobbled alleys, of rain-flecked streets, of
forgotten pubs.

He informs the way I think and feel. The searching for a
place to call his own.

Weeps.

It doesn't do much good to contemplate the past.

O, Sampson is the one for me,
The only one I love:
The man who first made love to me,
And called me turtle-dove.

Sings.

'O to be loved so gently,
O to be loved so true,
O to be loved so deeply
– as I, my dear, love you'.

Pause.

Then there was Kitty Norman.

CLARKE. 'The Northern Nightingale.'

ZENA. Her parents worked in a shop. They came to the theatre, time after time, knocking on the door.

CLARKE. They thought she had a voice. They saw a great career. Not music-hall but opera. They paid for her to have lessons. She fell in love. Her parents vilified the man and prevented her from seeing him.

Years later, of course, they met again. The visions with which he'd entranced her as a youth had ended in a second marriage. He was working in a garage. The engineer whose bridges would span the world, who would build machines to fly through the air at unprecedented speeds, who would revolutionise domestic life with robots, was a motor-car mechanic.

She blamed her parents for his fall.

'We each have a life to live,' she said. 'We must live it to the full.'

ZENA. She was always very bitter.

CLARKE. No.

ZENA. She was always very sad.

CLARKE. Not bitterness, Zee: conviction.
  Not sadness, Zee, but strength.

ZENA. She never had the voice.
  Kitty Norman was a fake.

CLARKE. She taught me how to love. 'There's something in

it for you,' she said. 'And something in it for me.' I was
twenty-one. She was forty-seven. In middle age she
became quite stout. 'A disused or a misused talent: you
must decide it for me, Clarke,' she said.

Like Sammy was for you, Kitty Norman was for me.
'Discount what I say,' she'd say, 'or you'll end up
something worse.'

Only recently have I understood how much poor Kitty
meant.

She'd sing arias she'd learned while still a child.

I tried another love.
I cried another tear:
They neither stopped my pain,
Nor drove away my fear.

They sounded grand.

Everything has been written,
Everything has been said:
Only the bad are living,
All of the good are dead.

Pause.

ZENA. Where, my dear, does that leave us?
CLARKE. Two might-have-beens.
ZENA. Two almost-weres.
CLARKE. The heirs of Sam and Kitty!
ZENA (*sings*). 'If you and I . . . '
CLARKE (*sings*). 'If I and you . . . '
ZENA (*sings*). 'If me and thee . . . '
CLARKE (*sings*). 'If we and us . . . '
ZENA (*sings*). 'Could love . . . '
CLARKE. Could love!
ZENA. Once we could dance the whole night through.
CLARKE. Love the whole night through.
ZENA. My love.
CLARKE. My dear.

Pause.

ZENA. Prissy never came to much.

CLARKE. 'The Boston Belle.'

ZENA. She came from Staines.

CLARKE. New York.

ZENA. She never went further west than Blackpool.

CLARKE (*pause*). It's true, of course, she was very light.

ZENA. Light!

CLARKE. She was once the partner to Wallace Coates. In addition to memorising dates and facts of absolutely no importance he would call up a member of the audience to blindfold him. Priscilla would then move through the auditorium, holding out rings and watches, pens and wallets which Wally would identify. He had worked out the act while a prisoner of war.

It was done, she said, by coded words.

In the end, of course, he went quite mad.

I learnt from her how to treat life as a whim.

ZENA. Not like me and you.

CLARKE. Not like you and I at all.

Ill-health caught up with Wally in the end. He developed a theory to do with growing plants.

ZENA. He died from weed-killer I was told.

CLARKE. His state of mind was something chronic. To do with being a prisoner, Prissy said.

Pause.

She turned to singing after that.

On top of which she learned to dance.

She's out there now. Most likely married. With not a mother and two ugly sisters but a mother-in-law and two children on her hands.

ZENA. How's your wife?

CLARKE. On tour.

ZENA. How's her hair?

CLARKE. Keeps falling out.

ZENA. Sends you money?

CLARKE. On the dot.

ZENA. Faithful?

CLARKE. Uses her discretion.
ZENA. Suspicious?
CLARKE. Not a bit.

A card from Blackpool came last week. 'A certain someone, whom you may know, has cast his eye in this direction.'

At home our rules are strict. No telephone calls. No letters. 'What starts on tour must end on tour.'

Sometimes, of course, it's possible to tell: a look in the eye, a tear.

Doughty old girl. At fifty-five you'd think she'd want a rest. But no. 'Love is a glorious game,' she says, 'when one hand's played you choose another.'

Even now she steals the show. Applause when she enters. At the end of the evening a special bow.
ZENA. I'm full of envy.
CLARKE. So you are.
ZENA. So many women in your life.
CLARKE. That's right.
ZENA. You and Etty.
CLARKE. Me and Ditty.
ZENA. You and Prissy.
CLARKE. 'A marriage with nothing in it is a marriage meant to last', Fenella says. We've been married now for fifteen years.

To those ladies whose possessions I am called in to assess I say, 'My dear, I am married to Fenella Marsden,' and though it doesn't discourage some, with those I most dislike I make it stick.

Pause.

How is Brendan?
ZENA. Has a beer-gut out to here. Goes on tour, of course, like Fenny. Hatred is the thing we have in common. Can't live with, and can't without. He's known, of course, for the loudness of his voice. '*Come here!*' in a pub when he sees me leaving. Puts his fist, at times, through doors. Has two words for everything. 'I wouldn't run on my legs after

you,' he often says, to which I answer, 'On what would
you run, in that case, wheels?' Fancies Fenny. 'I don't
know why,' he often says, 'the two of us shouldn't get
together.'

CLARKE. 'What do you think to Brendan Donoghue?'
Fenella often says. 'Do you think the two of us would hit
it off?' 'Brendan and you,' I say, 'are two of a kind.
There's no reason,' I tell her, 'why you shouldn't.'

They worked together once. 'Remember Brendan
Donoghue and Fenella Marsden: the mountain to
Mohamet,' I once heard in a pub.

ZENA. Keeps both of us in line.

CLARKE (*pause*) It does.

Pause.

ZENA. Something to fall back on.

CLARKE. Right.

ZENA (*sings*). 'What it is we are . . .

CLARKE (*sings*). 'What it is we fear . . .

ZENA (*sings*). 'Leaving you behind . . .

CLARKE (*sings*). 'Loving you, my dear . . .'

Pause.

Borelli is the one I never liked.

ZENA. Brussen brute.

CLARKE. Protruding ears.

ZENA. A very large mouth.

CLARKE. Such funny legs.

ZENA. Bowed.

CLARKE. Were they?

ZENA. A hairy back.

CLARKE. He had hair, my dear, all over.

Pause.

ZENA. I never saw.

Pause.

All we women in the cast could do – like women, my
darling, down the ages – was direct our thoughts to higher
things.

CLARKE. His body smelled.
ZENA. His breath was worse.
CLARKE. A dog.
ZENA. A beast.
CLARKE. I don't know how you stood it.
ZENA. A bulbous nose.
CLARKE. A bulbous brow.
ZENA. He never smiled.
CLARKE. Oh, no.
ZENA. He sneered.

All a girl could do was shake.

Such strength.

Pity you came in.
CLARKE. It was.
ZENA. I would have spared you that of all things, dear.

The baths I had. The washings-out.

'Here for the day,' you said, 'and not the night.'

All the way from Salford.
CLARKE. Plymouth.
ZENA. 'Girls at Sea.'
CLARKE. 'Sailors in Love.'
ZENA. Prissy was in that.
CLARKE. She was.
ZENA. When you and she got pally.
CLARKE. Very.
ZENA. Good job I didn't come.
CLARKE. It was.
ZENA. Pressing down with all his weight.
CLARKE. I'm surprised you never heard the door.
ZENA. Gave men in general a very bad name.

Borelli.

Pause.

CLARKE. The bad times you remember.
ZENA. The best times you forget.
CLARKE. Mother and father, Zee, were worse.

ZENA. The cries.
CLARKE. The screams.
ZENA. The shouts.
CLARKE. The groans.
ZENA. Borelli only happened once. Father happened every night.
CLARKE. Two rooms only.
ZENA. Theirs and ours.
CLARKE. Sister and brother!

Pause.

The only things I feel are what I feel through you.

The only feelings, Zee, I have.

I can't say more than that.
ZENA. My love.
CLARKE. I don't care if I die, as long as I'm with you.
ZENA. My dear.
CLARKE. Preparing for the worst
　Is how our life is cursed.
ZENA. It never is as bad:
　It's always something worse.
CLARKE. Feel this, feel that, feel nothing less –
ZENA. Pain is our paean of distress.
CLARKE. First breath: first pain.
ZENA. And then we rise –
CLARKE. God's purpose plain
ZENA. In creature's eyes:
CLARKE To find in death our final gain
ZENA. That what our God requires is pain.
CLARKE. Pain.
ZENA. We still have one another.
CLARKE. Yes.

Pause.

ZENA. Any new inventions?
CLARKE (*holds his head*). The engine slows.

You lie there on the couch.

I turn my mind to other things.
ZENA. Liar.
CLARKE. Cheat.
ZENA. What are you creating?
CLARKE. Love.

Pause.

ZENA. Michelle.
CLARKE. Cornhill.
ZENA. Don't remember.
CLARKE. No diaphragm.
ZENA. Red hair.
CLARKE. Dyed.
ZENA. Titian.
CLARKE. Made one or two films.
ZENA. Walk-on.
CLARKE. Chorus.
ZENA. See her?
CLARKE. Did.
ZENA. Painted.
CLARKE. Fingers.

Pause.

Borelli had a sister.
ZENA. Didn't.
CLARKE. We were on the midnight train.
ZENA. Never.
CLARKE. Actor's oath.
ZENA. Not worth a penny.
CLARKE. God's truth.
ZENA. Worth even less.

Pause.

CLARKE.
  I met him in the bar.
  'Candida,' he said, 'has been to see me.'
  'Who is Candida?' I asked.
  'Candida,' he said, 'is my twin sister.'
ZENA. Wife.

CLARKE. Sister.
ZENA. Wife.
CLARKE. He had no wife.

Pause.

'Life,' she said, 'is not worth living.'
ZENA. Is.
CLARKE. Isn't.
ZENA. She knew what he was up to.
CLARKE. Didn't.

'I realise,' she said, 'that this is not only the finishing but
the starting line. We realise that,' she said, 'before we
start. We always have to be in motion. We have no more
will than a clockwork mouse. We stop. We start. No
purpose why we move at all.'

'Above all else,' she said, 'we struggle. We dress up in our
comic clothes. Our trousers, shirts and suits and hats. Our
gloves and socks and boots and blouses.'

'Beneath it all,' she said, 'our clockwork pain.'
ZENA. Borelli's wife.
CLARKE. 'Fashion, the oil on which our hammers rise, our
cogs rotate, our wheels go round.'
ZENA. His wife.

Pause.

CLARKE. My original name was Bryan.
ZENA. I don't recall.
CLARKE. At the Registry you expressed surprise.
'I thought I was marrying Clarke,' you said.
'I find I'm marrying Bryan.'
ZENA.
Good old Bry!
Why should I sigh?
I'd rather die
than now deny
my

love for Bryan Harrison.

CLARKE. Harrison, too, of course, fictitious.

Pause.

ZENA. It was.

CLARKE (*sings*).
  'O singers love to sing,
  As lovers love to love:
  The tyrant on the wing
  Applauds the cooing dove.'

ZENA.
  Two ne'er-do-wells. Two almost-weres.
  Two almost-made-its, never-quites.
  Two almost-alsos, also-rans.

CLARKE.
  They also run who run away,
  But never quite so fast
  As those who run towards the day
  They know to be their last.

ZENA. How it all comes back.

CLARKE. It does.

ZENA.
  First you see it. Then you don't.
  First you sense it. Then it's gone.
  First you feel it. Then it moves.
  First you taste it. Then it dies.

CLARKE (*singing*).
  'Here are the reasons,
  Here are the spells –
  Why love has its seasons,
  Also its hells.'

ZENA. Candida was spoilt.

CLARKE. So was Borelli.

ZENA (*sings*).
  'He was my hero,
  For a while:
  He moved with grace,
  He moved with style.
  He had such manners,
  He had such airs –

He took me always unawares.'
CLARKE. A monster.
ZENA. As you are, too, at times.
CLARKE. O not at all.

Pause.

O not at all.

Pause.

ZENA (*sings*).
'Effete and gentle
All the while:
He had such grace,
He had such style.
Barbarity was not his suit:
He looked so kind –
But always mute.

O sadness comes,
O sadness dies:
I long for love,
Get only sighs.

May love return
When all is lost,
And never count
What it has cost.

O head aloft,
O feet of clay:
May love live longer
Than a day.'
CLARKE (*sings*).
'O love lives longer
Than a day:
A week at most
Then fades away.'
ZENA. Alec leaves me messages.
CLARKE. I don't know why you married.

ZENA. 'Where were you all last week.' Signed: 'Alec'.

CLARKE. My grandfather, Sir Thomas à la Fernley, manufactured sausages from a recipe he got from a man in the First World War.

ZENA. Sausages!

CLARKE. Civil-servant!

ZENA. At least I have an office.

CLARKE. In the Ministry of Health!

ZENA. What better Ministry to work for!

CLARKE. Without the wealth that I create you'd scarcely breathe at all. 'Fernleys Feed the Nation.' You can see it on our vans.

My mother's name was Merilyn.
My father called her 'Merry'.

'Merry! Merry!' he would call.

It made our home so happy.

ZENA. Like this place is at times.

CLARKE. It is.

Pause.

ZENA. Still eight years to run.

CLARKE. We ought to sell it.

ZENA. Why?

CLARKE. Get something back.

ZENA. We have got something back.

Pause.

CLARKE. It's been worth every penny.

ZENA. Daddy was a peer.

The only thing we had in common was a loathing of the status quo.

Mummy was a bore.

CLARKE. The gate of Caius.

ZENA. That summer night.

CLARKE. Annus Mirabilis.
ZENA. I shall have to dash.

Pause: neither moves.

Don't forget to ring.
CLARKE. I shan't.
ZENA. Cosy old flat.
CLARKE. Can't live without.
ZENA. Nor I.
CLARKE. Zena.
ZENA. So much fun.
CLARKE. Best of all worlds.
ZENA. So it is.
CLARKE. Best of all pals.
ZENA. So we are.

Pause.

Same time next week?
CLARKE. I'll ring you.

Pause.

ZENA. How long have we got?

Pause.

CLARKE. I've no idea.

Pause.

ZENA. You artists, dear, are all alike.

Here I am waiting:
Here I expire –
Lit like a furnace –
A flame without fire!
CLARKE. Darling.
ZENA. Darling.
CLARKE. Darling?
ZENA. Darling?

Pause.

CLARKE. Darling?
ZENA. Darling!
CLARKE. You okay?

ZENA *nods*.

CLARKE. Me, too.

Pause.

ZENA. I never liked this part.
CLARKE. Nor I.
ZENA. Stage Manager for how long?
CLARKE. Years.
ZENA. 'Caesar's Follies'?
CLARKE. Bit parts.

Pause.

You sometimes smile.
ZENA. I've noticed that.
CLARKE. Getting lighter.

Pause: light decreasing.

ZENA. Candid, cautious, careful Clarke.
CLARKE. Zany, zealous, zestful Zena.

Pause.

Read it, have you?
ZENA. Rang a bell.
CLARKE. Had an instinct.
ZENA. Heard about Beryl.
CLARKE. Good old stick.

On tour, in the evenings, there was nothing else
to do.
I didn't like drinking.
Nor did she.

Lay on the beach.
Sea crashing on the sand.

Portuguese.
ZENA. What nonsense, Clarke.
  She came from Kent.

  Joanna, too, I heard about.
CLARKE. Cut above the rest.
ZENA. She is.
CLARKE. Tea in bed. Morning papers.
  Loved doing things for other people.

  Pause.

  Thought of having babies.
ZENA. Not much fun.

Pause.

CLARKE. I heard about you and Gavin.
ZENA. Could write a book on what we ate.

  Mornings started at one p.m.

  'Debauchery suits me, Zee,' he said.
CLARKE. Good of him to tell you.
ZENA. 'Tis.
CLARKE. 'Too-Sober-Connolly' he's known at the club.
ZENA. Corcoran's.
CLARKE. A more civilised place it's hard to find.
ZENA. Wasn't O'Faolain murdered there one night?
CLARKE. Once.
ZENA. Wasn't it closed for rats in the kitchen?
CLARKE. Twice.
ZENA. Wasn't Corcoran fined for serving short?
CLARKE. There was a hole in the ladle, he said, at the time.
ZENA. Are you still going out?
CLARKE. I might.

  Pause.

  Zena, Zena.
  Always saner
  Than the zany Zena
  That I knew before.
ZENA. That's right.

CLARKE. The Clarke Harrison machine for passing time.
ZENA. Caring.
CLARKE. O, caring!
ZENA. Caring how we feel.
CLARKE. Caring we don't steal.
ZENA. Caring that we stay alive.
CLARKE. Caring that I have a wife.
ZENA. Caring that we never lose.
CLARKE. Caring that we care to choose.
ZENA. Caring that we care at all.
CLARKE. Caring that we never fall.
ZENA. Caring that we love and dance.
CLARKE. Caring that we have a chance.
ZENA. Caring that we sport and play.
CLARKE. Caring that we never say . . .
ZENA. Life in here is hell.

Pause.

CLARKE. Caring does not take away.
ZENA. The care that says we're here to stay.
CLARKE. Endlessly we sit and wait.
ZENA. Not caring how we celebrate.
CLARKE. As long as we survive.

Pause.

O Zena, Zena,
Always saner
Than the zany Zena
That I knew before.

Pause.

ZENA. Growing dark.
CLARKE. It is.

Pause.

ZENA. 'Jealousy Asunder.'
CLARKE.
'Better in our life to scan
What love can't do, not what it can.'

Pause.

Much pain?

ZENA. A little.

CLARKE. All that bustle.

ZENA. All that life.

CLARKE. All those people.

ZENA. All that strife.

CLARKE. Never knowing what we are.

ZENA. Never knowing what we feel.

CLARKE. Pinioned to a spinning wheel.

ZENA. Of terror and desire.

Pause.

CLARKE. Did that better, Zee, the last time.

ZENA. Yes.

CLARKE. Light coming up.

Light fading.

Pause.

ZENA. It is.

CLARKE. O Mother of God.

ZENA (*pause*). No idea, still, who you are.

CLARKE. Nor where we've been.

ZENA. Nor what we've seen.

CLARKE. Nor where we are.

ZENA. Nor what we do.

CLARKE. More like this.

His hands together.

ZENA. O more like this.

CLARKE. More like this.

ZENA. Together.

Pause: freeze: their two standing figures.

Light fades.

Methuen Contemporary Dramatists
include

Peter Barnes (three volumes)
Sebastian Barry
Edward Bond (six volumes)
Howard Brenton
  (two volumes)
Richard Cameron
Jim Cartwright
Caryl Churchill (two volumes)
Sarah Daniels (two volumes)
David Edgar (three volumes)
Dario Fo (two volumes)
Michael Frayn (two volumes)
Peter Handke
Jonathan Harvey
Declan Hughes
Terry Johnson
Bernard-Marie Koltès
Doug Lucie
David Mamet (three volumes)

Anthony Minghella
  (two volumes)
Tom Murphy (four volumes)
Phyllis Nagy
Peter Nichols (two volumes)
Philip Osment
Louise Page
Stephen Poliakoff
  (three volumes)
Christina Reid
Philip Ridley
Willy Russell
Ntozake Shange
Sam Shepard (two volumes)
David Storey (three volumes)
Sue Townsend
Michel Vinaver (two volumes)
Michael Wilcox